STUDIES IN IRISH LITERATURE, CINEMA AND CULTURE

**Series editor: Dr. Pilar Villar-Argáiz, Senior Lecturer in British and Irish Literature, the Department of English Philology, University of Granada**

1. Kathryn Laing and Sinéad Mooney (editors), *Irish Women Writers At the Turn of the 20th Century: Alternative Histories, New Narratives.*
2. Constanza del Río and José Carregal (editors), *Revolutionary Ireland, 1916–2016. Historical Facts & Social Transformations Re-Assessed.*
3. Adela Flamarike, *Women, Art And Nationalism in the Irish Revival. Presence And Absence.*
4. James Gallacher, *Bohemian Belfast and Dublin. Two Artistic and Literary Worlds in the Work of Gerard Keenan.*

STUDIES IN IRISH LITERATURE, CINEMA AND CULTURE
No. 3
Series editor: Dr. Pilar Villar-Argáiz

# Women, Art, and Nationalism in the Irish Revival

## Presence and Absence

# Women, Art, and Nationalism in the Irish Revival

## Presence and Absence

Adela Flamarike

*EER*

EDWARD EVERETT ROOT PUBLISHERS, BRIGHTON 2020.

*EER*

Edward Everett Root, Publishers, Co. Ltd.,
30 New Road, Brighton, Sussex, BN1 1BN, England.

*Details of our overseas agents and how to order our books are given on our website.*

www.eerpublishing.com

*edwardeverettroot@yahoo.co.uk*

Adela Flamarike
*Women, Art, and Nationalism in the Irish Revival*
*Presence and Absence*

*Studies in Irish Literature, Cinema and Culture series,* volume 3.

ISBN: 9781911454335 Paperback
ISBN: 9781911454366 Hardback
ISBN: 9781911454380 ebook

First published in England in 2020.



Cover and book production by Pageset Limited, High Wycombe, Buckinghamshire.

# Foreword by Liz Gillis

The "Decade of Centenaries" has provided the opportunity for us re-examine the history of the Irish revolution. New material is being constantly released from state archives which in turn, is bringing to light new information or stories that were overlooked. This is certainly true in relation to the role that women played in the revolution.

Amazing work has been done in this area, started long ago by historians Dr Margaret MacCurtain and Dr Margaret Ward and it has gone from strength to strength. The story of women in the revolution is no longer "hidden history" and the appetite from the public to know more is tremendous. School children are not just learning about Countess Markievicz or Grace Gifford, they are discovering stories about women from their own communities, what they did, how the conflict affected them. We are so lucky at this moment in time, because there is no longer any excuse to exclude women from the narrative. The Irish revolution could not have happened the way it did without the contribution of women.

While all of this work is welcome, it is only part of the story. The Irish revolution did not happen overnight. It was a manifestation of people coming together from all sections of society, from different backgrounds. It was not just a political revolution; it was also a cultural revolution. One influenced the other. Today, the role of women in the political revolution is firmly established in the general narrative, the same cannot be said of the importance of women in the cultural revival that took place in the late nineteenth century. Lady Augusta Gregory and Maud Gonne would be the names that people would know, but there were so many more women who contributed so much to this movement.

The connection between the Gaelic Revival and the Irish revolution has been well documented. The resurgence of interest in the Irish language, art, sport, literature, music, folklore etc. brought together a generation of men and women who were determined to change Ireland's future. Much emphasis has been placed on how literature, poetry and the theatre awakened a political awareness in young men and women at the time. Art was no less a powerful medium, a platform where ideas of nationhood were expressed through painting, illustration, etchings and drawings. Through art, a group of young women emerged, taking full advantage of the fact that they could go to college to study their craft. These women would help influence future revolutionaries; they themselves were witnesses of the revolution, while some of them were actual participants. Through their passion for art they left a legacy that we benefit from today.

Like the women of Cumann na mBan, their contribution to their craft and the importance of their work to the Irish art scene was overshadowed by that of their male counterparts in the years following independence. Not anymore. Through her work, Adela Flamarike is putting these Irish women artists back where they rightly belong. The women she has written about are the tip of the iceberg. They were trailblazers in their personal and professional lives, who let nothing stand in the way to creativity. Adela has done a tremendous job in telling their stories and by doing so she has given back to the Irish people a forgotten aspect of our past. She has done these women proud.

# Acknowledgements

Writing this book has been a beautiful and rewarding experience, and also a challenge. For their contribution and their help in the research for this book I would like to thank the Crawford Art Gallery in Cork, The Model – Home of The Niland Collection in Sligo, The Central Bank of Ireland, The University of Saint Vincent in Halifax (Nova Scotia, Canada), The Ireland's Great Hunger Museum (Hamden, CT.), Adam's and Whyte's Auctioneers, the staff at the Military Archives of the Irish Defence Forces, The Hugh Lane Gallery of Modern Art and especially the National Gallery of Ireland for giving me access to their wonderful library and archive collections. Many thanks as well to Elaine Sisson and Liz Gillis, for their advice and their kind words.

All my gratitude to the staff at Edward Everett Root Publishers, especially to John Spiers and Pilar Villar-Argáiz for their amazing work, as well as for their patience and support throughout this project.

I would like to thank my parents Viki and Javier, and my brother Diego for their encouragement. I'm also eternally grateful to all my good friends in Westport and Biurrun. Without their support this would not have been possible.

And finally, I would like to dedicate this book to all the women in my life. Especially to my mother, for her unconditional love. To Marisol, for her strength and affection. To Lucy Bracken, for her kindness. To Carolyn Claire Mitchell, for sharing her knowledge and her love of Ireland with me. To Natalia, for the friendship and the wonderful road trips around the west coast. Like the women in this book, you are an inspiration.

Westport, Co. Mayo, 2019

*"But where is the brush that could show anything*
*Of all that pride and that humility?*
*And I am in despair that time may bring*
*Approved patterns of women or of men*
*But not that selfsame excellence again"*

(W. B. Yeats
"The Municipal Gallery Revisited", *Autobiography)*

# Contents

## PART FOUR

# Introduction. Presence and Absence

In 1989, a group of women wearing gorilla masks burst into the New York Metropolitan Museum holding a banner with the image of the Neoclassical painter Jean-Auguste Dominique Ingres's *The Great Odalisque* (1814) also wearing an ape mask. Against a garish yellow background, a message in black letters: "Do women have to be naked to get into the Met. Museum? Less than 5% of the artists in the Modern Art Sections are women, but 85% of the nudes are female". Only a year earlier, the Museum of Modern Art of New York had held an exhibition entitled *An International survey of Painting and Sculpture*, in which only 10% of the exhibited artists were women. The Guerrilla Girls called themselves "the conscience of the artworld", and through their performance they criticised the lack of female representation in the artistic institutions. It has been thirty years since their irruption in the Metropolitan Museum, but things have not changed excessively.

This book is the result of two personal experiences, also related to the claims of the Guerrilla Girls. The first one happened during my time studying Art History in the University of the Basque Country in Vitoria (Spain), when I had to wait four years to even hear a female artist being mentioned in a class. This only happened during my last year in the university and the artist was, of course, the marvellous Mexican painter Frida Kahlo. Sadly, the absence of women artists in the Art History program did not surprise any of the –mostly– female students of our class. Women artists seemed to have been removed from the academic curriculum, as well as from every manual of art history that was recommended to us as a complement to our studies. The few ones that were mentioned, such as Frida Kahlo, Tamara de Lempicka or Sonia Delaunay, were never studied in depth unlike their male colleagues. They were mostly muses of, wives of, lovers of. Their contributions were dismissed, their circumstances were ignored and their experiences were overlooked.

The second experience occurred when I first arrived in Ireland in 2014 and I had to face a similar situation. When I became familiar with Irish art history, and particularly with the cultural scene of the nineteenth and twentieth centuries, I noticed a connection between the invisibility of women painters and the events of modern Irish history marked by nationalism and Catholicism. I found myself amazed by the difference of discourse between the paintings signed by women and those carried out by men. In their own way, women addressed the changes of their time and combined tradition and modernity, the past and the future, academicism and the European avant-garde. This artwork, developed during the so-called Irish Revival, offered a dialogue between two Irelands and, above all, provided new and unexplored perspectives about the country's recent past, the tumultuous years that led to the foundation of the Irish Free State in 1922 and the transition to a modern Ireland. This book is thus based on the thesis that the specific experiences lived by women during the turn of the century led to the development of a very particular art that proposes another point of view about Irish cultural nationalism. The Revival in particular and Irish culture in general have played (and still do) a key role in Ireland's process of self-definition and in its search of a national identity, especially in the years surrounding the foundation of the Irish Free State. In this journey, the female voice has been systematically silenced by a patriarchal artistic canon developed within a Catholic and nationalist discourse.

Irish nationalism embraced the image of the woman-nation as the main symbol of the fight against the British occupation, and depicted Ireland as a vulnerable damsel in need of the protection of brave Irish men against the British threat. This rhetoric was combined with the processes of colonialism, independence and the reconstruction of the nation – and all of them were played over the female body. As this book will examine, discourses of purity, sexuality, fertility and motherhood were developed by Irish nationalism and the Catholic Church, which decided that Irish women's only duties in society were to give birth to the sons who would fight for Ireland and to raise the daughters who would secure the continuation of the Irish race, the Gael. The control over the female body, both by the State and by the Church, has affected Irish women's lives, experiences and reproductive rights up to the present day. In 1928, only a few years after the foundation of the Irish Free State, a Dublin bookseller was taken to court, prosecuted and fined for selling an obscene book. The book was *Family Limitation*, by Margaret Sanger, sex educator and an advocate of birth control who opened the first clinic issuing contraceptives in the United States. The Criminal Law Amendment Act of 1935, while not forbidding the use of contraception within the Republic of Ireland, prohibited the sale or import of contraceptive devices and pills until 1978. Ireland did not legalise contraception by prescription until 1979, with the passing of the Health (Family Planning) Act. By then, other more progressive European countries had already decriminalised homosexuality, legalised abortion and liberalised the access of unmarried women to contraception.[1] The latter was not fully legalised in Ireland until the passing of the Health (Family Planning) (Amendment) Bill of 1993, when Ireland became the last country in Europe to do so. Ten years earlier, in 1983, the Eight Amendment of the Constitution Act recognised equal status to the life of the mother and the unborn: "The State acknowledges the right to life of the unborn and, with due regard to the equal right to life of the mother, guarantees in its laws to respect and, as far as practicable, by its laws to defend and vindicate that right".[2] The Eighth Amendment forced thousands of Irish women and girls, who could afford it, to travel abroad to get an abortion, mainly Britain. Abortion had first been banned in Ireland in 1861 by the Offences Against the Person Act, still active after Irish independence. In May 2018, Ireland voted 66.4% to 33.6% to remove the Eighth Amendment, with other two million votes cast. The turnout of the referendum (64.5%) was one of the highest ever recorded in Ireland. The referendum bill was signed into law by President Michael D. Higgins in September 2018, becoming the first act to make elective abortion legal in Ireland from January 1st 2019. However, there are still some issues regarding people's access to abortion in Ireland, such as the time limits and a mandatory waiting period, the refusal of medical practitioners to provide abortion services on grounds of conscience, the ambiguity of the Act regarding people's access to abortion after twelve weeks, or the criminalisation of anyone who helps a pregnant person to obtain an abortion outside the provisions of the Act.[3]

The control over the female body became central to the rhetoric of the Irish Revival and the nationalist movement. Influenced by the Victorian ideology of the separate spheres, Irish women were expected to remain in the household and to be passive and quiet, controlled and dominated by others. However, not all women followed the rules: Irish women played a central role both in the private and the public sphere, as well as in the political and cultural events of the nineteenth and twentieth centuries. Many women mentioned in this book were also deeply involved in the nationalist struggle at the turn of the century, which often clashed with their activities within the suffragist movement or their artistic subversion of the nationalist discourse. The implication of women in the social and political struggle was not limited to the upper and middle classes, and it included every social stratum, from the bourgeoisie to the poorest classes of Irish society. Some women had not even been born in Ireland, and not all of them were Catholic: there were Protestants, Quakers, Jewish, and also atheist who collaborated with the cause by organising memory masses, raising funds for the families of the deceased, travelling to England to visit the prisons and speaking out about the injustices committed in their country.[4] Their efforts, however, were ignored once independence was gained. De Valera's 1937 Constitution confined women in the home, banned abortion and divorce, and restricted women's access to the labour market. Subsequently forgotten, these women have only very recently begun to be significantly quoted in the history books. The studies about women's contribution to Irish history, however, are often labelled as "feminist studies", while those events led by men are simply classified as "history". This has favoured the development of a science that merely records past events from a male perspective while ignoring women's experiences, leading to a biased and subjective history that consciously excludes half of the population.

Irish women of the turn of the century witnessed the consequences of the British occupation in Ireland, the rise of nationalism, the War of Independence and the Civil War as well as the creation of the Irish Free State. All these events coexisted with important changes that deeply affected women's lives, such as their incorporation to the workforce, the access to education, the rise of feminism and the right to vote. The critical changes regarding women's place in society that took place in the nineteenth and twentieth centuries came together in the growth of a cultural blast. Women's dilemmas, thoughts and hopes were addressed in painting, sculpture and applied arts. However, female artwork was scarcely valued by Irish historiography and, although the studies about women artists of the Revival are flourishing nowadays, there is still a long way to go. During the twentieth century, the Irish cultural establishment marginalised women artists, a situation that was common to most European countries. As the art historian Linda Nochlin stated, art criticism has perpetuated the concept of "male genius" while describing any skilled female artists as a rare and exceptional figure.[5] This idea only started to be challenged in the 1970s thanks to the efforts of many feminist art historians who worked tirelessly for the gradual recovery of knowledge about the practice of women artists and their contribution to the history of art. In Ireland, this awareness of the female artistic production is particularly significant because of their leading part in the arrival of modern art to the cultural scene. The 1987 exhibition "Irish Women Artists: From the Eighteenth Century to the Present Day" (National Gallery of Ireland and the Douglas Hyde Gallery, Dublin) was the first and, up until today, one of the most important initiatives that aimed to understand the contribution of women artists in modern and contemporary Ireland.[6] This comprehensive exhibition was exhaustively expounded in the catalogue edited by Jenni Rogers, Wanda Rayan-Smolin and Elizabeth Mayes. Another significant show of female artists was Adam's fifth Summer Loan Exhibition entitled "Irish Women Artists 1870–1970", which took place in Dublin in 2014. Amongst the authors that have supported the implementation of a gender perspective in the study of Irish art are the editor James Steward (*When Time Began to Rant and Rage. Figurative Painting from Twentieth-Century Ireland*, 1999), Jeanne Sheehy (*The Rediscovery of Ireland's Past: the Celtic Revival 1830–1930*, 1980), Maria Connolly and Paul Finucane (*Journeys Through Line and Colour: Forty Irish Women of the Twentieth Century*, 2010), Éimear O'Connor (*Irish Women Artists 1800–2009*, 2010), Fintan Cullen (*Sources in Irish Art. A Reader*, 2000), or Síghle Bhreathnach-Lynch, who has examined the importance of landscape art and gender in the construction of an Irish identity (*Art, Nation and Gender. Ethnic Landscapes, Myths and Mother-Figures*, 2003 – with Tricia Cusack; *Ireland's Art, Ireland's History. Representing Ireland, 1845 to Present*, 2007).

The present book examines the contexts, the lives and the artwork of several female artists born before 1900, who studied and worked during the Irish Revival and the years surrounding the foundation of the Irish Free State. Their art cannot be fully understood without taking into consideration their influences, their milieu, and the socio-political events that conditioned their artistic careers. In order to do so, this book has been divided into four chapters that complement each other. The first one, "Brief Overview: History, Art and the Role of Women in Ireland" outlines the influence of the Celtic era and the Middle Ages in the visual arts of the Irish Revival. Following the first Viking raid of Ireland in the ninth century, the constant invasions of the island had important consequences on Irish art. The political and economic instability prevented Ireland from enjoying a continuous and homogeneous aesthetic development. This, however, also paved the way for a rich cultural scene that, during the Irish Revival, embraced many different areas and genres. Irish art at the turn of the century rooted in the Celtic motifs of pre-Christian Ireland, which encouraged the development of Abstract art in the country in the first decades of the twentieth century. Medieval manuscripts and metalwork inspired the stained-glass revival of the nineteenth and twentieth centuries, which emphasised the use of national materials, designs and workforce. Likewise, the structure and ideals of medieval guilds were followed by the many cooperatives founded throughout Ireland in the nineteenth and twentieth centuries. The figures of the three Irish patrons, St. Patrick, St. Colmcille and St. Brigid of Kildare, which combined the Celtic pagan tradition with the Christian faith, also served as an inspiration for women artists in their particular portrayal of the Irish identity.

This first chapter analyses as well the influence of Victorian ideology in the Irish society of the turn of the century. The concept of separate spheres was challenged by the New Woman writing, which led to a change in the concepts of class, gender and nation in Ireland. The nineteenth century witnessed an increasing demand for women's rights regarding education, work and citizenship. The foundation of schools and colleges for women encouraged them to pursue a career and to earn a living, while their access to the workforce and the development of the cottage industries anticipated the development of the Arts and Crafts Revival led by Irish women. Feminist issues such as the suffragist cause or women's control over their own body engaged –and often clashed– with the nationalist struggle. Irish women found themselves compelled to choose between the fight for independence or the vote, between nationalism and feminism. Socio-political dichotomies and dilemmas were often addressed by women artists in their artwork. The political context conditioned both their creative manner and their subject-matters. Their milieu influenced the way in which they pursued their careers as professional women artists in the public sphere and within a male-centred artistic tradition.

Finally, this first chapter examines the importance of early movements such as the Antiquarians or the Gaelic League in the development of the Irish Revival. It addresses the connection between literature and visual arts by offering an overview of the foundation of the Abbey Theatre. Visual arts were highly influenced by literature and theatre, which focused on reversing the negative stereotypes of Ireland and its people. Irish drama developed an idealised vision of the west of Ireland that would inspire artists such as Paul Henry, A.E. Russell, Lilian Lucy Davidson, Jack Yeats and Grace Henry amongst others. Myths and legends were being translated, published and staged, inspiring the paintings and illustrations created by Beatrice Elvery or Constance Markievicz. The collaboration between art and literature in the Revival reached its highest point in the guilds and industries created throughout the country. One of the most influential guilds was the Cuala Industries, founded and managed by the Yeats sisters.

The second chapter, "Irish Women and Art", discusses the female allegories developed by Irish cultural nationalism, which were embraced both by literature and art and became central to the nationalist discourse. These allegories established concepts of motherhood and femininity in relation to the nation and the Irish race, and exposed the secondary place that women occupied in the Irish nation. The processes of colonisation and decolonisation were played over women's bodies, and reinforced gendered notions about women's role in Irish society. The strong influence of the Catholic Church following the foundation of the Irish Free State brought the figure of the Virgin Mary to the spotlight, which alluded to women's sexuality and the State's control over the female body. The beautiful and young peasant women were gradually substituted in the canvas by old and haggard characters, more suitable to the Catholic rhetoric of pure, asexual motherhood. However, as a consequence of the Irish socio-political conflict, these allegories were to be challenged, questioned and replaced. Women artists like Margaret Clarke or Mainie Jellett did not conform to the nationalist imagery that relegated them to the role of passive mothers. Instead, many painters carried out alternative depictions of Mother Ireland, offering a possibility of transgression and liberation inspired on the same nationalist rhetoric that aimed to confine them in the domestic sphere.

This second chapter also expounds the efforts placed by Irish artists to restore a national identity that had been destroyed by the British colonisation. The ideal of the west of Ireland was central in the paintings of the Revival, and served as the background for many scenes by key artists such as Aloysius O'Kelly, Paul Henry, Lilian Lucy Davidson, Grace Henry or Letitia Marion Hamilton. The nationalist rhetoric was faithfully illustrated by Aloysius O'Kelly and Paul Henry through their representations of female peasants, thatched cottages and costumes of the west. Unlike them, William Orpen worked for the redefinition of Irish art. His legacy needs to be addressed, as he left a deep mark in a whole generation of Irish artists, including the women mentioned in this book. Jack B. Yeats became the meeting point between modern art and the spirit of the

Revival. His representation of the nationalist rhetoric was deeply influenced by the writing of John Millington Synge and Irish literature. Subsequently, the chapter addresses the apparent lack of women artists at the turn of the century. Banned from artistic training and life classes, excluded from official exhibitions, disregarded and patronised, women were responsible for the foundation and development of the many amateur clubs that flourished throughout the country. These associations helped to dignify the status of the female, amateur artist and, at the same time, encouraged other women to pursue a career in the arts. The gender discrimination present in the artistic establishment encouraged those who could afford it to travel to the continent, where women enjoyed a more integral artistic training while, at the same time, absorbed the modern trends that they would later bring to Ireland, becoming pioneers of Abstract art in their own country. However, the arrival of the twentieth century took longer in Ireland than elsewhere. Sarah Purser became the first woman to be elected full member of the Royal Hibernian Academy, and this only happened in 1924. It was not until 1950 that the modern trends were accepted in Ireland, and painters like Mainie Jellett had to face the rejection in their own homeland before becoming the leaders of a new artistic era in their own country through initiatives like the Irish Exhibition of Living Art.

The third chapter, "Presence I. Painters", explores the lives and careers of several women artists who depicted in a very personal manner the political and social issues of their time. Beatrice Elvery and Margaret Clarke's paintings and illustrations explored the theme of the Madonna with Child and turned into a unique portrayal of the nationalist rhetoric. Through two very different styles, Lilian Lucy Davidson and Mary Swanzy illustrated the connection between the peasantry and the land. While Davidson spent most of her life in Ireland, Swanzy travelled the world depicting the exotic landscapes of Samoa or Hawaii and remained more distant –if still associated– from Irish subject-matters. Their work addressed the colonial issue from a different perspective, far from the voyeuristic, male-gaze employed by many occidental artists. Constance Markievicz, Kathleen Fox and Estella Frances Solomons depicted the contribution of Irish women to the nationalist cause, which they experienced first-hand. Solomons sheltered nationalist leaders in her studio and portrayed them; Fox wandered the streets of Dublin during the Easter Rising carrying out sketches of the struggle; and Markievicz's cartoons became a depiction of the life of republican women during the war. The arrival of Abstract art in Ireland came by the hand of Mainie Jellett and May Guinness, two pioneer artists who combined Modernism and Irish heritage in a body of work that was initially rejected by the Irish public.

Women's rights –political, social or cultural– were not given, but gained; and even though all these women ended up becoming successful artists, their involvement in the cultural scene was not easy. Some artists, like Margaret Clarke, remained in Ireland and developed a body of work more influenced by the Irish academic tradition than by modern trends. Those who stayed in Ireland were also involved in the foundation of diverse associations as an alternative to male-only artistic circles; they supported women's artistic practice, campaigned for women's access to higher education and fought for a deeper understanding of Irish art and its diverse nature. Those who could afford it travelled to countries like France or Belgium, where they had access to a more complete artistic training and could attend life-drawing classes. Most of the artists examined in this book belong to this second category, and also share a well-off Anglo-Irish Protestant background except for Estella Solomons –who was born to a Jewish family– or Lilian Lucy Davidson –who came from a more humble family that led her to portray the harsh conditions of the inhabitants of the west coast of Ireland. None of those who travelled lost sight of their Irish roots during their time abroad. When they returned to Ireland, they brought with them the European modern trends, which they combined with Irish subject-matters and a nationalist spirit, developing a new concept of what national art should point to. They became leaders of modern art and the Avant-Garde in Ireland, and their work represented an inflection point in the history of Irish art.

The fourth chapter, "Presence II. The Arts and Crafts", explores the influence of the English Arts and Crafts movement on Irish applied art, and the peculiarities of the movement in Ireland. Studies about the Irish Revival still focus, to a great extent, on literary work; indeed, poetry and drama were the preferred vehicles for the expression of nationalist ideas. However, visual arts were also paramount in the evolution of the Cultural Revival, and so their recognition has become a necessity in order to gain a better picture of what the Irish Revival truly meant. Important studies about the impact of Irish applied art at the turn of the century have been carried out by Jeanne Sheehy (the aforementioned *Rediscovery of Ireland's Past: the Celtic Revival, 1830–1930* is a major study on the influence of the arts in the Revival and vice versa), Paul Larmour (*The Arts and Crafts Movement in Ireland*, 1992), Nicola Gordon Bowe (*The Life and Work of Harry Clarke*, 1994; *The Arts and Crafts Movements in Dublin and Edinburgh, 1885–1925*, 1998, with Elizabeth Cumming; *Wilhelmina Geddes: Life and Work*, 2015) and more recently Vera Kreilkamp (*The Arts and Crafts Movement: Making it Irish*, 2016). Fine arts, and particularly easel painting, were mistrusted due to their association to the British colonial culture. Applied arts, on the other hand, already had a tradition in Ireland, and soon became the visual means of expression of the nationalist rhetoric within the visual arts. Even though the Irish Arts and Crafts movement was deeply inspired by the same movement born and developed in England, in Ireland it became closely associated with national identity and the political struggle. As applied arts were considered a minor category within the artistic hierarchy and a more "feminine" field, once again women were responsible for the growth of a pivotal and highly influential movement in the history of Irish art. Inspired by the Home Industries, many Irish women founded and directed countless projects and enterprises associated with the Arts and Crafts that enriched the artistic scene while, at the same time, creating job opportunities for working-class women who needed to earn a living. This chapter addresses two artistic adventures led by Irish women who, through their own guilds, encouraged a taste for Irish heritage, educated other women and offered them the opportunity to pursue a professional career. These two initiatives are the Dun Emer Guild and Cuala Industries run by the Yeats Sisters and Evelyn Gleeson– and Sarah Purser's An Túr Gloine, a stained-glass cooperative studio.

The body of work of all these female artists –painters, illustrators or craftswomen– is part of Ireland's legacy, a testimony of experiences that have only started to be taken into account very recently. All of them carried out a quiet but critical revolution in every aspect of Irish art. Most of them took part in the foundation of the Hugh Lane Gallery of Modern Art in Dublin –paramount in the arrival of modernism in Ireland– and advocated a new direction in Irish art. But, most importantly, their genuine portrayal of the socio-political context set an example for the following generations. Pioneers, strong and independent, they confronted the conservative society that wanted them absent from the public sphere. They subverted the history of their own country, their past and their present in order to build their future. This book is a modest effort to recognise their presence, and to recover a little part of a lost memory.

# NOTES

1. Brian Girvin, "An Irish Solution to an Irish Problem: Catholicism, Contraception and Change, 1922–1979", *Contemporary European History,* University of Glasgow, 27, no. 1 (2018): 1–22.

2. "Eighth Amendment of the Constitution Act 1983", Irish Statute Book, accessed on April 29th 2020, http://www.irishstatutebook.ie/eli/1983/ca/8/schedule/enacted/en/html

3. "Abortion law in Ireland", Abortion Rights Campaign, 2019,accessed on April 29th 2020, https://www.abortionrightscampaign.ie/abortion-law-in-ireland/

4. Sinead McCoole, *No Ordinary Women. Irish Female Activists in the Revolutionary Years, 1900–1923.* (Dublin: O'Brien Press, 2015), 17.

5. Linda Nochlin, "Why have there been no great women artists?" In *Women, Art and Other Essays,* ed. Linda Nochlin (London: Thames and Hudson, 1989), 145–177.

6. Katy Deepwell, *Dialogues: Women Artists from Ireland* (London and New York: IB Tauris, 2005), 4.

# Part One

# Brief Overview: History, Art and the Role of Women in Ireland

The visual arts of the Irish Revival cannot be understood without taking into consideration certain elements that paved the way for the rise of the cultural revolution that took place between 1830 and 1930. The first one is Ireland's insularity and its distance from the continent which, along with its mountains and stunning cliffs, complicated the access to the island in the past. This led to a rich Celtic culture that became the base for the visual arts of the Irish Revival.

The Celts arrived in Britain and Ireland around 500BC and, within a few hundred years, Ireland's Bronze Age had disappeared giving way to the Iron Age and La Tène culture, which is often regarded as characteristic of Celtic society and the cultural foundation of Celtic Ireland.[1] However, one must not forget that both the Neolithic and the Bronze Age in Ireland were also highly developed cultures, and that the Celts also absorbed the influences of the non-Celtic and non-Indo-European societies that had settled in Ireland before their arrival.[2] The Irish language was likewise shaped by pre-Celtic languages, and major Celtic sacred sites were cult centres long before the coming of the Celts. One notable example is the Hill of Tara, one of the richest archaeological sites in Ireland which holds monuments from the late Neolithic and Bronze Age. According to the legends, the High Kings of the pre-Norman period of Ireland were crowned on top of the stone pillar called the *Lia Fáil* (the Stone of Destiny). The idea of the High Kings of Ireland being chosen by the gods in the sacral place of Tara became a recurring theme in Irish mythology, one of the main subject-matters in the literature and the visual arts of the Revival. The goddesses of fertility and sovereignty, Medb and Eithne, represented the female aspect of the Kingship of Tara. The site held ceremonies of sacral kingship represented by the symbolic union between the king and the Goddess of Sovereignty, whose blessings ensured the prosperity of the reign, the people and the land. The role of women in Celtic societies, the power of Celtic goddesses in mythology, and the connection between the female and the land were also addressed by the female artists of the Revival, who through their art questioned the Victorian notions about femininity, womanhood and a woman's place in the Irish contemporary society. Because of its connection with Celtic mythology and with a past free from British colonisation, sacred places like the Hill of Tara became the base for the development of a landscape art in the Revival that linked nationalism with the land and with antiquities.[3]

Although there is archaeological evidence of contact between Ireland and the Roman Empire, its extent remains still controversial.[4] Even though the influences of Britain, the Roman Empire and the Christian culture brought important changes to the country, the absence of Roman invasions in Ireland allowed the survival of native languages and cultures that in other countries had disappeared due to their Romanisation. The Celtic artistic legacy also gives an idea of the values, beliefs and structure of their societies. Metalwork in bronze, precious metals or iron served as the inspiration for the stained-glass Revival and also for the development of Abstract art in Ireland. Although examples of Celtic art in Ireland prior to the fifth century are scarce, almost all Celtic remains from the sixth century onwards can be found in Ireland and northern Scotland. Earlier art was presumed to be secular, while during the beginning of the Medieval period it became deeply influenced by the Christian faith. The two main figures who brought Christianity to Ireland were Palladius in the South, and St. Patrick, who was mainly active in the north. The conversion of the Irish to Christianity was a slow and complex process that had started with several Christian communities in 431, when Palladius was appointed first bishop of Ireland.[5] The missionary church developed with relative ease and, by the sixth century, Christianity had been embraced by the Irish learned classes, although a great deal of pagan belief survived into the Middle Ages and afterwards. Irish Christianity evidenced a Celtic influence personified in the figure of St. Colmcille and St. Brigid of Kildare, whose monastery and cathedral were amongst the most popular pilgrimage centres in Ireland until at least the twelfth century.

Often compared to the Virgin Mary and known as the Mary of the *Gael*,[6] St. Brigid became an important figure in the imagery of the Irish Revival. In the work of artists such as Margaret Clarke (*Mary and Brigid*, 1917) or Mainie Jellett (*The Virgin of Éire*, 1940s), St. Brigid's connection with the Celtic goddess Brí served to illustrate the pre-Christian culture in which women played active socio-political roles. They were included in political and religious life and had more privileges regarding marriage and divorce than women of Greek, Roman and other societies. The roles of men and women were not based on the superiority of one sex over the other, but offered a more equalitarian reasoning. They held a better position in society and enjoyed more freedom and protection under the law.[7] While the Roman law dictated that, through marriage, a woman became her husband's property, Celtic societies considered marriage a partnership between a man and a woman. Texts written by Latin and Greek authors stated that Celtic women had the right to choose their husbands, and they could not be married without their consent. The dowry system was different depending on the Celtic groups, but both husband and wife were expected to contribute to the marriage with an equal sum and, in case of divorce, each of them got their original contributions back, as well as its profits. This economic independence protected women in event of a divorce or a husband's death. In Celtic communities, women also served as rulers and diplomats, druids, priestesses, poets and healers, and did not need their husband's consent to conduct business. But, despite all this, we must not forget that the Irish Celtic structure was undoubtedly a patriarchal one and that, with a few exceptions, queens generally ruled only as the wives of kings. The rulers of the *tuath* (tribes) were men who, for the most part, had the ultimate power in politics and the household. Women worked with men in the fields and in the farms, wove the wool and sewed clothes and linens. According to medieval laws, the daughters of kings should be taught sewing and weaving, two of the most valuable jobs for a woman. And, ironically, needlework became one of the most preferred crafts of the Irish Revival amongst those artists and businesswomen who spoke out about their wishes and their roles in society. In Celtic cultures, only motherhood was above the needle, for kinship was the basis of Irish society.[8] Indeed, this emphasis on family, motherhood, kinship and race was to become a key feature in Irish society, particularly in the nationalist rhetoric of the turn of the century.

The combination between Celtic tradition and Christian beliefs resulted in a flourishing culture that appointed Ireland as the centre of spirituality during the early Middle Ages. This was a key feature of the visual arts of the Irish Revival, which focused on the Celtic aspect of Irish Catholicism and combined Christian subject-matters with Celtic designs and spirituality (e.g. *Decoration*, by Mainie Jellett, 1923). Celtic structures were absorbed by Irish Christianity, which focused on monasticism and led to the foundation of important culture centres that replaced the druidic schools.[9] Ireland became a conservatory of language, literature and Celtic art. Irish art, centre-less during its pre-Christian period, was now to be unified and redirected. Through this new guidance, Irish culture flourished and survived another five hundred years. During this time too, Ireland witnessed the creation of three works that went on to become key in the artistic scene of the Irish Revival: the Book of Kells, the Tara Brooch and the Ardagh Chalice. The Book of Kells is now undoubtedly one of the main achievements of Irish Celtic art, an illuminated manuscript of the Four Gospels in Latin of the New Testament and dated from the second half of the eighth century. It has been associated to St. Columcille and his large monastic confederation in the island of Iona, Scotland. When the monastery was raided by the Vikings during the first years of the ninth century, the monks travelled to Kells (Co. Meath), where the manuscript was probably finished. Made from vellum (calf skin) and meticulously painted by hand, the illustrations contained in the manuscript were used as an alternative form of narration. On each page, the first letter is bigger than the rest, carefully and brightly decorated with the distinctive patterns of Celtic art, and some of them have also been transformed into different objects. Figures from the Celtic bestiary and spirals embellish the pages painted in a great range of colours, including different tones of mauve, yellow, blue, green and red. The Book of Kells created a portrait of the entire cosmos and offered a symbol of the connection between the divine and nature by bringing humanity to the centre of the attention.[10] Both aesthetically and symbolically, the Book had an important influence on stained-glass artists such as Harry Clarke and even on textiles, as displayed on the Honan Chapel in Cork.[11] The Book also inspired the fine arts of the Revival, especially on those artists who, influenced by European Modernism, explored Cubism and Abstract art. One of them was the aforementioned Mainie Jellett (1897–1944) who, in her essay "A Word on Irish Art" (1942), wrote:

> The similarity of ideals between much present-day non-realistic art and the Celtic art of the Book of Kells, the metal work and the High Crosses is very striking. The sense of filling and decorating a given space rhythmically and harmoniously, one of the first principles of Cubist painting and subsequent non-realistic schools, is clearly shown in Irish work. The forms are all enclosed and held within the limits of their outside shape; there is a wonderful play of interlaced rhythmically-organised movement running through all. The realism, if any, is secondary to the element of form considered in pure relation of one shape to another.[12]

The second item, the Ardagh Chalice, dates from the eighth century and it is considered one of the finest examples of Irish metalwork. Even though it is clearly influenced by Roman tableware, its method of construction is Irish.[13] Despite its plain design, the chalice is delicately adorned with designs of the Cross as well as with the names of the Apostles engraved in the silver. The decorative panels offer geometrical designs and animal decorations, characteristics of Celtic art of La Tène. Its pattern of spirals, zig-zags and basic forms follows the contour of the area to be decorated, which is characteristic of early Celtic art. The third item, the Tara Brooch, was as well created during the eighth century, a time that has been proved to be a high point in Irish medieval craftsmanship. This penannular brooch has often been compared in its artistic quality to the Ardagh Chalice, and it is considered the finest secular metalwork of the period in Ireland. Although the brooch has been seen as particularly Irish –it is indeed close in style to the Ardagh Chalice– and has exerted a strong influence in the arts and designs of nineteenth and twentieth century Irish art, its design is basically Roman.[14] A recurrent element of this masterpiece is the triskele, a triple spiral used in symbolic places and for important figures of Celtic society. The rediscovery of the Tara Brooch and the Ardagh Chalice during the nineteenth century was an important step in the development of a national culture based on Ireland's past. Round towers, Celtic crosses, metalwork and manuscripts provided new symbols for the emerging Irish national identity that would influence both the fine arts as well as the Irish Arts and Crafts movement, thanks to the early work carried out by the antiquarians.

However, the conditions that allowed Ireland to flourish artistically and to become one of the hearts of Classical and Christian culture were soon to be replaced by anxieties and war. Following the arrival of the Vikings in the 795, Ireland's political weakness and the eternal rivalry between the different kings allowed constant invasions until the first years of the eleventh century. Culture and art declined, but the invasions were not sufficient to destroy Irish art, which survived especially through the Celtic High Crosses, Ireland's main sculptural contribution to the history of art. Following the Anglo-Norman invasion, Irish art suffered the consequences of the introduction of Romanesque and Gothic art through the arrival of Benedictine and Cistercian monks, who adapted the Irish Church to the Roman Tradition and made considerable changes in the Irish artistic direction.[15] Due to the instability, the Irish society did not have the conditions nor the means for the development of the arts, which eventually became a Protestant domain.[16] The colonisation isolated Ireland and deprived it from the influence of the Renaissance art. Both Gaelic and Catholic traditions perished. Nationalism became stronger following the campaigns for the rights of the Catholics at the end of the eighteenth century, and the mid-nineteenth century witnessed the creation of a pivotal organisation in the development of the Revival: Young Ireland, a nationalist cultural and social movement led by Thomas Davis, Charles Gavan Duffy, John Mitchell and John Blake Dillon. The founder members also edited a newspaper called *The Nation*, which became the voice of the organisation. Inspired by other European nationalist movements, they projected their own vision of a united Ireland built on its religious and ethnic diversity –the Young Irelanders came from both Protestant and Catholic backgrounds– as well as on the Gaelic tradition. In July 1848 they carried out an armed rebellion, which ended tragically with two of the insurgents killed few days later. Its legacy, however, resided in its romantic idea of nationalism and its use of Ireland's cultural past as well as contemporary art for political ends.

## Two Separate Spheres

In her essay "Is Female to Male as Nature is to Culture?" (1974), Sherry B. Ortner questions the universal conditions and structures that have led every culture to give women a second-class status within every society.[17] Her dissertation –one of the seminal works in feminist academic anthropology– explains how female subjugation has been common to all cultures, yet diverse and at different levels. Evidence for this statement can be found in elements of cultural ideology that explicitly devalue women and their roles, functions, products and social context, as well as in symbolic elements or socio-political structures that exclude women from the highest levels of powers in a community. According to Ortner, behind this universality of female subjugation we find that every society has identified women with a concept that has also been devalued in and by every culture, for being considered less than culture itself: nature. While women are associated to nature, men are identified with culture, which claims to be superior because of its ability to *transform* nature and turn it to its purposes. Women have thus been confined in the domestic context of the family, a private sphere that has contributed to exclude them from the cultural milieu because of their constant association with children and the notion that this sphere is opposed to the public entity (society). The universality of female subordination indicates the complexity of the problem and the depth of its roots.

Irish women of the turn of the century were still judged by the theory of the separate spheres developed during the Victorian era, which also affected women's experiences throughout the twentieth century. The feminine ideal in Victorian society was addressed by Coventry Patmore in his narrative poem entitled *The Angel in the House* (1854). The image of an ideal chaste woman who gladly conforms to her duties within the private sphere goes back to the age of Enlightenment, when reason was seen as a universal category free from desire and passion. Two separate spheres were established: the private (nature) and the public (the political realm). Women's exclusion from the public domain meant that the rights of citizenship were controlled by men, who disqualified women from political life. Women were denied the status of full citizenship and, in many Western countries, they remained "second class citizens" who lacked political and civil rights until the twentieth century. However, the American and the French revolutions had also opened up new ideas about politics and the role of the individual within the state, and the eighteenth century witnessed the beginning of new discussions about women's rights and their place in society. Although writing was considered a potentially subversive activity for women during the eighteenth and nineteenth centuries, many early feminist female authors criticised gender inequality through their work. In 1791, Olympe de Gouges (1748–1793) published her *Declaration of the Rights of Woman and of the Female Citizen* as an answer to the 1789 *Declaration of the Rights of Man and of the Citizen* set by the French National Constituent Assembly in 1789. The first article asserted that women are equal to men in every aspect of both private and public life, and they were thus entitled to the same citizenship rights: "Woman is born free and remains equal to man in rights. Social distinctions may only be based on common utility". De Gouge's manifesto condemned that the French Revolution had forgotten about women's participation in the struggle, and urged women to take action in order to remedy those injustices committed against them. Because of her feminist agenda and her writings on slavery, she became one of the first individuals who supported a wider respect for the rights of all humans.[18]

While Olympe de Gouges fought for the rights of women in France, Mary Wollstonecraft (1759–1797) did the same in England. Her *Vindication of the Rights of Woman* (1792) was a revolutionary work of literature which still has influence in contemporary feminism and in the fight for human rights nowadays. In this document, Wollstonecraft advocated for women's right to education and reclaimed it as the main way for a woman to become financially independent and on an equal footing to men. An improved education, she stated, would allow women to be also capable workers in diverse professions. The difference between Wollstonecraft's *Vindication* and other early feminist writings lied in her idea that an improvement in women's status would benefit the entire society. Sadly, her legacy lost strength with the eruption of the Romantic movement and following her husband Godwin's publication of a controversial memoir after her death.[19] During this very same century, Romanticism stated that female inferiority was based on natural and biological reasons. Once again, women were reduced to the mere condition of female, passionate and non-rational beings whose only duties in society were to get married and bear children.

Nevertheless, the call for a new role for women developed by authors like De Gouges or Wollstonecraft made an impression in French and British societies; also in Ireland, although here female public visibility was strongly shaped by patriotism and there was not much concern with women's rights. However, feminist ideas were discussed in the country during the eighteenth century, both in private as well as in the press to a limited extent.[20] The concept of the separate spheres was confronted by the figure of the New Woman, a feminist ideal that developed during the nineteenth century. The Woman Question, addressed by Mary Wollstonecraft in her *Vindication of the Rights of Woman*, had a deep effect in Victorian feminists in England, such as the author Harriet Martineau, and suffragettes like Millicent Garrett Fawcett, one of the leading figures of the National Union of Women's Suffrage Societies. There were also several Irish editions of Wollstonecraft's *Vindication*, and her work was known to some Irish women at the time. One of them was the author Maria Edgeworth (1767–1849), who also advocated education for girls. In her writings, she criticised the mismanagement of the estates and the abuse carried out by the Ascendancy landlords in Ireland. Issues like nationalism, gender and race are also explored in other works such as Belinda (1801), *Essays on Irish Bulls* (1802), or *The Grateful Negro* (1804). Her work is an example of how, in nineteenth and twentieth-century Ireland, the fight for women's rights overlapped with other struggles such as the Land War or the Home Rule, the Anglo-Irish War and the War of Independence. During this time, the Western countries had witnessed the development of the ideas and practices of citizenship, but universal suffrage only allowed men to vote, and citizenship was masculine in its origins. Democracy has also been a gendered term throughout history, and thus it is not surprising that revolutions, struggles for national independence and social movements went on to become one of the main vehicles in the fight for women's rights.

The issues examined by Wollstonecraft and Edgeworth were also addressed by the Irish writer Sarah Grand (1854–1943) in her article "The New Aspect of the Woman Question", published in 1894. In this article Grand used the concept of the New Woman referring to a whole generation of women that confronted the ideal of the Angel in the House by demanding the vote, advocating social reform and working in the public sphere. She protested against the hypocrisy of the Victorian society that demanded women to be virtuous while overlooking the moral of their male counterparts. Grand was as well expelled from the Royal Naval School where she was studying for leading groups that supported Josephine Butler's protests against the Contagious Diseases Acts of the 1860s through the Ladies' National Association (LNA). Her status and career as a professional writer were already a statement to the Victorian society in which she grew up: she did not conform to remain in the private domain and, instead, she decided to explore her context and develop her ideas through literature.[21] According to Sally Ledger, the New Woman was "variously, a feminist activist, a social reformer, a popular novelist, a suffragette playwright, a woman poet; she was also a fictional construct, a discursive response to the activities of the late nineteenth-century women's movement".[22] The term New Woman, although first used by Sarah Grand, was popularised by the author Henry James to refer to all those women who, like the Irish artists explored in this book, received an education, attended university and challenged the patriarchal roles of their world. The New Woman shared its context with issues like socialism, imperialism, anti-colonialism and Darwin's theories of evolution, and was influenced by all of them.[23] Indeed, the nineteenth century was a period of great changes in which the concepts of sexuality, gender and homosexuality were being discussed and women began to speak out about their own desire. Embracing art and reality, the New Woman Fiction in literature addressed themes such as marriage, maternity and education by the hand of authors such as Maria Edgeworth or Elizabeth Barrett.

Tina O'Toole has observed that the hybrid national identity of Irish New Woman writers like Sarah Grand was crucial in challenging normative constructions of gender at the turn of the century.[24] Their writing was preceded by other subversive movements led by Irish women such as the Match Girls who, tired of the poor working conditions in the Bryant and May match factory in London, carried out a successful three-week strike in 1888. The Match Girls Strike followed the steps of the Ladies' Land League driven by Anna Parnell in the early 1880s, a "radical opening up of the political sphere to nationalist women".[25] Both movements provided role models for the emerging figure of the New Woman in the writing of Irish authors like Sarah Grand, George Egerton, L.T. Meade, Hannah Lynch or Katherine Cecil Thurston. Religious issues and important events such as the Great Famine inspired their perspective on the

New Woman themes which, eventually, led these authors to create subversive modes of femininity and to address nationalist concerns through their writing. The Land War fiction of George Moore and Rose Mulholland offered a new depiction of women's involvement in the nationalist struggle, and the influence of Anna Parnell in the work of Hanna Lynch provide role new role models for the new generations of feminists. Their writing led to a change in the concepts of, class, gender, sex and also nation. The Irishness of these New Woman writers and the nationalist context were pivotal in the subversion of hegemonic discourses, and encouraged them to question the nationalist rhetoric about motherhood, family and sexuality in novels whose main characters, resembling the Match Girl and the Land League woman, were influenced by feminist ideas, spoke out about their rights and were willing to fight for them.

Even though very few women of this new generation rejected marriage and motherhood completely, the New Woman was opposed by the conservative members of the society and the churches, who considered them degenerate and immoral. Conservative literature and visual culture proposed a war of sexes where women were portrayed as destructive and evil. The New Woman was also criticised by some feminists and suffragettes who claimed that this new generation had no interest in politics or education, only in pleasure and entertainment. They were associated to the Decadent movement, an artistic and literary trend developed in France in the late nineteenth century that had Oscar Wilde as its main figure in England and Ireland. During his time as editor of the *Woman's World* between 1887 and 1889, Wilde requested articles on "higher education, women's careers, suffrage, the status of women in society, dress reform, the history of women, and the notable women of the past, including prominent Sapphists".[26] But, with the decline of the Decadent movement and following Oscar Wilde's sentence for "gross indecency", the figures of the New Woman and the Dandy also weakened.[27] However, its legacy continued throughout the twentieth century. More and more women avoided marriage or decided to get married at a later age. They placed their education first, fought for women's suffrage and became professionals who worked outside the home. They also supported the military effort in the First World War, a contribution that was ignored once the war was over and women were asked to return to their duties in the household. But the seed had been planted, and things were about to change rapidly in the next decades.

The implementation of the Irish National School System in 1831 was a response to the different socio-political factors in Ireland such as the widespread poverty or the struggles of the British Empire to control its closest colony. It also aimed to prevent religious denominations from using the schools to their advantage and from influencing the future generations with their own faith.[28] However, the possibility of using education as an agent of assimilation, politicisation and implementation of colonial values in order to make Ireland more easily governable led to the development of alternatives to the fee-paying illegal Hedge Schools and philanthropic initiatives. Established by the British Government in 1831, National Schools were originally multi-denominational, but the timing coincided with the rise of power of the Catholic Church and with the 1829 Catholic Emancipation. Soon, the majority of the schools under the Irish National System were run by and for Catholics, and they offered an education based on strict gender roles.[29] The Irish national education followed the Victorian ideal of women relegated to the private sphere, confined in the home and expected to devote their lives to the care of their husbands and children. Women's intellectual skills were said to have a lower development capacity, and only Primary education was open for both boys and girls. Women of middle and upper-class background were not expected to focus on work or a career, and female domestic duties would not require further knowledge.[30]

The nineteenth century witnessed great changes regarding women's education, mainly because the struggle of unemployed women, the expansion of convent schools and several campaigns for reform led by female activists. The fight for improvement on the education of middle-class girls was directed by women of Protestant backgrounds, and started in England with the foundation of the Queen's Institute in London in 1841, which aimed to offer a better education to the governesses and improve their status. Following the path started in London, Anna Jellicoe founded the Queen's Institute in Dublin in 1861. In the decades following the Famine, the number of single women with limited income and in need of a career had increased, and the Queen's Institute focused on providing Irish women with technical training so they could undertake paid employment. However, many middle-class women who attended the Queen's Institute lacked the most rudimentary education, and also the range of careers suitable for genteel women was very restricted.[31] As a result, the scope of the project was always very limited. In 1866, the Alexandra College in Dublin was created "for the sound and liberal education of gentlewomen".[32] With the support of Trinity College, Alexandra College focused on a more academic education and became the first university-style institution for Irish women with a view to sitting university examinations. The Intermediate Education Act of 1878 was an important turning point in improving educational standards in order to provide a good basis for university education. It set up a system in which schools were financed according to the students' success in their examinations. Initially, this act aimed only at boys, but the canvassing led by the Belfast Ladies' Institute ensured that women would also benefit from it. The system improved the finances of female schools and, most importantly, proved that girls could also obtain high academic results and benefit from higher education.

The second stage in the reform of women's high education came also by the hand of the Protestant with the passing of the Royal University Act of 1879. The act dissolved the Queen's University and replaced it with the examining board of the Royal University of Ireland, which offered degrees to every individual who passed its examinations. However, while university degrees were now potentially granted to both men and women, the reality was very different. The Intermediate Education Act and the Royal University Act had been passed within a year of each other, and it took several years to implement the reforms in girls' schools so they could take the university examinations. The number of women obtaining degrees was small and they also had to face much greater opposition. Trinity College did not accept women in its ranks until 1904, becoming the last university in Ireland to do so.[33] In order to take advantage of the changes in education, women had to seek private tuition and they thus needed economic resources. The content of the education offered to girls and women did not change excessively either, and the subjects were still related to domestic duties and the private sphere. Even when universities opened their lectures to women, they were deliberately excluded from the corporate aspects of college. Although female illiteracy decreased over the century, women's education only reinforced the Victorian ideal of the "angel in the house", and they were still expected to put their careers aside to become wives and mothers. Yet, the achievements paved the way for the change of women's role within Irish society. The success of female students in the exams of institutions like the Royal University wrecked the conservative idea that women were not biologically suited to receive the same education as men. Many women who obtained a degree came from a middle-class background and pursued arts, an area considered particularly suited to the female character, which in part explains the high female participation in the visual arts of the Irish Revival. Many women focused on teaching, and influenced a whole generation of artists. Others went on to carry a revolution within the cultural scene of the turn of the century.

As well as their intellectual capacities, women's workforce was less valued than men's labour during the nineteenth and twentieth centuries. However, female employment was often essential in the domestic economy. Traditional gender roles limited the areas of employment middle-class women could access to. Generally, women from more prosperous middle and upper-class backgrounds did not have to contribute to the family income or to the domestic duties. Those who were forced to support themselves focused on teaching, governessing and nursing. In the pre-industrial period, women's labour was divided in three main areas: the work in the farm, domestic service and, especially, the textile industry, which became an important supplement to the domestic economy in pre-Famine Ireland and even at the turn of the century, when it still remained a major form of employment.[34] Factory work mostly concentrated in the spinning mills, and the linen industry became Ireland's main manufacturing industry in the eighteenth century. This also encouraged a great interest in embroidery, printing, fine cambric and thread making. They employed only a minority of women who were often marginalised and seen as temporary workers, for they were expected to get married, have kids and focus on domestic duties. Necessity led low-class women to take up jobs at extremely low wages, and female work became synonymous with low status and low wage occupations.[35] By 1900, the pre-Famine economic structure of working in the home in order to earn an income survived only amongst the craft workers, a fundamental factor in the growth of the Arts and Crafts movement addressed in the fourth chapter of this book entitled "Presence II. The Arts and Crafts". However, the female members of the families often worked anonymously: the census did not reflect their true level of participation in the workforce, and a woman's money was considered an asset to the family earnings. This created a biased reality of the female role within the workforce and distorted their contribution to the Irish economy.

The solitary and seasonal employments available for women, along with the low level of political consciousness, made it difficult for women to organise themselves into trade unions during the nineteenth century.[36] Women did, however, fight for the improvement of their conditions on several occasions, often with the help of middle-class feminists but also on their own.[37] The Irish National Teachers' Organisation –the oldest "white collar" or professional union–[38] represented women national school teachers since its foundation in 1868. However, female concerns were always relegated to a second category when there was a conflict of interest such as the Marriage Bar, which obliged women national teachers to retire on marriage between 1933 until its abolition in 1973. The Irish women Workers' Union was established in 1911 as a sister organisation to the Irish Transport and General Workers' Union with Delia Larkin as its first general secretary. Amongst those who attended the IWWU's first meeting was Constance Markievicz, who stated that the union "would not only give women a greater voice in the workplace, but would also help to win them the vote and improve their status in society".[39] The union wished to improve the situation of working-class women, but did not unconditionally support equal pay or the right of married woman to work. Helping working-class women through the trade unions was not a fight for the right of women to full citizenship, but an act of charity in a time when philanthropy had become an essential part of middle-class women.

In the second half of the nineteenth century women had begun to play an important role in public life. Philanthropy had become the principal –although unpaid– occupation of many middle-class Irish women in the nineteenth century. Through their work in these societies, women gained a wider sense of identity and community, which encouraged them to help the poor and the disadvantaged. They did not content with being mere helpers in male-run societies, and proved to be capable of organising committees, raising funds, writing reports and working as accountants. Their contribution in charitable work brought many women to a higher awareness about social injustices, and encouraged them to claim their right to take part in the political process as the only alternative in the creation of a better society for everyone. Nineteenth-century Irish political organisations such as the Irish Republican Brotherhood or Young Ireland rarely accepted female participation within their ranks. The structures of these organisations were based on traditional gender concepts;

specific roles were assigned for both men and women, and the latter were often subordinated to their male companions. Nevertheless, women were always involved in politics, in one way or another. They took part in riots during election times, played a part in secret agrarian societies and worked for nationalist organisations as couriers, providing safe houses for those on the run or raising funds for the cause even outside Ireland.[40] Aware of the fact that they would not be allowed to participate publicly in politics, they also founded their own political organisations and played an essential role in the development of a national sense of identity in Ireland.

The first time Irish women became formally involved in nationalist politics was through the foundation of the Ladies' Land League,[41] set up in 1881 by Anna Parnell thanks to the mediation of Michael Davitt, founder of the Land League and secretary of the Irish Republican Brotherhood. Both Anna and her sister Fanny supported their brother's involvement in the Land League movement. However, at the height of the Land War in 1880, the Land League was banned and the government imprisoned most of its leaders. Charles Parnell and Michael Davitt were amongst them. The Ladies' Land League led by Anna Parnell took over their work, encouraged country women and men to be active in withholding the rent, supported boycotts, provided accommodation for evicted tenants and held public meetings that often turned into direct action in order to stop the evictions. They also edited and distributed the weekly newspaper *United Ireland*, running the press themselves when the male staff remained imprisoned. The radicalisation of the Ladies' Land League caused its persecution in December 1881, when the organisation was banned and some of its members were jailed. Charles Parnell had been doubtful about the creation of the Ladies' Land League from the very beginning and he dismantled both the Land League and the Ladies' on his release in May 1882. However, they Ladies' Land League also found support in some of the key figures of the Land League movement such as Michael Davitt or Andrew Kettle. According to Tina O'Toole, "through the interaction of Anna Parnell's public speeches, along with her contemporary journalism, and that of other members of the Ladies' Land League, a discursive space was created within which Irish women could openly address issues of national politics and public affairs".[42]

At the turn of the century, nationalist women found a unique leader in the figure of Maud Gonne (1866–1953). A lifelong political activist, Maud Gone opposed the Anglo-Irish Treaty, was active in the Women's Prisoners Defense League and created the female nationalist organisation Inghinidhe na hÉireann (Daughters of Erin) in 1900, which had a specific cultural purpose. Even though Inghinidhe na hÉireann barely lasted fourteen years, it proved to be ahead of its time by influencing both women and men, and by canvassing for the Irish cause years before the foundation of Sinn Féin by Arthur Griffith in 1905. The organisation supported women's suffrage, but it prioritised the Irish independence and objected to the vote being granted by a "hostile parliament".[43]

The members focused on restoring national customs, culture, language and Irish-manufactured goods. They also supported the access of lower-class children to education, aware of the fact that these boys had traditionally provided recruits for the British Army.[44] Inghinidhe founded schools were children of the poor classes were taught Irish history and language, subjects that were not part of the curriculum in the government schools of the time. They wished to "combat in every way the English influence" which was "doing so much injury to the artistic taste and refinement of the Irish people".[45] They founded a small drama company which recreated events of Irish history, song or legends, and in 1902 they subsidised a play written by W.B. Yeats and Lady Augusta Gregory, *Cathleen ni Houlihan*, a pivotal play in Irish theatre that deeply influenced the Rising and its leaders. The play, set in the Irish Rebellion of 1798, tells the story of an old woman dressed in an old cloak who laments that her "four green fields –the four provinces of Ireland: Ulster, Munster, Leinster and Connaught– have been taken away from her. She exhorts a young man to give his life for the love of his country and she is reborn as a young and beautiful queen for him. Inghinidhe's newspaper, *Bean na hÉireann* (Woman of Ireland), also published designs and articles by Constance Markievicz, one of the most committed members of the organisation and whose illustrations matched the newspaper's motto of "militancy, separatism and feminism".[46] Like Markievicz, many of the prominent women of the nationalist movement such as Helena Molony, Louise Gavan or Grace Gifford started off in Inghinidhe na hÉireann.

In 1913, the Ulster Volunteers were preparing themselves to resist the Home Rule Bill while the Irish Volunteers gathered strength to counter the British force. The republican paper *Irish Freedom* claimed that "there is nothing unwomanly in active patriotism",[47] but the inaugural meeting of the Irish Volunteers made clear, one more time, that women would not participate on equal terms as men.[48] Cumann na mBan (The League of Women) was set up as the women's auxiliary part to the Irish Volunteers in order to help revolutionary men throughout the war and the first years of the Free State. While many working-class women joined Inghinidhe na hÉireann, Cumann na mBan was mainly formed by middle-class and professional females. The founding member Agnes O'Farrelly claimed in her inaugural speech that "each rifle we put in their hand will represent to us a bolt fastened behind the door of some Irish home to keep out the hostile stranger. Each cartridge will be a watchdog to fight for the sanctity of the heart".[49] This statement, however, also addressed the role of Cumann na mBan as subordinate to the volunteers executive, despite being funded as an independent organisation. Countess Markievicz was one of the harshest critics with traditional female roles within nationalist organisations, and declared that these women "attached to national movements are there chiefly to collect funds for the men to spend. These Ladies Auxiliaries demoralise women, set them up in separate camps and deprive them of all initiative and independence".[50]

Women were determined to participate in the Irish struggle, proved by their actions in the Easter 1916. Within the ranks of the Irish Citizen Army, women were treated equally with men. To the complaints about female participation in the event of an uprising, James Connolly responded that "if none of the men turned out, the fight would go on with the women".[51] A large number of Volunteers and members of the Irish Citizen Army, both male and female, marched through the centre of Dublin on April 24th 1916 and occupied several buildings throughout the city. At first, the members of Cumann na mBan were turned away from many posts but, when the news filtered back to the leaders, a mobilisation order for Cumann na mBan was sent out and commandants were obliged to accept female collaboration. The role played by Constance Markievicz, Second-in-Command in the Rising, was remarkably portrayed in Kathleen Fox's *The Arrest* (1916). However, the participation of Cumann na mBan in the Rising also highlighted its limitations and the subordinate role that women were expected to play within the nationalist movement.

Women's campaigns for the access to higher education and better employment opportunities, as well as their powerful performances in the Land War and in the nationalist struggle, increased the demand for women's rights to parliamentary vote. The first explicit appeal for women's franchise was written by the socialist William Thompson and the author Anna Wheeler in 1825, in a publication that criticised the husbands' control over the children and wives' property. The suffrage movement was taken over in the 1870s by two women who were already active in campaigns for women's education: Isabella Tod and Anna Haslam. These early societies were composed mainly of small groups of Protestant and Non-Conformist women who already had experience in philanthropic organisations. They focused on meetings, petitions to the Parliament, on lobbying politicians and sending letters to the press. While Ana Haslam and her husband Thomas remained pacifists in their views and their campaigns, Frank and Hanna Sheehy-Skeffington believed that militant action was the only way for women to achieve the vote. In 1908 they established the Irish Women's Franchise League (IWFL), a more aggressive and militant suffrage group that followed the path initiated by the British Women's Social and Political Union (WSPU) formed in 1903 by Emmeline Pankhurst. The IWFL's newspaper, the *Irish Citizen* (1912–1920), stated their opposition to any use of physical force with the exception of a just war or a just rebellion, and addressed their belief that a better and fairer society would only be achieved through the votes of women.

The number of suffragette associations proliferated in such way that in 1911 Louie Bennett and Helen Chenevix set up the non-party and non-military Irish Women's Suffrage Federation to coordinate all the initiatives. However, in November 1912 the Women's Suffrage Bill and Women's Suffrage Amendments to the Home Rule Bill were rejected by the Irish Parliamentary Party, and when the Home Rule Bill was eventually passed in 1914, it did not include women's suffrage either. These caused a rise of militant action that interacted with the struggle for independence and also with the trade union movement. Loyalties were divided, dilemmas had to be faced, and disagreements arose amongst those women who prioritised the vote and those who put independence first. Inghinidhe na hÉireann opposed to a vote being granted by a "hostile parliament", and Constance Markievicz discouraged women to join any suffragist movement that did not actively support the Irish independence, stating that women's equal rights would follow naturally once independence was gained.[52] The socialist and feminist Helena Molony also prioritised the freedom of Ireland because, she stated, "there can be no free women in an enslaved nation".[53] Both unionist and nationalist women were disapproved for their submissiveness to male-dominated structures. Hanna Sheehy-Skeffington encouraged Irish women to put the suffrage campaign first because otherwise women would always play a subordinate role, and the new state would root in patriarchal structures.[54] She criticised nationalist parties for giving women only the role of wives and mothers rather than citizens, and she was not wrong. The majority of the republicans believed that the right to vote should not be discussed until Ireland had its own government.

When the Representation of the People Act passed in 1917, parliamentary vote was granted to women over thirty "who were householders, the wives of householders, were possessed of a £5 occupation qualification or were graduated".[55] In the elections of 1918, Constance Markievicz became the first woman elected to Westminster although, like all her Sinn Féin colleagues, she never took her seat. Apart from Markievicz, the only other female candidate was Winifred Carney, also from Sinn Féin. Despite the result of the elections, there was still a long way to go, as the IWFL pointed out: "under the new dispensation the majority sex in Ireland has secured one representative. This is the measure of our boasted sex equality. The lesson the election teaches is that reaction has not died out with the Irish Party – and the IWFL which has been so faithful to feminist ideals, must continue to fight and expose reaction in the future as in the past".[56] The right to vote was finally granted in 1922 with the creation of the Irish Free State, when every man and woman over the age of 21 was allowed to vote. Great Britain would still have to wait another six years to be granted the same right.

However, after the implementation of the universal suffrage, a series of Acts were seen by women as a setback on female citizenship: the Juries Act of 1927, the Marriage Bar in 1932 and the Conditions of Employment Act in 1936, amongst others. The exclusion of women from the workplace and the public sphere was reinforced by De Valera's 1937 Constitution and the Article 41, which stated that:

> 1.1. In particular, the State recognises that by her life within the home, woman gives to the State a support without which the common good cannot be achieved.

1.2. The State shall, therefore, endeavour to ensure that mothers shall not be obliged by economic necessity to engage in labour to the neglect of their duties in the home.

Despite the promise of advances regarding women's rights, this was never captured in the Constitution and, as a response to the attacks on female citizenship, several women's organisations were established. Amongst them were the National Women's Council, the Irish Women's Social and Progressive League, or the Joint Committee of Women's Societies and Social Workers Against the 1937 Constitution. De Valera's conservationism and the traditionalist stance of Irish society with respect to women's rights were exemplified in the fact that women had no part in framing the draft of the Constitution. Feminist organisations refused to support a legal document that reinforced women's role as homemakers and mothers over public and political life. The Constitution also revoked the declared equality of the sexes of the 1916 Proclamation, which had consequences in the participation of women in the political and intellectual life. Maud Gonne criticised what she felt as a betrayal of the principles of the 1916 Proclamation:

> We have a Proclamation of the Republic –a noble, clear concise document– as our charter of liberty. It has been endorsed by the whole nation. The substitution of another document is a weakening of our national position. If, when Ireland is free, a more detailed constitution were needed, the articles concerning women and the articles providing for special courts [art. 38.3] in Mr. de Valera's draft constitution would damn it in my eyes.[57]

The family –centre of the Irish society, symbol of resistance, and transmitter of nationalist ideas– became also the basis of the 1937 Constitution. This had long-lasting gender implications, as citizenship for women was defined in terms of their roles as wives and mothers.[58] The Constitution banned abortion and divorce, confined women in the home and restricted their access to the labour market. It also recognised "the special position" of the Roman Catholic faith,[59] whose assumptions about a woman's place in society matched those of the Irish government. The majority of women did not support feminists in their campaigns for women's rights, which was predictable. As devout Catholics, many Irish women accepted their "natural" role as mothers and home-makers.[60] The discrimination of women barely changed until the 1960s and 1970s, when these attitudes began to be openly and generally challenged. The connection between modernisation and feminism was illustrated in 1990 with the election of Mary Robinson as the first woman president of the Republic. The Thirty-Four Amendment of the Constitution (Marriage Equality) Act and the Thirty-Six Amendment of the Constitution of Ireland (Repeal of the Eighth Amendment) were passed in 2015 and 2018 respectively. Both amendments were approved by popular referendum, a clear example of the rapid advances that have taken place in Ireland in the last few years regarding civil rights.

## The Irish Revival

"All changed, changed utterly: a terrible beauty is born".[61] With these words, W. B. Yeats described in "Easter 1916" the sentiments of a disturbed Ireland in the aftermath of the Easter Rising. In his poem, the nationalist leaders were portrayed not only as heroic revolutionaries, but also as cultured men of letters. And it is indeed inarguable that literature and art played a crucial part in the events leading to the foundation of the Republic of Ireland. Between 1830 and 1930,[62] the cultural movement known as the Irish Revival proved that troubled times can also lead to creative outbreaks with social and political effects.[63] Ireland's struggles and dilemmas were addressed in art, drama and literature, and Irish culture portrayed the development of a whole range of political and social trends, from nationalism or the working-class struggle, to unionism, republicanism or feminism. Often associated to the Revivalist movement in Scotland, Wales, the English regions and Brittany, Ireland's cultural revolution is also known as The Celtic Revival. However, although the term Celtic distinguished the movement from the more modern English urban society, it has often been contested for concealing its Irish and nationalist nature.[64] Influenced by the rising of the nationalist spirit throughout Europe during the nineteenth century, Irish artists and writers immersed themselves in the search of a national identity based on the Irish tradition as the counterpoint to the British discourse. National culture constituted the means to reshape the identity of a country conquered and oppressed for centuries, and art and literature became the vehicles of expression of political beliefs based on a modern reinterpretation of Ireland's past, its myths, its legends and its folklore.

The movement was initially embraced by a small circle of scholars, antiquarians and artists such as George Petrie, Frederick William Burton or Henry O'Neill who, partially motivated by the European interest in landscape and travels, documented and studied the landscape and antiquities of Ireland. One of the pioneers in Irish antiquarian studies was Margaret Stokes, who edited and illustrated publications on Irish antiquities, architecture and heritage, and made important contributions to the study of medieval Irish culture with books like *Early Christian Art in Ireland* (1887), one of the earliest modern studies of Irish medieval art. Her illustrations for Samuel Ferguson's *The Cromlech of Howth: A Poem* (1861) made her one of the earliest artists to reproduce the work of the Book of Kells. The nineteenth century also witnessed the discovery of two important objects held in the National Museum of Ireland, the Tara Brooch and the Ardagh Chalice, which contributed to the growing interest in the golden age of Ireland. However, the Revival found its main vehicle of expression in literature, thanks to the unbroken tradition of folklore and storytelling in the Irish-speaking areas of the country: the Gaeltacht. Much Irish medieval literature in Gaelic was being translated for the first time, and during the century several societies, such as the Irish Archaeological Society or the Ossianic Society, were established with the purpose of preserving the Irish language and making those texts available. However, many of these early institutions, concerned with antiquarian and folkloric studies, aimed only to revive Gaelic as a literary language and as a tool for historical research,[65] and not for its everyday use.

Irish spoken tradition was not addressed until the creation of the Gaelic League in 1893. The League was, in name, non-political and non-sectarian, and wished to involve people of different backgrounds and beliefs in the revival of the Irish language and literary culture. However, most of its members did participate in the nationalist movement and played an active role in the Easter Rising, which led to the persecution of the organisation in September 1919. The League's Manifesto addressed "the necessity for de-anglicising the Irish nation" in order "to keep the Irish language alive where it is still spoken, which is the outmost at present we can aspire to".[66] In 1902, Jeremiah O'Donovan claimed that the Gaelic League's goal was "the creation of an Irish Ireland" by the "spread of true national ideas. Once those ideas are grasped, a development of Ireland from within, embracing language, literature, art, industries and music will necessarily follow".[67] The organisation was a big success, and by 1905 it had 550 branches throughout Ireland that ran language classes and Irish-speaking social gatherings, concerts and lectures. However, it was never too concerned with fine arts.[68]

The Gaelic League was the first male cultural organisation in Ireland to admit women to full membership, which challenged some of the stereotypes and prejudices regarding women's rights in Ireland.[69] With the progress on women's education and employment opportunities, the Gaelic League offered them a platform where they could put their skills and experience to use. Alice Milligan (1866–1953), although hardly remembered nowadays, was one of the most important members of the Gaelic League and a very influential figure in the social, cultural and political life in Ireland. Along with her friend, the journalist Anna Johnston, Milligan edited the *Northern Patriot* and produced the newspaper *The Shan Van Vocht* (the Poor Old Woman). Both newspapers published poems, plays and stories promoting Irish culture, which Milligan believed was the key for the success of the Irish cause. But the powerful role played in the Gaelic League by women like Alice Milligan clashed with the traditional gender roles often advocated by its members, male or female. The Gaelic League praised the private sphere as the place for nationalist pedagogy, a milieu where women's only duties were motherhood and domesticity. These ideas were supported by important female figures of the League such as Mary E. Butler who, despite her prominent role as a member of Sinn Féin and the

Gaelic League Executive, reclaimed a passive role for Irish women. Writing allowed women to take part in the Gaelic League and the Irish Revival to a certain extent, but those who wished a more active role in the Irish cause were always forced to found their own political and cultural organisations.

The very same year the Gaelic League was founded, W. B. Yeats published his book *The Celtic Twilight*, a collection of poems that became the generic name for the entire Irish Literary Revival. This book became Yeats's first effort to fill with culture the political vacuum left after the turbulent years of the Famine, the rebellions, the fight for the Home Rule and especially the death of Charles Stewart Parnell.[70] The artistic scene became the place for innovation, action and experimentation where artists and writers redefined the idea of nation, identity and national history. The writers involved in the Revival focused on reversing the negative clichés and stereotypes of Ireland and its people, and presented the Irish as a spiritual and antimaterialistic race, linked to the earth and nature. They contributed to a new sense of national identity through their literary work based on Irish mythology and history, and by exploring the links between the past and the present of their country. Thanks to Ireland's rich and wide oral tradition, Irish authors found a genuine source that allowed them to develop a national literary practice independent from the British tradition. The landscapes and the atmosphere of the West of Ireland turned into the ideal scenario for the recreation of the Irish idyllic and mythic life, and the authors' evocative depictions of the land became a catalyst for many readers and also artists who were determined to travel and paint the most remote places of the West. The pre-Christian way of life and Irish folklore encouraged a sense of unity in Ireland despite the diverse, and often clashing, trends that coexisted within the Irish cultural, social and political arena.

Through these new appreciations, traditional poetry and drama developed into the emblems of Irish cultural nationalism by the hand of writers such as Standish O'Grady, A.E. Russell, Edward Martyn and Lady Gregory, who often shared a Protestant background and were instrumental in the growth of Irish national literature in English. The main figure of the Literary Revival was W. B. Yeats (1865–1939), whose work in poetry and drama addressed the dilemmas of a young Irish writer influenced by the British tradition, and explored the strains between Irish nationalism and his own desire of personal and artistic fulfilment. W. B. Yeats's family was deeply involved in the Revival: his father, John B. Yeats, was a painter who became famous for his portraits of Irish nationalist leaders, and his brother Jack B. Yeats became one of the leaders of the Irish artistic modernism. His two sisters, Lily and Lolly Yeats, established one of the most important initiatives of the Arts and Crafts Movement within the Irish Revival, the Cuala Industries. Yeats's interest in folklore was the basis for the redefinition of Irish identity, and was addressed in his four anthologies *Fairy and Folk Tales of the Irish Peasantry* (1888), *Stories from Carleton* (1889), *Representative Irish Tales* (1891) and *Irish Fairy Tales* (1892). He had been critic with the use of Irish literature for political reasons by certain organisations and individuals: "Young Ireland had sought a nation unified by political doctrine alone, a subservient art and letters aiding and abetting [...]. All the past had been turned into melodrama with Ireland for blameless hero and poet".[71] However, his interest in the Irish tradition took on a more political significance when he began to take part in the nationalist circles during the 1880s and 1890s: "There is no great literature without nationality, no great nationality without literature".[72] The figure of Parnell and his ideal of Ireland remained a constant presence in the life and work of Yeats who, during his time in London, focused on setting up nationalist literary organisations that would be the basis for a cultural revival with political aims. He founded the Irish Literary Society in London (1891) and the National Literary Society in Dublin (1892) with Douglas Hyde and John O'Leary amongst its founding members, and Evelyn Gleeson as its first secretary. The National Literary Society wished to "afford a centre of social and literary intercourse for persons of Irish nationality, and to promote the study of the Irish language, Irish history, literature, music and art",[73] and it even offered Irish language classes before the League was established. Like the Gaelic League, these societies insisted on their independence from politics, but found impossible to keep the national culture separate from Irish politics. Even Yeats participated in several republican campaigns such as the opposition to the celebration of Queen Victoria's jubilee in Ireland in 1897 or the commemoration of the 1798 Rising. His greatest achievement was the establishment of a distinctively Irish national theatre along with Lady Augusta Gregory, an author who went on to become one of Yeats's most generous patrons and a lifelong friend until her death in 1932.

Lady Gregory had soon forged a deep connection with the Irish workers of the Coole Park state and with the peasantry of the West of Ireland, which turned into a major theme in her writing. Following the death of her husband Sir William Henry Gregory in 1892, Lady Gregory turned the Coole Park state into a meeting point for some of the most important nationalist authors of the time. Her widowhood became her most creative period as an artist, translator, editor and also as manager of literary organisations. Lady Gregory was amazed by Ireland's myths and folklore, and her adaptations of Irish legends became an attempt to educate the Irish public in national mythology in a moment when theatre and literature were considered a central part of the educational role of the arts. The nationalist tone of her writing encouraged the public to reflect on every aspect, negative or positive, of the history of their country, and her exploration of different genres, from comedy to drama, fantasy or tragedy, was always based in her beloved Ireland. Unlike Yeats's symbolist theatre, Lady Gregory wrote realist plays portraying the genuine character of the Irish peasantry and its particularities. Her vast knowledge of the Irish language and folkloric literature was encouraged by Yeats and, although she was well aware that she was an author in her own right, she also acknowledged Yeats's part in her career as a dramatist: "If I had not met Yeats" –she wrote–, "I believe I should still have become a writer, because my energy was turning to that side, and I had got a certain training in the editing of the *Autobiography* and the *Letter Box*. But I might have never found opportunity or freedom; I might have become [at most] a writer of middle articles in literary papers".[74]

But Lady Gregory's career was impressive not only for the amount of plays she wrote, but for her originality and her principles. Her writing was deeply influenced by the ideas of John Ruskin, who also had an effect on her political and social views. She was involved in the Cooperative Movement and in the Home Industries Movement, which provided employment for poor women and developed the Arts and Crafts Movement in Ireland from a nationalist perspective. Like many authors of the time, Lady Gregory supported Ruskin's belief that art should play a central role in any project that aimed to encourage artistic taste in Ireland and to improve the life of Irish people, and her social and political ideas impregnated her writing and influenced the Revival. She also challenged the traditional and strict gender roles of the Irish nationalist culture. As Anthony Bradley and Maryann Valiulis remarked, Ireland had, "of course, long been gendered –by the political nationalist metanarrative and the cultural nationalism of traditional history and literature– as a woman victimised by the colonizing English male. For an equally long time, the lives of actual Irish women were arguably colonised by Irish men, at the same time as both genders were colonial subjects of England".[75]

Declan Kiberd also argued that "in the literature of the emerging nation, women reverted to being a site of contest rather than an agent of her own desire. No nationalism in the world has ever granted women and men the same privileged resources of the nation-state".[76] The Revival was based on the belief that those works written by men would engage in issues of national importance, while female writers would focus on domestic, personal and private subject-matters. The life and career of Lady Gregory, however, defeated this argument. Although she never made any public statement about a woman's place in the public sphere, Lady Gregory's plays became known not only for their social criticism, but also for exposing the patriarchal nature of Irish nationalism that denied women an active role in the foundation of the Irish nation.[77] Her writing explored the lives of strong women and revealed the impact of nationalism in the traditional allegory of the woman-nation, one of the most important concepts in the imagery of the Revival.[78] Her plays reclaimed a fair representation of peasant women's stories, and her female characters challenged the Revival's practice of idealising women. Taking over the masculine milieu of the nationalist history and Irish legends, Lady Gregory questioned the social restrictions of her time and subverted traditional gender roles, fighting the patriarchal aspects of the Revival and offering new possibilities for an independent Ireland.

Lady Gregory contributed quietly but constantly to the development of a national theatre in Ireland. She has often been quoted as Yeats's collaborator in the Irish Literary Theatre, despite her leading role in the dramatic movement. An example of her invisibility was the authorship issue of *Cathleen ni Houlihan*. Despite the evidence that proved Lady Gregory as the author of most of the words of the play, Yeats was listed as the play's writer due to his more famous name. This prevented Lady Gregory from receiving the credit she deserved until very recently.[79] In his essay "An Irish National Theatre" (*Samhain*, 1903), Yeats explained how he "had a very vivid dream one night" and had "made *Cathleen ni Houlihan* out of this dream",[80] while privately confiding to Lennox Robinson that Lady Gregory's contribution to *Cathleen* was so great that "the authorship of the play should be ascribed to her".[81] Even though Yeats did not always credit Lady Gregory as she should have been credited, they both seem to have overcome disagreements, proved by their long collaborative career and friendship. Described as "the woman behind the Irish Renaissance",[82] this description exemplifies how Lady Gregory has been, until very recently, overshadowed by her male colleagues and reduced to a mere "mother-muse" of Yeats, in spite of her independent success, her substantial contribution to the Irish cultural scene and her leading role in the Irish Literary Theatre and the Abbey Theatre.

The summer of 1897 was the first of many summers that Yeats spent at Coole Park with Lady Gregory, where their conversations about Irish literature and folklore shaped one of the most important adventures of the Irish Revival: the Irish Literary Theatre. The Irish playwright and political activist Edward Martyn, who found difficulty in presenting his work in England, supported the project also financially. Founded in 1899, the Literary Theatre was an attempt to establish a distinctively Irish national theatre by combining Ireland's rich tradition with more modern European theatrical methods, independent of the commercial stage. Although many of the early plays of the Irish Literary Theatre portrayed scenarios and characters from ancient myths and legends, they were always linked both with the past and the present, addressing Irish themes in ways that had not been explored before. However, not all the responses to the innovative dramatic movement were positive, and soon difficulties arose. Yeats's *Countess Cathleen* was attacked for its heresy and blasphemy, and criticised for its lack of patriotism, which proved how quickly the theatre could become a place for national debate in Ireland. Disagreements arose, especially between Edward Martyn, who was deeply influenced by Ibsen's realism, and Yeats, who wished to surpass Realism in order to explore more symbolic paths.

The Irish Literary Theatre became the Irish National Theatre Society in 1902. Controversies were to begin soon. That very same year, the company staged A.E. Russell's *Deirdre* and Yeats's and Lady Gregory's *Cathleen ni Houlihan*, with Maud Gonne as Cathleen. These early representations scandalised Ireland's strong religious beliefs and encouraged the political ambitions of the nationalist sector. In 1916, Yeats suffered a crisis of conscience, believing that *Cathleen* might have encouraged the events of the Rising. In his late poem "The man and the echo", he wondered: "Did that play of mine send out / Certain men the English shot?".[83] However, the genuine methods of the Literary Revival and its less conventional theatre caught the attention of both the public and the critic from its beginnings. Yeats was a well-known poet and Miss Annie Horniman, an English admirer of Yeats, gave her financial support to the project, which allowed the members to afford their own space. The Abbey Theatre opened its doors on December 27th 1904, with Yeats, Lady Gregory and John Millington Synge as directors of the company. The Theatre went on to become the headquarters of the Irish Revival and, in the old Mechanics Institute, the leaders of the literary revolution represented the plays that they could not stage in any other place. The key element in their representations was the figure of the peasant, which was "elevated to a position of great importance in national life, as creator and guardian of the oral tradition that gave Irish literature its power and uniqueness".[84] The Theatre became a place for political expression and experimentation where comedy and character predominated. The peasantry and the West of Ireland became the perfect antithesis to modern life which, for Yeats, Synge, Gregory and Hyde, was associated to materialism, uniformity and the breaking of tradition. The countryside's Catholic roots influenced the tone of literature in the Revival, although the authors also highlighted the pagan beliefs that had survived in the Gaeltacht in order to "bring upon the stage the deeper emotions of Ireland".[85] The authors of the Literary Revival explored the diversity of Irish identity, and engaged in eternal debates as to whether literature should be involved in politics and whether Irish authors should be influenced by the European trends and to what extent.

Art and literature became the centre of national identity, but this was not without controversy. John Millington Synge's depiction of an unfaithful Irish woman in *The Shadow of Glen* (1903) was received as an insult to Ireland. The problematic set the stage for a deeper conflict with the nationalist community. In 1907, *The Playboy of the Western World* gave the Abbey Theatre its masterpiece, the best example of the link between the past and the present, tradition and modernity. His play sent a message about the nature of the violence in Ireland, and became a critique of the images of the Revival, its heroes and their deeds and, like most of Synge's subversive comedies, its critic views of the folk tradition caused upset within the nationalist circles in a time when national feelings were extremely idealised and any criticism to what Irishness meant was considered outrageous. Sean O'Casey's Dublin Trilogy brought the struggle of the Dublin poor to the stage of the Abbey Theatre, and also questioned the heroism of some Irish patriots. The work of both Synge and O'Casey, although part of the Revival, became also a criticism of the Irish culture,[86] and the ongoing riots led Yeats to declare: "I thought you had tired of this, which commenced fifteen years ago [a reference to John Millington Synge's *The Playboy of the Western World*]. But you have disgraced yourselves again. Is this going to be a recurring celebration of Irish genius?"[87]

The Abbey Theatre became a rich source of inspiration for the visual artists of the Irish Revival. Irish myths, the peasantry and national identity were also addressed by painters and craftsmen and women in the turn of the century. Inspired by the success of Irish drama and literature, the art collector and director Hugh Lane aimed to encourage a higher appreciation of national art. In 1904, he organised *Works by Irish Painters*, an exhibition held at the Guildhall Art Gallery in London that included artworks by Irish artists from the eighteenth and nineteenth centuries. In the catalogue of the show, he claimed:

> There are some many painters of Irish birth or Irish blood in the first rank at this moment, that extreme interest is being taken in this bringing together of sufficient specimens of their work to enable students of art to discover what common or race qualities appear through it. There is something of common race instinct in the work of all original Irish writers of today, and it can hardly be absent in the sister art.[88]

# NOTES

1. Lloyd Laing and Jennifer Laing, *Celtic Britain and Ireland. Art and Society* (London: Herbert Press, 1995), 11.

2. Donnchadh Ó Corráin, "Prehistoric and Early Christian Ireland", in *The Oxford History of Ireland,* ed. Robert Fitzroy Foster (New York: Oxford University Press, 1989), 2.

3. See Julia M. Wright, *Representing the National Landscape in Irish Romanticism* (New York: Syracuse University Press, 2014)

4. Laing and Laing, *Celtic Britain and Ireland,* 11.

5. Ó Corráin, "Prehistoric and Early Christian Ireland", 9.

6. Aodh de Blacam, "Mary of the Gael", *The Irish Monthly,* vol. 67 (August 1939): 577.

7. See Jean Markale, *Women of the Celts* (Vermont: Inner Traditions, 1986).

8. Margaret Schaus (ed.), *Women and Gender in Medieval Europe. An Encyclopaedia* (New York and London: Routledge Revivals, 2006), 409.

9. See John Ryan, *Irish Monasticism. Origins and Early Development* (Dublin: Irish Academic Press, 1986).

10. Bruce Arnold, *A Concise History of Irish Art* (London, Thames and Hudson, 1977), 31–32.

11. See Nancy Netzer, "Cloths of Ireland's New Golden Age": Creating Textiles for the Honan Chapel", in *The Arts and Crafts Movement. Making it Irish,* ed. Vera Kreilkamp (Chicago: University of Chicago Press, 2016), 101–116.

12. Mainie Jellett, "A Word on Irish Art", in *The Artist's Vision: Lectures and Essays on Art,* ed. Eileen MacCarvill (Dundalk: Dundalgan, 1958), 103.

13. Arnold, *A Concise History of Irish Art,* 21.

14. Arnold, 21.
15. Arnold, 47–48.
16. Arnold, 55.
17. Sherry B. Ortner, "Is female to male as nature is to culture?", in *Woman, culture, and society,* eds. Michelle Zimbalist Rosaldo and Louise Lamphere (Stanford, CA: Stanford University Press, 1974), 68–87.
18. Bonnie G. Smith, *The Oxford Encyclopaedia of Women in World History* (Oxford: Oxford University Press, 2008), 393.
19. Ghislaine McDayter, "On the Publication of William Godwin's Memoirs of the Author of a Vindication of the Rights of Woman, 1978", *BRANCH: Britain, Representation and Nineteenth-Century History.* Ed. Dino Franco Felluga. Extension of Romanticism and Victorianism on the Net. Web. Accessed on May 7th 2020, https://www.branchcollective.org/?ps_articles=ghislaine-mcdayter-on-the-publication-of-william-godwins-memoirs-of-the-author-of-a-vindication-of-the-rights-of-woman-1798
20. Maria Luddy, "Feminism", in *The Princeton History of Modern Ireland,* eds. Richard Bourke and Ian McBride (New Jersey: Princeton University Press, 2016), 470–489.
21. See Ann Heilmann and Stephanie Forward (eds.), *Sex, Social Purity and Sarah Grand. Vol. 1* (London: Routledge, 2000).
22. Sally Ledger, *The New Woman. Fiction and Feminism at the Fin de Siècle* (New York: Manchester University Press, 1997), 1.
23. Ledger, 1.
24. See Tina O'Toole, *The Irish New Woman* (London and New York: Palgrave Macmillan, 2013).
25. O'Toole, 74.
26. Ann Heilmann, "Wilde's New Women. The New Woman on Wilde", in *The Importance of Reinventing Oscar: Versions of Wilde During the Last 100 Years,* eds. Uwe Böker, Richard Corballis, Julie Hibbard (Amsterdam: Rodopi, 2002), 142.
27. Ledger, *The New Woman,* 94.
28. Tom Walsh, "The National System of Education, 1831–2000", in *Essays in the History of Irish Education,* ed. Brendan Walsh (Dublin: Palgrave Macmillan, 2016), 8.
29. Maria Luddy, *Women in Ireland, 1800–1918. A Documentary History* (Cork: Cork University Press, 1995), 89.
30. Luddy, 89–92.
31. Helen Rappaport, *Encyclopedia of Women Social Reformers. Vol. 1* (California: ABC-CLIO, 2001), 336.
32. Quoted in Maria Cullen and Maria Luddy, *Women, Power and Consciousness in 19th Century Ireland* (Dublin: Attic Press, 1995), 139.
33. Luddy, *Women in Ireland,* 91.
34. Luddy, 157.
35. Mary E. Daly, "Women in the Irish Workforce from Pre-Industrial to Modern Times", in *The Irish Women's History Reader,* eds. Alan Hayes and Diane Urquhart (London: Routledge, 2001), 195
36. Luddy, *Women in Ireland,* 161.

37. Maria Luddy, "The Labour Movement in Ireland, 1800–2000", in *The Field Day Anthology of Irish Writing, vol. 4: Irish women's writing and traditions,* eds. Angela Bourke et al. (Cork: Cork University Press, 2002), 548–565.
38. Eoin O'Leary, "The Irish National Teachers' Organisation and the Marriage Bar for Women National Teachers, 1933–1958", *Saothar,* 12 (1987): 47.
39. "A Brief History", Irish Women Workers Union, accessed on May 8th 2020, https://womenworkersunion.ie/history/
40. Luddy, *Women in Ireland, 1800–1918,* 239–240.
41. Sean J. Connolly, *Oxford Companion to Irish History* (New York: Oxford University Press, 1998), 453.
42. O'Toole, *The Irish New Woman,* 86.
43. Quoted in McCoole, *No Ordinary Women,* 26.
44. Connolly, *Oxford Companion to Irish History,* 271.
45. Nancy Cardozo, *Maud Gonne* (London: Victor Gollanez, 1979), 188.
46. Karen Steele, *Women, Press and Politics During the Irish Revival* (New York: Syracuse University Press, 1997), 110.
47. Quoted in Margaret Ward, "Marginality and Militancy: Cumann na mBan, 1914–36", in *The Irish Women's History Reader,* eds. Alan Hayes and Diane Urquhart (London: Routledge, 2001), 59.
48. Ward, 59.
49. McCoole, *No Ordinary Women,* 28.
50. *Irish Citizen,* 23 October 1915. Quoted in Ward, "Marginality and Militancy", 59.
51. McCoole, *No Ordinary Women,* 31.
52. McCoole, *No Ordinary Women,* 26.
53. Joe Cleary, "Postcolonial Ireland", in *Ireland and the British Empire,* ed. Kevin Kenny (Oxford: Oxford University Press, 2004), 274.
54. McCoole, *No Ordinary Women,* 26.
55. Luddy, *Women in Ireland,* 244.
56. Rosemary Cullen Owens, "Votes for Women", in *The Irish Women's History Reader,* eds. Alan Hayes and Diane Urquhart (London: Routledge, 2001), 42.
57. Maria Luddy, "Irish women's opposition to the 1937 draft constitution", in *Transactions of the Royal Historical Society,* vol. 15, ed. Aled Jones (Cambridge: Cambridge University Press, 2005), 180.
58. See Caitriona Beaumont, "Women, Citizenship and Catholicism in the Irish Free State, 1922–1948)", *Women's History Review,* vol. 6, no. 4 (1997): 563–585.
59. Niall Meehan, "Article 44 Reconsidered", History Ireland, vol. 27, no. 1 (January/February 2019), 44.
60. Beaumont, "Women, Citizenship and Catholicism", 578.
61. William Butler Yeats, *Selected Poems and Four Plays of William Butler Yeats,* ed. Marcha Louis Rosenthal (New York: Scribner, 1996), 84.
62. See Jeanne Sheehy, *The Rediscovery of Ireland's Past. The Celtic Revival, 1830–1930* (London: Thames and Hudson, 1980).

63. See Declan Kiberd, *Inventing Ireland. The Literature of the Modern Nation* (1995); *The Irish Writer and the World* (2005); *Handbook of the Irish Revival: An Anthology of Political and Cultural Writings 1891–1922* (ed. with P.J. Matthews, 2015).
64. Michael McAteer, "Celtic and Irish Revival", *Oxford Bibliographies,* accessed on May 8th 2020, https://www.oxfordbibliographies.com/view/document/obo-9780199846719/obo-9780199846719-0025.xml
65. Connolly, *Oxford Companion to Irish History,* 225.
66. Douglas Hyde, "The Necessity for De-Anglicising Ireland", in *An Irish Literature Reader. Poetry, Prose, Drama,* eds. Maureen O'Rourke Murphy and James MacKillop (New York: Syracuse University Press, 2006), 139–149.
67. O'Growney Memorial Lecture, September 29th 1902, published as Gaelic League pamphlet no. 26, 2.
68. Sheehy, *The Rediscovery of Ireland's Past,* 98.
69. Maria Luddy, "Gender and Irish History", in *The Oxford Handbook of Modern Irish History,* ed. Alvin Jackson (Oxford: Oxford University Press, 2014), 205.
70. Jonathan Allison, "Yeats and Politics", in *The Cambridge Companion to W. B. Yeats,* eds. Marjorie Howes and John Kelly (Cambridge: Cambridge University Press, 2006), 185–205.
71. William H. O'Donnell and Douglas N. Archibald (eds.), *The Collected Works of W. B. Yeats. Autobiographies. Vol. 3* (New York: Scribner, 1999), 172–173.
72. Quoted in Richard Allen and Harish Trivedi, *Literature and Nation. Britain and India 1800–1990* (New York: Routledge, 2000), 79.
73. "History", Irish Literary Society, accessed on May 8th 2020, https://irishlitsoc.org/home/about/history/
74. Lady Augusta Gregory. *Seventy Years: Being the Autobiography of Lady Gregory,* ed. Colin Smythe (New York: Macmillan, 1976), 390.
75. Antony Bradley and Maryann Gialanella Valiulis (eds.), *Gender and Sexuality in Modern Ireland* (Massachusetts: University of Massachusetts Press, 1997), 6.
76. Kiberd, *Inventing Ireland,* 406–407.
77. Noelle Bowles, "Nationalism and Feminism in Lady Gregory's 'Kincora', 'Dervorgilla', and 'Grania'", in *New Hibernia Review / Iris Éireannach Nua,* vol. 3, no. 3 (Autumn, 1999): 116.
78. See Judith Hill, *Lady Gregory. An Irish Life* (Dublin: The Collins Press, 2011).
79. David Holdeman, *The Cambridge Introduction to W. B. Yeats* (Cambridge: Cambridge University Press, 2006), 42.
80. W. B. Yeats, "An Irish National Theatre", in *The Collected Works of W. B. Yeats. The Irish Dramatic Movement, vol. VIII,* eds. Mary FitzGerald and Richard J. Finneran (New York: Scribner, 2003), 33.
81. James Pethica, "Our Kathleen: Yeats's Collaboration with Lady Gregory in the Writing of Cathleen ni Houlihan", in *Yeats Annual* no. 6, ed. Warwick Gould (London: Macmillan Press, 1998): 15.
82. Mary Lou Kohfeldt, *Lady Gregory: The Woman Behind the Irish Renaissance* (London: Andre Deutsch, 1985).

83. William Butler Yeats, "The Man and the Echo", in *Collected Poems of W. B. Yeats,* ed. Richard J. Finneran (New York: MacMillan, 2008), 372.
84. Marjorie Howes, *Yeats's Nations: Gender, Class and Irishness* (Cambridge: Cambridge University Press, 1996), 39.
85. Quoted in Owens and Radner, *Irish Drama,* 2.
86. Cóilín D. Owens and Joan N. Radner (eds.), *Irish Drama, 1900–1980* (Washington: The Catholic University of America Press, 1990), 122–188.
87. Anthony Roche, *The Irish Dramatic Revival, 1899–1939* (London: Bloomsbury, 2015), 2.
88. Hugh Lane, "Exhibition of Works by Irish Painters: London Guildhall (1904)", Catalogue preface. Quoted in Fintan Cullen, *Ireland on Show: "Art, Union and Nationhood"* (New York: Routledge, 2016), 153.

# Part Two

# Irish Women and Art

# Female Allegories in Irish Cultural Nationalism

Symbols and allegories have played a pivotal role in the rhetoric of Irish cultural nationalism. The Revival witnessed the development of national emblems such as the shamrock and the harp, the rising sun of the Fianna, the round tower, the aforementioned Celtic and early Christian crosses, the wolfhound or the ruined chapel and, although most of these images already existed,[1] they were awarded a privileged space in the visual iconography of the turn of the century. According to Gabriella Elgenius, these symbols were, "as far as nationhood is concerned, a significant element of the nation-building process, as it authenticates boundaries".[2] Nationalist imagery was addressed by Thomas Davis in *The Nation*, as well as by important history artists like Daniel Maclise, and especially by the Irish Arts and Crafts Movement. A key feature of Irish cultural nationalism was the political use of the allegorical female figure. This highlighted the secondary place women occupied in Irish society in the nineteenth and twentieth centuries. Women were not subjects, but objects. They were linked to the land, as guardians of the race, mothers of the nation and religious icons.

In Ireland, like in many other European countries, the feminisation of the land became one of the dominant images in the nationalist discourse. Irish nationalism poeticised the fight for independence, and portrayed it as a romantic story about the liberation of Éire (which was rendered as passive and female) from the hands of her male oppressor, England. This discourse was not new in the Irish tradition. From the Celtic goddesses of the Pre-Christian era to the more nationalistic figure of Éire, or the chaste Virgin Mary, Ireland had always been a woman eternally associated with the land. She was "to be worshipped, wooed and won, if necessary by death";[3] she was raped, colonised, praised and fought for. And, above all, she was voiceless. As the poet Eavan Boland remarks:

> the heroine, as such, was utterly passive. She was stamped, as a rubbed-

> away mark, on silver or gold; a compromised regal figure on a throne. Or she was a nineteenth-century image of girlhood, on a frontispiece or in a book of engravings. She was invoked, addressed, remembered, loved, regretted. And, most important, died for. She was a mother, or a virgin [...]. And she had no speaking part.[4]

As a consequence of the English colonisation, the image of Ireland as a Celtic goddess of sovereignty was replaced in the eighteenth century by a passive, helpless female figure, particularly with the development of the Aisling poetry. This poetic form portrayed Ireland as a mythologised and beautiful woman who appears to the poet in a vision and laments her woes, caused by the absence of her rightful spouse. She yearns for the return of the exiled Stuart line, whose place has been usurped by the British. From then on, the Irish nationalist imagery based its discourse on the idea of a raped land, on the concept of Otherness and on the issue of sexual fidelity; and, even though Irish nationalism reinforced the image of a chaste Ireland as a passive victim of the coloniser, female sexuality became a very important part of its rhetoric. As Elizabeth Grosz observes, patriarchy, in an attempt to preserve the "contradictory role of mother (as pure and as a seducer)", divided its features into two types of women, "either virgin or whore, subject or object, asexual or sexual with no possible mediation".[5] The Catholic Church had also portrayed women as either chaste, pure and untouchable, or as immoral prostitutes, and Marianism in particular became a "badge of national identity"[6] at the beginning of the twentieth century.

The Aisling tradition passed into Anglo-Irish literature through translations. In 1837, James Clarence Mangan wrote "Dark Rosaleen", a translation of the Aisling poem "Róisín Dubh". Mangan wrote the poem in the form of a love lament that narrates the sufferings of the motherland, portrayed as a mystical and beautiful woman. Published in *The Nation* in 1846, Mangan's poem became one of the most important texts in Irish literature, and a symbol of the Irish struggle against the British. Fusing the erotic with a national and romantic sentiment, it encouraged readers to fight for their country with the same ardour as they would protect their lovers, while at the same time stating the necessity of bloodshed in the battle for freedom. The poem planted the seed for other important personifications of the nation such as Éire, Mother Ireland and later the Virgin Mary.

Female iconography was characterised by its fluidity, for all these allegories were modified depending on political interests both by the colonised as well as by the colonisers.[7] The feminisation of the Irish land by the British can be traced back to Edmund Spenser (1552/53) and his colonial tract entitled *A View of the Present State of Ireland.* It was highly critical of Irish life and presented the Irish as a "feminised, culturally barbaric and economically intractable society".[8] This idea developed during the nineteenth century, when stereotypical gender roles were used by the British to maintain their control over Ireland.[9] The Irish were often portrayed as passive people, incapable of governing themselves and in need of guidance, all characteristics traditionally associated with female nature. The colonial rhetoric presented Ireland as a "virgin land awaiting the English impression",[10] and developed a metaphor of rape of the land as a positive concept.[11] Especially towards the end of the nineteenth century, British magazines like *Punch* published cartoons that represented Hibernia as a young, virginal girl with her hair tied up and decorated with clovers, often threatened by ape-like Fenians. England, however, was personified by John Bull –Hibernia's father or husband– who symbolised the British male power, or by Britannia –Hibernia's strong sister–. In these illustrations, Britannia often appears dressed in an armour with a symbolic military headgear, or portrayed as an imperial ruler in ancient dresses, an image of Pallas Athena that also exemplified the interest in Neo-Classicist art amongst the British well-off society from the eighteenth century onwards.[12] Hibernia, on the contrary, is frequently dressed in more humble clothes, a sign of the lower status of the Irish people.

As a response to these negative colonial stereotypes, Irish nationalist publications praised Charles Stewart Parnell and other members of the Home Rule as heroes and protectors of the country, and portrayed the figure of Éire as a more independent –although also suffering– woman with dark hair and dressed in ancient clothes too. The image of the helpless maiden is vanished in illustrations like *Her First Work* (*The Weekly Freeman and National Press*, 1900, author unknown), where Ireland is holding a sword and a shield decorated with an Irish harp and with the inscription "United Irish League". She appears fighting a snake –the symbol of the British landowners– that, in turn, is attacking an Irish peasant. "His rescue must be my first work" –Éire states–, "the rest will inevitably follow". The cartoon *The Last Obstruction to Freedom* (*The Weekly Freeman*, 1892) proposes the same idea of a strong nation. Éire is dressed in an ancient tunic embroidered with shamrocks, and wears a green cape covering her right shoulder. She appears accompanied by an Irish wolfhound, and holds the sword of "national unity". She has just defeated the coercive strategies by the government of Lord Salisbury during the Land War, and now she is ready to fight the last obstacle in the way of Home Rule: the nationalist factions.

Even though the use of allegories was very common in Western cultures during the nineteenth century –Columbia in America, Marianne in France or Helvetia in Switzerland amongst others–, in Ireland it became more than an artistic resource. As Patrick Pearse wrote: "When I was a child, I believed that there actually was a woman called Erin, and had Mr. Yeats's *Cathleen ni Houlihan* been then written and had I seen it, I should have taken it not as an allegory, but as a representation of a thing that might happen any day in any house".[13] Female allegories of the land reached their highest expression

Fig. 1. Lily Williams, ***Hibernia***, n.d. Pastel, 65.5 x 42 cm.
Image courtesy of Adam's Auctioneers

in the cultural production of the Irish Revival. Lily William's (1874–1940) painting *Hibernia* (fig. 1) illustrates this concept of Ireland as an anonymous woman –we can barely see her features– who becomes an eternal symbol of national awakening. The figure, resolute and alert, and covered in the tricolour flag, ignores the viewer and focuses her attention on writing on a paper that she is holding on her lap. Augustus Nicholas Burke follows the same line in *A Connemara Girl* (1870), a portrayal of a young and beautiful colleen wearing a green skirt and a dark shawl that recalls a devotional Christian imagery. She is portrayed gathering heather in a Connemara hill overlooking the sea. This mythical and sentimental representation of the West of Ireland, along with the girl's naked feet and the goats around her, symbolised a sacred earth as well as the deep connection between the Irish peasantry and their environment.[14] William's *Hibernia* and Burke's *A Connemara Girl* are visual examples of the idea of Ireland as a young woman, an image that went on to become one of the main subject-matters of the Literary Revival thanks to authors such as Patrick Pearse himself or W. B. Yeats. Nineteenth and twentieth-century ballads and literature illustrated the British colonisation of Ireland as the violation of a mother who then exhorts her sons to fight the invader and to avenge her suffering in order to restore her freedom and her purity. The foreign occupation, the nationalist fight and the reconstruction of the Irish nation were processes that were played over women's bodies, and the myth of Mother Ireland as a rape-victim perpetuated the idea of the Irish woman as a passive defenceless sufferer whose only salvation was masculine action. The gender-based imagery of the Irish Revival was developed by the nationalist discourse and then projected into the socio-political arena, which had important consequences in the lives and rights of Irish women regarding citizenship and the control over their bodies.[15]

Following the Irish Famine, Mother Ireland and the Virgin Mary were often associated in literary and artistic imagery. Both figures were constructed around the dichotomy between the virgin and the whore (Madonna/Magdalen), a remnant of Victorian ideology.[16] Based on this polarity, maternity became the centre of discourse in the Revival, which aimed to promote "the mother Church of Catholic revival; the motherland of national revival; the mother tongue of Celtic revival".[17] The idea of motherhood as the main duty of Irish women, praised in Yeats and Lady Gregory's *Cathleen ni Houlihan* or Patrick Pearse's *The Mother*, can also be found in the artwork of well-known painters such as Aloysius O'Kelly or Séan Keating. O'Kelly's *Expectation, West of Ireland* (1881) shows a young beautiful mother as a peasant Madonna and a child beside a window. The scene is placed inside a traditional cottage in the West of Ireland. Both the representation of the West and the portrayal of the peasantry are related to traditional values, and every detail in the canvas symbolises the promise of a new state and a new life: from the mother with the child, to the flowers in bloom placed beside the bright window, to the bowl full of potatoes representing prosperity.[18] The role of the young mother in the painting is clear. As Mary Butler proclaimed in 1859 in the *Dublin University Magazine*, the mother is "the educator of the race. The child is the father of the man. The nation is the result of motherhood".[19] O'Kelly proposes here a portrayal of Mother Ireland guiding her son to manhood. Her main duty in society is to give birth and nurture the soldiers who will later fight for her and maintain the Irish tradition. Séan Keating addressed the same idea in *An Allegory* (1924), a representation of the wake of the Irish Civil War where two men, symbolising the two sides of the war, bury the Irish flag. They appear surrounded by a cleric and a businessman, a man (a self-portrait of the artist himself) slumped against a tree, and a mother with a child. The last two figures are the only ones interacting with each other, as the mother is fixing her clothes after having breastfed her child. While praising motherhood, Keating's painting also emphasises the role of the Irish woman in the New State as a healer. She embodies the idea of regeneration –a power already associated with women in the Gaelic mythology of the pre-colonial era–, and the promise of a different future for the nation.[20]

One of the most famous icons of Éire was created by Sir John Lavery (1856–1941), a leading member of the Glasgow School of Painting who became famous for his portraits, landscapes and wartime depictions. Although none of his two wives were strictly Irish, Lavery portrayed both of them as the quintessence of Irishness. *An Irish Girl* (1890) shows his first wife, Kathleen MacDermott, as an exotic Irish beauty with dark hair, pale skin and dressed in a cloak and emerald green clothes. After her death in childbirth, Lavery discovered that MacDermott's name was actually Annie Evans, and her background was Welsh. According to Fintan Cullen, this illustrated how "the whole idea of being Irish had become something enviable, something to aspire to and even worth faking".[21] However, it was the portrait of his second wife, Hazel Lavery, that went on to become a symbol of Ireland, a great example of how the political and the patriarchal came together in the creation of a nationalist cultural discourse. *Portrait of Lady Lavery as Kathleen Ni Houlihan* (fig. 2) was commissioned in 1927 by the Note Committee for the new Irish Free State banknotes issued in 1928. In order to create a symbolic portrait of Éire, Lavery reworked a picture of his American wife Hazel, created in 1909, and portrayed her as Cathleen ni Houlihan, the legendary heroine made popular after W. B. Yeats and Lady Gregory's play. Hazel Lavery was depicted as a peasant woman dressed in green clothes, the antithesis of the contemporary fashions associated with England and the European continent. She appears supporting her chin in her hand and resting her arm on an Irish harp with Celtic ornaments. Like many other artists of the time, Lavery used the West of Ireland as the background for his subject-matters.

Lavery's Éire, like Maclise's Aoife, is represented as passive and submissive, in line with the nationalist discourse that advocated a subordinate role for women

Fig. 2. Sir John Lavery, ***Portrait of Lady Lavery as Kathleen ni Houlihan***, 1927.
Oil on canvas, 75'5 x 62.5. L. 14776
On loan from the Central Bank of Ireland. Photo © National Gallery of Ireland.

in the new state. The painting was reproduced on Irish banknotes between 1928 and 1975, and then as a watermark until the introduction of the Euro in 2002. Lavery himself quoted William Cosgrave, then head of the Cumann na nGaedheal government, as saying that "every Irishman, not to mention the foreigner, who visits Ireland, will carry one [banknote] next to his heart".[22] Hazel Lavery became the face of the nation, well known not only in Ireland but also abroad. By then, Irish portraits had become embodiments of national identity.

Another artist whose artwork brought female portraiture to a new level of significance was William Orpen. In 1907 he carried out a portrait of one of her students entitled *Young Ireland: Grace Gifford*, first exhibited at the Royal Hibernian Academy in 1908 under the title *Young Ireland Knocking*.[23] Gifford was involved in the nationalist movement, campaigned for the suffragist cause and became a member of the Irish Women's Franchise League. She was as well the author of the *Kilmainham Madonna*, painted in the cell of the jail where she was arrested for seven months during the War of Independence. Gifford's husband, Joseph Mary Plunkett, was also imprisoned in Kilmainham Jail in 1916 for his part in leading the Easter Rising. The couple got married in the prison chapel hours before he was executed. Thomas M. Coffey described Gifford as a "muse" during the rebellion, a woman "who he [Plunkett] loved as if she were Cathleen ni Houlihan herself, the manifestation of the Irish ideal in womanhood and nationhood –beautiful, sanctified, romantic and not quite attainable".[24] Although influenced by the Irish cultural nationalism, Orpen's portraiture stands far from the image of Ireland as a "pure unitary race, rural-based, Irish-speaking and Roman Catholic",[25] and offers a different concept of Irishness. He proposed an Irish identity that embraced other images of Ireland as well as people from diverse social and religious backgrounds most notably in *Young Ireland Knocking*. This portrait of a sophisticated Grace Gifford in Edwardian-style dress highlights diversity as one of the main characteristics of Irish identity.

The image of a young female as an allegory of a glowing country is also addressed in other symbolic paintings such as *Ruth and Boaz* (1907) –also modelled by Grace Gifford–, and *Gardenia St. George*. In *Bridgit, a Picture of Miss Elvery* (1908–1909) Orpen carried out a three-quarters portrait of the artist Beatrice Elvery, highlighting her pale skin and her long bright red hair so characteristic of the stereotyped Celtic women. Orpen portrayed Elvery as Brigit, the Celtic goddess, but also as Saint Brigid, Ireland's female patron saint. This was one of the two allegorical portraits of Elvery carried out by Orpen, who also depicted her in the rather sensual painting entitled *The Colleen* (1908).[26] The painter Margaret Clarke was another one of the students of the Metropolitan School of Art who modelled for Orpen in 1909. The painting, entitled *An Aran Islander*, was criticised for its theatricality and it was indeed very different from the realist and honest self-portraits carried out by Margaret Clarke. In William Orpen's artwork, the artists Beatrice Elvery, Grace Gifford and Margaret Clarke became symbols of their country and the quintessence of Irishness, images that they would later subvert through their own artistic practice.

However, Ireland was not only personified by beautiful young colleens and virgin maidens. The other extreme was also evident wherein old haggard women symbolised the nation. The former represented hope and the future, the latter, the abuses of the past.[27] The image of the haggard woman was inspired by literature and folklore and rooted in the character of the Shan Van Vocht (the Poor Old Woman) from a traditional song of the Irish Rebellion of 1798. Like Cathleen Ni Houlihan, who encouraged the self-sacrifice of men for the nation, the Shan Van Vocht appeared as a beautiful young queen only to true patriots. This figure became particularly popular within landscape painters. Paul Henry's portrayal of old women of the West of Ireland celebrated the strength and perseverance of the Irish peasantry, inhabitants of a hostile environment represented by Henry's immense and desolate landscapes. His artwork revealed the harsh life of elderly peasant women, which fascinated the artist. Henry himself stated that he had yet to see "people who worked so hard for so little to gain. It meant incessant toil with the spade".[28] The painter and his wife, Grace Henry, shared their interest in the life and the landscape of the West of Ireland. However, Grace offered a different and more contemporary perspective of the peasantry, especially in respect of women. Her painting entitled *Top of the Hill* (1920) addressed the lifestyle of the communities of the countryside by depicting a happy encounter between three women in Achill, Co. Mayo. Leaving business aside for a while, they seem to be enjoying a break and a chat. Also, paintings like *Potato Sowers* (n.d.) or the melancholic *Lady of the West* (1912–1919) stand in contrast to Paul Henry's romanticised portrayal of the peasant life. Grace's work illustrated the role of women in the isolated communities of the West, focusing on their hard work and offering a more honest view of everyday life scenes.

The old woman gradually replaced the young colleen during the first decades of the twentieth century, especially after the foundation of the Irish Free State. This was a reflection of the demographic structure of the Irish rural society and its depopulation but, more importantly, it demonstrated that the construct of femininity by the Church and the State idealised an asexual motherhood while denying women an autonomous sexuality.[29] The portrayal of young women in a wild landscape had started to be problematic, as they had become a symbol of uncontrolled sexuality. Gradually, their place was taken by old women that represented female fulfilment both in the nation and in the home. They were considered the guardians of tradition and folklore, the asexual incarnation of pure motherhood, and the guides responsible for nurturing a whole generation of Irish children. However, the allegory of the peasant woman did not stop there. During the 1920s, the female figure practically disappeared in Paul Henry's landscape painting. Substituted by representations of Irish traditional cottages, the woman's presence was understood to remain within the walls, confined in the household as a symbol of the family unit and the rural way of life –the Gaelic ideal.[30] Strongly associated to family and tradition, nationalist female role models inevitably marked the history, life and experiences of Irish women. As Ruth Roach Pierson states, "there is an inverse relationship between the prominence of female figures in the allegorisation of nation and the degree of access granted women to the political apparatus of the state".[31] The poet Eavan Boland has criticised the continuous use of images that perpetuated traditional gender-based stereotypes, especially in Irish literature:[32]

> In all of this I did not blame nationalism. Nationalism seemed to me inevitable in the Irish context, a necessary hallucination within Joyce's nightmare of history. I did blame Irish poets. Long after it was necessary, Irish poetry had continued to trade in the exhausted fictions of the nation, had allowed those fictions to edit ideas of womanhood.[33]

Female allegories were central in the search for a national identity carried out by Irish artists. From Daniel Maclise's history painting, Aloysius O'Kelly's depictions of peasant customs and Paul Henry's landscapes, to Séan Keating's overtly nationalist themes, all of them insisted on the idea of Irish women as mothers of the Gael, in charge of reproduction. Female sexuality was portrayed as a male property and, like motherhood, was linked to political aims. For their part, female artists used their art to question and subvert fixed constructs of gender. Their artistic career was not an easy one, and Irish women artists struggled to find their place within Irish culture. Amongst those artists who challenged gendered visual imagery were Margaret Clarke, who offered an alternative view of the Madonna and the Magdalen; Lilian Lucy Davidson, whose intimate depictions of peasant women did not possess sexual connotations; and Mainie Jellett, who demanded a change in the Irish artistic establishment through her abstract representations of the Virgin Mary. They embraced the images of a female land as their own expression of identity, which eventually had an effect in the socio-political context and led to a change in the status of visual allegory. Although traditional and conventional, the discourse that confined women in the domestic sphere offered a possibility of transgression and liberation.

## In Search of Irishness

As mentioned before, poetry and literature became the main vehicles of expression of the Irish Revival thanks to the unbroken tradition of folklore that had survived in the rural areas of Ireland and the *Gaeltacht*. Unlike oral lore, music or dancing, Ireland did not have a continuous tradition of fine art as a result of centuries of invasions, occupations and economic instability.[34] The Irish Literary Revival found its visual counterpart on applied art, which was already part of the Irish folklore and could more easily incorporate the nationalist iconography. The Gaelic League became interested in certain aspects of applied art, as they began to be considered a potential factor of improvement for cottage industries in rural areas. Also, the Abbey Theatre employed members of the Arts and Crafts movement who worked in the production of costumes and set designs, as well as in the decoration of the theatre itself, which included stained-glass from Sarah Purser's cooperative An Túr Gloine, and metal-works from Youghal.[35] However, despite the fact that the Revivalist movement had a more apparent effect on applied art, Irish painting was not oblivious to the nationalist influence during the nineteenth and twentieth centuries. Irish fine artists aimed to follow the accomplishments of the Arts and Crafts movement and the Literary Revival and, by combining the British tradition –praised by the official artistic institutions– with Continental influences and the subject matters of the Revival, the Irish artistic scene flourished.[36] Painting was essential in the creation of a nationalist imagery and, at the same time, it became a chronicler of the emergence of Irish modern society and the foundation of the Irish Free State. Through a great variety of style and techniques, the artists portrayed their own vision of the themes of the Revival, from historical events and mythological passages to portraits of nationalist leaders, landscapes of the West of Ireland or the life of the peasantry.

Despite its location in the European periphery, all kinds of trends and artists moved freely in and out of Ireland until the nineteenth century. With the pass of the Act of Union in 1800, the abolition of the Irish Parliament began to cause economic difficulties for the Dublin Society of Painters by reducing the demand of portraits and landscapes. This, along with the devastating effects of the Great Famine, forced many artists to travel to London in order to continue their careers.[37] On the other hand, Ireland witnessed an increasing interest for small-scale landscapes, history and antiquarian subject-matters as well as for scenes of the daily life. Irish artists used their work to criticise the wealthy colonial class that had monopolised the artistic patronage by demanding paintings of their great mansions built in Irish land.[38] As an answer to the British depiction of Ireland as a wild country inhabited by primitive people, Irish painters and scholars published drawings of their travels around the country, where they praised its rich visual tradition, its distinctive iconography and its people's customs. One of these scholars was George Petrie (1790–1866), "the father of Irish archaeology, one might say father of Irish history, and of the study of Irish art and music".[39] During his time as member of the council of the Royal Irish Academy, the institution went on to become one of the main points for the documentation of Ireland's heritage. Petrie reorganised its museum and added spectacular acquisitions such as the Cross of Cong, the Tara Brooch and the Ardagh Chalice. His achievements, along with the whole antiquarian movement that took place in Ireland between 1830 and 1840, have been considered the first stage of the Revival, and the starting point of a serious interest in documenting Irish antiquities.[40] The antiquarians built the basis for the next generation of Irish painters who would focus their interest on the search of Irishness.

With the growth of a nationalist sentiment, visual arts celebrated Ireland's past as an effort to restore the national identity. This had already begun in the eighteenth century with artists such as Vincent Waldré (1742–1814) or James Barry (1741–1806), who believed that the best way to find an Irish identity was to concentrate on cultural accomplishments and historical events. The efforts for the reconstruction of a national identity led to a new perception of the visual arts, and depicting Irishness became not only a necessity, but also a desire. This interest was addressed in the artwork of Daniel Maclise (1806–1870) who, highly influenced by the work of George Petrie, carried out a number of sketches of architectural remains, studies of Irish antiquities and pieces of Celtic jewellery. Like James Barry, Maclise's ambition was to become a great history painter, and his successful career culminated in his large mural decorations painted in the Houses of Parliament in the 1860s. His masterpiece *The Marriage of Strongbow and Aoife* (ca. 1854) portrays the wedding of the Norman invader Strongbow with the daughter of Dermot MacMurrough, Aoife, as the personification of Celtic Ireland. Maclise's monumental picture depicts the union between Strongbow and Aoife as the formal establishment of Norman foothold in Ireland. Even though the painting was requested by the Commissioners of Fine Arts for the decoration of the Conference Hall of the Houses of Parliament at the Palace of Westminster, Maclise's treatment of the painting appears to be more sympathetic to Ireland by depicting a sacrificial scene with a submissive bride and a background of dead, wounded and captured Celtic warriors.[41] Strongbow places his foot upon a fallen Celtic cross, and an elderly musician falls over a broken Irish harp, a symbol of the lost tradition of the Celts.[42] Aoife, with a hand over her chest, bows her head and bends her knees before Strongbow as a sign of submission.

Like Maclise, many Irish artists had left the country in order to make a living in London. Yet, a group of artists remained in Ireland and decided to establish an Irish academy of painters founded on the model of the Royal Academy of London. Inaugurated in 1823, the Royal Hibernian Academy became the main institution for Irish visual arts and held annual exhibitions from 1825 until its destruction by a fire during the 1916 Rising. The Academy was to be the guardian of the Irish artistic tradition, and offered its male students a strictly academic training. However, Ireland was also inevitably influenced by the Modernist movements that were shaking Europe at the time. After the Art of Union, patronage was no longer monopolised by the landed gentry, and the emerging middle and professional classes began to participate in the sponsorship of the arts.[43] The new trends and the many exhibitions held throughout the nineteenth century culminated with the Irish Industrial Exhibition of 1852, which offered a sample of the artwork of the Old Masters as well as a great collection of contemporary European art. Yet, modern artists saw themselves ostracised by a Cultural Revival which, obsessed with the promotion of a Gaelic identity, focused its efforts mostly on literature and poetry. The artistic production of the previous century was associated in the public psyche with the Anglo-Irish Protestant Ascendancy, and was not well appreciated within nationalist circles. Modern art was also perceived as foreign and Protestant, and so it was ought to be avoided.[44] In order to create a national school of art based on the model of those of the European continent and within the principles of the Revival, Irish painters appropriated the imagery of pre-colonial Ireland and its Celtic motifs as a distinctive feature, and insisted on the depiction of basic geometrical forms, interlaced animals, knots and spirals represented not only in painting, but also in sculpture and decorative arts. The Irish medieval manuscript *par excellence*, the Book of Kells, influenced many artists of the turn of the century, especially those female painters who worked with Abstraction.

A national feeling began to flourish amongst Irish artists working in Ireland and abroad, but this was not exclusive of Ireland. Through the Romantic Movement, the European nationalist movements encouraged artists to look back to the style and themes of the Medieval era. In Ireland, visual arts became highly influenced by the nostalgia for the country's period of glory: the Celtic era, the early Middle Ages and the Gaelic heritage.

In 1843 Thomas Davis, leader of Young Ireland, called for the foundation of a national school of painting parallel to the literary activities of the Irish Revival. Young Ireland, although more interested in the Arts and Crafts movement as the voice for nationalist ideas, also aimed to exploit contemporary fine art for political ends. "National art is conversant with national subjects", Davis wrote. "We have Irish artists, but no Irish art or national art. This ought not to continue, it is injurious to the artists and disgraceful to the country".[45] In his essay, Davis encouraged Irish artists to embrace national subjects as the only way to achieve a sense of national pride and identity. While not necessarily following Davis' lead, artists addressed the concept of Irishness in their own way through diverse genres, media and styles. At the end of the nineteenth century, nostalgic scenes of rural Ireland and sentimental depictions of the Irish peasantry became more and more popular. Just like in literature, the West of Ireland became prominent in the artistic imagery of the visual arts, allowing Irish painting to produce something characteristic of its country without having to fall back on Celtic art. The changeable colours of the West of Ireland and its particular light, along with the wildness of the Atlantic sea, became the background for the portrayal of the Irish peasantry and its strong connection to the land. Nationalism developed the idea of Ireland as a desolate but beautiful country inhabited by Gaelic-speaking people, as the counterpoint to the urban and modern background of the English-speaking and Protestant British colonisers. Rooted in the nineteenth century romantic ideas about primitive places and traditional lifestyle, these images of Ireland and its inhabitants came to be the visual way to reconstruct the Irish identity.

Aloysius O'Kelly (1853–1936) was one of the many painters who carried out a portrayal of a dignified peasantry with the landscapes of Clare, Donegal and Connemara as their main settings. He was recognised for his allegorical paintings of Ireland where he addressed the harsh conditions of the rural communities and the fight for social justice that would lead to the politics of the Land League. He depicted the traditions and customs of the Irish peasantry in paintings like *Mass in a Connemara Cabin* (1883), where the artist recalls the times of oppression and fear when Catholics were forced to hide their religious practices inside their cabins. This change of location was adopted by the popular tradition. *Mass in a Connemara Cabin* was the first painting of an Irish subject matter not taken from history or mythology exhibited in the venue since its foundation in the early eighteenth century.[46] It illustrates a contemporary Irish rural experience, a mass given for a group of people gathered in a cottage in Connemara. Utensils like the butter churn represent the daily life of those gathered in the cabin and the strong connection of the people to their customs. The tradition of making butter at home is also portrayed in O'Kelly's *Kitchen, West of Ireland* (early 1880s) which portrays an Irish woman using the butter churn in the kitchen. Because O'Kelly often worked the characters in order of importance, the figures of the seated man and woman in the background are less defined, while the standing woman making the butter is the most detailed one, as she appears working in her domain. Both the small churn and the kitchen are signs of humility, as Irish farms often had a separate room for dairying.[47] O'Kelly was the first artist to offer a different vision of the West of Ireland, portraying an emergent nation through the Irish peasantry and far from the romantic and primitive ideals of his predecessors. He abandoned the traditional Celtic emblems of Irishness such as the round tower, the wolfhound or the harp, and substituted them for images of a dignified peasantry through their daily life. The West became a symbol of the resistance of the Gael, where the Gaelic customs were to be preserved. O'Kelly's paintings are an example of the connection between the people and their environment, a theme explored by Séan Keating during the twentieth century.

Those artists who travelled to Paris, Antwerp or Brittany learnt to paint from nature and let their styles to absorb the influences of the French impressionists. This was the case of Paul Henry (1867–1958), who went on to become the most influential and the archetypal Irish landscapist of the twentieth century. His artwork of flat surfaces and simplified shapes evidences the trace of Paul Cezanne and Paul Gauguin, as well as the realism of Jean Françoise Millett, whose *Angelus* (1857–1859) and *The Gleaners* (1857) echoes in one of Henry's best-known paintings, *The Potato Diggers* (1912). The painting portrays two peasant women wearing the characteristic red skirt and the shawls covering their head and shoulders. One of them is digging potatoes, hiding her face from the viewer, while the figure on the right, standing up, takes a break and rests the rake between her hands. In the background, the hills of Connemara and the blue sky of Ireland, guardians of the traditions of the peasantry. While studying in Paris, Henry met Grace Mitchell, whom he married in London in 1903. The couple moved to Achill Island (Co. Mayo) in 1912, where the local landscape became the main theme of his art. Through landscape painting, artists like Paul Henry not only expressed the spiritual, cultural and social values of the nation, but also addressed people's places and roles within it. Henry painted scenes of the daily life in the West, of peasants digging potatoes, cutting turf or harvesting seaweed. He reduced the Irish landscape to its essentials of sky, bog and turf, and portrayed the traditional way of life in a post-impressionist style. Irishness was to be found amongst the farmers and fishermen of the West, as well as in their wives, mothers and daughters. This romantic vision of the West was supported by Michael Collins:

> Today, it is only in those places that any native beauty and grace in Irish life survive [...]. In the island of Achill, impoverished as the people are, hard as their lives are, difficult as the struggle for existence is, the outward aspect is a pageant. One may see processions of young women riding down on the island ponies to collect sand from the seashore, or gathering in the turf, dressed in their shawls and in their brilliantly-coloured skirts made of material spun, woven and dyed by themselves as it has been spun, woven and dyed, for a thousand years [...].It is only in such places that one gets a glimpse of what Ireland may become again.[48]

The symbolism of the petticoats and the red skirts can be understood in the context of the biological role given to women in the rural communities of the West of Ireland. In a time when the suffrage movement gathered strength, Henry's paintings like *The Potato Diggers* (1912) or *The Watcher* (1911) became part of the group of paintings that helped confining women within the space of rural nature and domesticity. While Henry's early paintings portrayed the daily life of the Irish peasantry, his work increasingly turned into pure landscape representations in which the only reference to their inhabitants was symbolised by the traditional thatched cottages. The cabin became the romantic symbol of the rural families of the West, in which the role of the woman was that of the mother and nurturer of future generations. She had become the guardian of the culture and traditions of the Gael.[49] The idealised images of these thatched cottages are also a depiction of women's imprisonment in the domestic sphere, which agreed with the Irish nationalist ideology especially after the foundation of the Irish Free State. The landscape turned into a metaphor for the banishment of women from the public sphere. And, even though Henry claimed to be apolitical, his imagery was politically charged with the ideal of a national identity. His landscape fitted perfectly the aspirations of the newly created Irish Free State. The cottage was a symbol of the national tradition and the family unit. Women's destiny was to be fulfilled within the home, where their duties and activities were limited. Motherhood, health and rural family values were praised by landscapists as the basis for the nation, and challenged more active political roles for women. Their place in the nation was in the centre of the family, not in the centre of society.

William Orpen (1878–1931) was to have a profound influence in Irish art of the twentieth century, thanks to his time teaching at the Metropolitan School of Art from 1902 until the outbreak of the First World War. He had attended the London's Slade School of Art and Design, one of the most advanced art academies in Britain thanks to its drawing master, Henry Tonks, who insisted on the importance of the study of the live model and on a meticulous draughtsmanship. But Tonks, highly influenced by the work of the Old Masters, also opposed to Modern Art and to opening the Slade's curriculum to the new trends. Unlike his master Tonks, Orpen longed for a redefinition of Irish art based on international trends that would lead Irish artists to define their own cultural identity. His philosophy permeated his artistic career as well as his teaching in the Metropolitan School of Art, where he introduced a new era of painting. Following the ideas of Henry Tonks, he focused on introducing international standards and a more rigorous study of the life model in artistic education. He proposed the employment of international visiting teachers and encouraged students to explore the work of contemporary international artists rather than focusing only on the techniques of the Old Masters. Orpen worked tirelessly to reconfigure the visual arts in Ireland, but became frustrated with the immobility of Irish arts and disappointed with the conservatism of the Revival, which, he thought, was an impediment for cultural regeneration and for the reconstruction of an Irish national identity. Between 1913 and 1916, he painted *Sowing New Seed (for the Board of Agriculture and Technical Instruction for Ireland)* (1913), *Western Wedding* (1914), and *The Holy Well* (1916), three large-scale allegorical pictures addressing his frustration and satirising everything nationalism had stood for. Ironically, he did so through the use of nationalist elements such as the Irish peasantry, the holy well or the high cross. The three paintings created a satirical critique of the conservative Ireland who rejected modern trends and focused on the past without looking to the future.

Séan Keating (1889–1977) was Orpen's favourite pupil and his most beloved disciple, and was well aware of his master's satire of Ireland. He travelled with Orpen to London as his assistant and model. Keating painted in a realist manner –similar to his master's–, with strong drawing skills and an academic approach to painting. However, as a nationalist, Keating believed his duty was to help define Irishness and the motherland through his work. He was inspired by a trip to the Aran Islands in 1914, where he saw the islanders as the personification of the ideal Gael, the type of men needed for the new nation. The artist's left-wing nationalism was excellently exposed in his allegorical painting of the Irish working-class entitled *Men of the West* (1917). In a social-realist style, Keating depicted three men close up, uniformed in the typical clothes of the Aran Islanders with baggy woollen trousers and waistcoats. Finished in 1915, the painting became a prediction of the events of the following year. Unlike Orpen's satirical trilogy or Lavery's ambiguous sympathies, *Men of the West* clearly is a nationalist picture that displays the painter's ideology. Catherine Marshall and Fintan O'Toole described the painting's exhibition in the Royal Hibernian Academy in 1917 as an "act of political defiance",[50] as it was shown in the Academy's temporary home after the original building was destroyed during the Easter Rising. The canvas became an iconic image of Ireland. From 1916 onwards, Keating focused on portraying Ireland's military struggles in paintings like *Men of the South* (1921–1922). Artworks such as *The Race of the Gael* (1939) or *An Aran Fisherman and His Wife* (1914–20) also insist on the idea of the repossession of a female land, historically perceived as to be controlled. They are a representation the ideal nationalist society, in which the man was encouraged to be strong and "active in the affairs of the country" while

Irish women were to "inculcate their children (especially their sons) with love of country, of Gaelic traditions and of freedom".[51] Although very different to the more obviously political *Men of the West*, Keating's Aran hardworking peasants are surrounded by an aura of heroism and infiniteness; he has turned them into a symbol of Irishness.

The meeting point between the spirit of the Revival and Modern Art was found in the paintings of Jack B. Yeats (1871–1957), the son of John Butler Yeats and brother of Williams. From 1898, he concentrated almost exclusively on Irish subject matters, especially after his *Sketches of Life in the West of Ireland* were exhibited in Dublin and London the following year. Through his early work, he explored a very particular concept of Irishness, mythologising the Irish landscape while evocating the daily life of its inhabitants in a descriptive manner. He, however, did not take a romantic view of the Irish peasantry, nor did he portray it as a picturesque postcard. He painted people as they were, with their circumstances and their uniqueness. As Thomas MacGreevy wrote, he "filled a need that had become immediate in Ireland for the first time in three hundred years, the need of the people to feel that their own life was being expressed in art".[52] His narrative scenes of deep, individual characters set in the West of Ireland have often been compared to John Millington Synge's literary characters. This is not accidental, as Jack himself admired Synge deeply. The West and the Gael had become very important elements of the national identity, and they were the emblems that Jack would base his artwork on. *The Man from Aranmore*, an early painting of 1905, turned into an iconic image of Irishness and an example of Jack's characters of depth, individuality and pride. The figure is not idealised or romanticised, but showed as he is. And the landscape is not a simple landscape anymore. In Jack's artwork, the background becomes the domain of the character. It is now the territory of the peasantry, its natural surroundings.

By 1910, Jack was considered the "most Irish" of the Irish painters.[53] His subject matters became more obscure and his technique more experimental. His manner displayed the new directions Irish art was pointing to. From the 1920s onwards, his style changed radically and moved to a more symbolic approach, but the influence of European Expressionism in his work faced an adverse reception in Ireland.[54] This radical change in Jack's style has been read by different authors as a reaction to Ireland's political situation and the artist's experiences within it.[55] Jack was not politically active then, but described his duty for Ireland stating that "the true painter must be part of the land and the life he paints. The artist may travel all the roads of the world and may paint picture of what he sees, but he can never be part of these roads as he can of the roads of his own land".[56] His *Bachelor's Walk, In Memory* (1915) was described by Thomas MacGreevy as "one of the most beautiful and moving pictures the artist ever painted".[57] It shows a girl leaving her offering in the memorial for an event that took place in 1914 when the British Army opened fire against the crowd, leaving three dead and thirty-two wounded. The soldiers claimed that they shot in self-defence as they had been attacked by the mass. Normal life goes on in the background, a boy passes the flower girl and a horse with a cart goes down the quay.

Representing contemporary events of the Irish struggle became even more important after the Easter Rising. For many artists, painting was now the way to describe the sentiment of the Irish people and their national concerns in an eloquent and direct manner. An important portrayal of the people of Dublin during the early years of the Irish Free State is Yeats's *Communicating with Prisoners* (1924), an experimental representation of a historical event in Ireland. It praises the solidarity between Irish women by painting a group of seven women and a boy listening to a group of republican women imprisoned in Kilmainham Jail by the Free State Government for their involvement in the Civil War. The people in the crowd are mothers, sisters or daughters of those imprisoned by their own people. The women have broken the windows of the jail to wave and shout messages to their friends below. The poster of a Santa Claus, stuck in a colourful billboard on the left side of the canvas, along with the clothes of the women, suggest a modern Ireland that clashes with the lack of freedom of the prisoners. In this painting, Jack gives an honest view of those chaotic years, and highlights the role of women in the Irish struggle for independence. This message, whoever, contrasts with the ideal of a woman's place within the conservative Irish Free State, better represented in Jack's anonymous flower girl in the aforementioned *Bachelor's Walk* who, on the side of the political events, her only duty is to mourn the losses.

Jack B. Yeats painted the landscape, the peasantry and the rebels, but also the tinkers and the beggars. He was considered earthier than his brother W. B. Yeats, who was utterly absorbed by the magic and the legends of the country, and its native mysticism. He shared this interest with another great artist of the Revival, George William (A.E.) Russell (1867–1935). He was fascinated by mythology and folklore, and his personal view of the Irish land and tradition was captured in the canvas. In his paintings, the Irish gods and goddesses are always larger than the human characters, and they are usually painted in bright hues. Like in *The Stolen Child* (n.d.) or *A Spirit or Sidhe in a Landscape* (n.d.), the divinities often wear classical vestments and are portrayed in rural landscapes with hills, rivers or trees. Influenced by his contemporaries, he also painted the Irish landscape as a whole in works such as *Man in a Cabbage Field* (1908) or *The Potato Gatherers (n.d.),* yet Russell's images dealt with the concept of harmony with nature in a more symbolic and spiritual way. Russell himself described his wish to draw on native mysticism and visions of a Celtic past within the creations of the Irish Revival:

> The Celtic Renaissance in Ireland [...] has come about [...] through the almost simultaneous awakening of a number of Irishmen to a higher ideal of beauty and perfection in their art than hitherto; and just because they have a more perfect means of expression, the Celtic spirit is much more

> apparent, for that is something which cannot be analysed or gained by thought, or by making use of any particular set of symbols. It already exists and is the heritage of all, and whenever the mind is subtle and plastic enough to yield to its protean influence, it shapes the human imaginings into harmony with its own ideals so that they express the dreams long hoarded in the Celtic fancy.[58]

Opposed to the Revivalist aim of a Gaelic-speaking Ireland that he considered a "narrow" aspiration, he saw himself as someone who would "gladlier hail / The firstborn of the Coming Race / Than the last splendour of the Gael".[59] Russell was familiar with the harsh environment and poverty of rural Ireland, and criticised the focus of Irish society on militaristic and political matters. Although very little has been written about his painting and his role within the Irish art history, he was one of the only two Irish artists of the period that stayed and painted almost exclusively in Ireland.[60] About his work, Joseph Holloway stated that "if ever the Celtic spirit of dreaminess and longing for something that is neither land nor sea was transplanted onto canvas, here that longing and dreaminess surely was".[61]

A.E. Russell, along with William Orpen, Walter Osborne, John Lavery and many others, supported Hugh Lane's campaign for the establishment of a Modern Art gallery in Dublin, which became one of the most important projects of the artistic Revival. However, the efforts to support the new artistic trends in the country were very limited. It was Evelyn Gleeson who opened the debate about artistic superiority and reclaimed the role of visual arts within the nationalist movement and in the reconstruction of an Irish identity:

> I have been told by a good authority, Herr Spiess, a well-known Swiss expert and Director of the Industrial Museum at Basle, that our artistic side has never been systematically explored [...]. By Irish art I mean Gaelic art –it must either be Gaelic or nothing. All else is imitation: though we might take suggestions from other lands [...]. Here then we stand on the verge of an immense question, –the problem whether it is possible to revive Gaelic ideas in our material surroundings –our tables, our chairs, our silver, our inkstand, our various kinds of stuffs. Something has been done in this direction, chiefly owing to the Language Movement. But infinitely more could be done. And, of those who are Gaelic Leaguers, I would ask –Cannot one nationalise through the eyes as well as through the ears?[62]

The visual arts developed during the Revival, although diverse, had some characteristics in common due to its historical and political context. Yet, at the same time, the cultural movement witnessed the arrival of different techniques and styles that portrayed Irishness in many different ways and perspectives. Irish artists created a unique imagery of the Irish nation and its people and, although some authors reckon that painting after 1900 became less nationalistic,[63] national themes and dilemmas were the main subject-matter of those artists who painted before and after the foundation of the Irish Free State. These artists had to face the dichotomy between Modern art and tradition, which led, in the end, to more complex creations that enriched the Irish artistic scene. But in the gendered imagery and hierarchy of the cultural nationalist discourse, female artists often felt displaced. Still facing the consequences of Victorian ideology, Irish women's access to artistic training and exhibitions was highly difficult. They were banned from the academies, overlooked, and patronised. Their fight for artistic training and the obstacles they faced in order to become professional artists left a deep mark in their artwork.

## Overcoming Obstacles: Irish Women and Artistic Training

In 1971, the American art historian Linda Nochlin published in the *Art News Magazine* her article "Why Have There Been No Great Women Artists?", where she stated that, if there has been no female equivalent to Michelangelo or Rembrandt, Delacroix or Cezanne, Picasso or Matisse, it is not because women biologically lack artistic talent, but because social and institutional factors have prevented women's skills from developing.[64] From the Renaissance until the late nineteenth century, 'high art', such as history, religious or mythological painting, was based on the study of the nude and human anatomy. While artists, ateliers and private academies often employed female models, this was forbidden in almost all public schools until 1850. Women found even more obstacles, as their access to either male or female nude models was restricted. However, they were allowed to model nude, which exemplifies their place in the world as an object to be observed and not as a maker of art. They had to wait until 1893 to be able to attend the life class at the Royal Academy of London, and even then the model had to be "partially draped".[65] This meant that women artists had to explore other genres considered less important, such as portrait, landscape or still life, leading to the so-called "gendering of the genres".

Within these restrictions, female artists explored their social status, challenged traditional roles and subverted the concept of "femininity". Women saw themselves barred from artistic training and professional careers due to their association to nature as opposed to reason and culture, traditionally attributed to men. The "natural" milieu of the woman was the intimate, private sphere, exemplified in the little stories of women illustrated by Dutch painting, in the representation of the West and the Irish peasantry already explored, or in the Impressionist painting which always portrayed women within the domestic and familiar space. In art, as well as in real life, women were conditioned by the concept of the separate spheres, and confined in the domestic domain of the home and the family. The public space was the realm of men and, for women, to enter it meant unforeseen risks. The "public visibility" necessary for success in the Irish artistic scene belonged only to men, who were seen as the only gender capable of developing a more complex and theory-based art practice, opposed to female amateur craftwork. Women tended to focus on the lives and experiences of women, often related to the domestic space, natural surroundings and motherhood.

Moralistic concepts of pure womanhood, the praise of domestic life and the influence of Christian ethics impregnated even more the already gendered visual imagery. In nineteenth-century Ireland, women were considered the guardians of culture, heritage and domestic affairs. Accordingly, upper-class families supported their daughters' efforts to develop their artistic skills only to a certain extent, as this was considered an accomplishment suitable to their role of custodians of the cultural identity and social status.[66] Middle and upper-class women were expected to have a good taste for clothing and home decoration, as well as an ability for "less elevated" artistic genres such as watercolour landscapes, miniature, embroidery or pottery. However, women were never expected to develop their skills any further. According to Jeanne Sheehy, there was a considerable social pressure for upper-class women not to become artists, and very few of them described themselves as such.[67] Women often depicted subject-matters that were closer to them, like domestic scenes of the household work, motherhood, family or children. Their interest in local landscape, domestic animals or plants led, however, to a great knowledge of natural history, zoology and botany for many women. They contributed quietly to the study of natural history and, although several women like Ellen Hutchins or Alice Jacob became published authors, most of their work was never exhibited or published.[68]

Those women who were determined to pursue a career in the arts or explored "male" artistic genres faced obstacles such as the difficulty of access to artistic training, the lack of job opportunities and exhibition, and an eternal condescension. Irish art embraced the concept of a "feminine art", delicate and, above all, amateur. The exception was the daughters of artistic families, who were often encouraged to pursue a career in the arts, and found it easier to establish themselves professionally, even before the nineteenth century. Thus, at least until the mid nineteenth century, women who were any successful as professionals generally came from families of artists,[69] like Caroline Clayton or Clementina Robertson. However, their practice was closely supervised by the male members of the family, which predetermined the kind of work they carried out and often forced them to remain unknown through their shared name.[70] Even in the twentieth century, traditional views about femininity and motherhood were still strong in Ireland and, while there number of women attending art schools increased, many put marriage and family first, as it was expected of them. The career awarded to women was to look after their husbands and children.

After the Act of Union, London had become the main centre for Irish artists. Patronage was scarce in Ireland; few women possessed the necessary wealth to assemble a collection of art, and those who could did not displayed any especial interest in the works of female artists. Patronage for Irish women artists came from the Art Unions, the Art Clubs and the amateur sketching and watercolour societies founded and promoted by women from the late nineteenth century onwards. These clubs, along with the art classes conducted for women in the private schools that flourished in Dublin at the time, allowed female artists to participate in the public sphere on a limited basis.[71] The sketching clubs aimed to develop both watercolour and drawing, frequently underrated by the Royal Hibernian Academy exhibitions, and wished to enrich and develop the arts. In 1870, a group of six women from Co. Waterford (Pauline Prochazcka, Harriet Keane, Frances Keane, Henrietta Phipps, Fanny Currey and Fanny Musgrave) founded The Amateur Drawing Society. Their aim was the "mutual improvement in painting and drawing and the cultivation of a taste for art".[72] In 1887 the Society became the Watercolour Society of Ireland, attracting many watercolour painters who distanced themselves from the Royal Hibernian Academy that prioritised oil painting over watercolour. Amongst them were Paul Henry, A.E. Russell, Jack B. Yeats, Nathaniel Hone or Sir William Burton, which evidenced the male enthusiasm for these successful amateur societies. By 1892, the committee of twelve included seven women, amongst them the leading watercolourists Rose Barton (1856–1929) and Mildred Butler (1858–1941).

In 1872, a Miss Deane (possibly related to Thomas Deane, RHA), along with some other ladies, founded the Ladies' Sketching Club in Dublin, where amateur artists could exhibit their work.[73] This society was created due to the necessity of a more favourable setting than the Royal Hibernian Academy for the exhibition of watercolours. A year later men were admitted to the club, which changed its name to the Dublin Amateur Artists' Society until it was integrated into the Dublin Sketching Club. In 1886, the Dublin Art Club was founded by a group who seceded from the Sketching Club, including Walter Osborne, and had links with many British naturalist painters who had studied in the Continent. The membership was divided between working members (fifty), non-working members (twenty), corresponding members (ten) and lady members (limited to ten), which evidences the status of women in this club. Unfortunately, a common feature in these societies is the lack of records. From the Dublin Amateur Artists' Society there is not even a catalogue left, and most of the information comes from press reports. However, what we do know is that these pioneering adventures were gladly taken up by men who regretted that "there was no society where artists and people of artistic temperament could meet socially in the evenings for discussion and improvement".[74] These societies often defended women's interests with prices and scholarships, organising exhibitions and fighting the discrimination from official organisms. Women showed a remarkable ability to compensate for their lack of resources in the assembly and reshaping of their immediate visual experience. However, these clubs were not totally independent; they included men and judging committees from the beginning, and did not have the financial stability that allowed men's clubs to enjoy permanent premises.

Even though these clubs encouraged other women to pursue a career in the arts, official artistic training during the nineteenth century was offered by academies of art that had been established since the eighteenth century throughout Europe, based on the model of the French Académie Royale de Peinture et de Sculpture founded in 1648.[75] The relationship between art academies and women was always contradictory because, despite the fact that some women were accepted in these institutions, they never enjoyed the same level of privilege than their male colleagues. They were banned from life-drawing classes, from teaching and from art competitions, and they were only accepted as honorific members. In nineteenth-century Ireland, most female artists shared similar backgrounds and came from well-off Protestant families that were more eager to encourage their artistic abilities than Catholic working-class families.[76] For those women growing up in more progressive and intellectual households who wished to pursue professional artistic careers, the problem was not the parental or financial pressure to contribute to the family business but the opportunities for training and practice.

The inequality and discrimination of the Academies was captured in Johan Zoffany's painting *The Portraits of the Academicians of the Royal Academy* (1771–1772). Amongst the founding members of the Royal Academy of Arts set up in London in 1768 there had been two female artists: Angelica Kauffman (1741–1807) and Mary Moser (1744–1819). Zoffany's canvas represents one of the life classes of the Academy in which the academicians, surrounded by copies of ancient sculptures, are gathered around two male models. However, in this group portrait, the female founding members Moser and Kauffman have been relegated to be represented by their portraits on the wall, instead of being portrayed with their colleagues as they deserved. Despite their successful careers and their participation on the foundation of the Academy, Moser and Kauffman were not represented as *creators* of art, but as *products* of art, object of contemplation for the male artist due to their gender. Artistic institutions, based on the same gendered model, hindered women's access to their schools, banned them from the life-class on moral grounds, and excluded them from full membership.[77] The most prestigious fine-art educational institutions in Great Britain and Ireland (the Royal Academy of Arts in London, the Royal Scottish Academy in Edinburgh and the Royal Hibernian Academy in Dublin) developed, like all other European academies of art, as institutions explicitly devoted to the promotion of the male professional artistic career, and many schools did not admit women until the end of the century. A campaign for equal opportunities for women in the Royal Academy Schools was launched by the Society of Women Artists in 1859. A year later, the artist Anna Laura Herford became the first female student of the RA School, after having signed her drawings only with her initials.[78] Although in the RA schools women were allowed to draw from casts in the Antique Class and to paint from the draped model, they were always separated from male students in a room of their own, and remained banned from studying the nude model.

In Dublin, The Royal Hibernian Academy was established in 1823 in order to ensure academic standards in Irish art and to offer education in fine art painting. By 1826 the Academicians opened their first exhibition. The institution gave more status to history, mythology and religious paintings than to portraits, landscape, genre painting or still life. It did not admit any woman into their schools until 1893, the same year the Royal Academy introduced a life class for women,[79] and this only happened on the insistence of Walter Osborne due to the difficulty in recruiting male students. However, as soon as the school opened its doors to women, men practically ceased to attend, as they refused to work with "privileged amateurs" and with the daughters of the upper-class society of Dublin who did not depend on their work to earn a living. Despite the fact that Sir William Abney suggested that "some of the best artists in Ireland are ladies", and that it would be beneficial for the Royal Hibernian Academy to elect them as associates,[80] Sarah Purser had to wait until 1924 to become the first female artist to earn the full membership of the institution, followed by Margaret Clarke in 1927. The Academy was also challenged when, by the hand of female artists, the modern trends began to embrace the Irish artistic scene, although this happened later in Ireland than in the Continent. Traditional methods continued to be taught throughout the first half of the twentieth century until student protests forced change in the 1960s and Academicism gave way to a more individual artistic expression.

Artistic training for women began to change in the nineteenth century when the control of the schools of the Royal Dublin Society passed to the newly established Department of Science and Art based in South Kensington (London) in 1854. When the Dublin Society was founded in 1731, there was a great emphasis on copying prints and drawings, as well as on drawing from plaster casts of antique sculpture and from the live model. The Society did not aim to compete with the Academy or with the private art schools, but it wished to offer applied-art training in the aspects of commercial design and illustration rather than to prepare the students to pursue a career in painting, sculpture or architecture. In 1739, the Dublin Society began to award prizes for painting and sculpture, which were open to both women and men although with distinctions. Women who were awarded prizes were never invited to attend and draw the outline of a head –something that men did– and, when the Society began to offer drawing classes in the 1740s, all the pupils were male. When, under the South Kensington system, the Dublin Schools reluctantly opened their doors to female students, their training only reached the earliest stages of the official curriculum, which in great part predetermined their amateur status.[81] Even those women who excelled in their training were prevented from progressing to a professional status through their ban from anatomy and life-drawing classes. These two subjects offered students the opportunity to learn to draw the human body from a nude model and to develop the ability to manipulate the expressive potential of the figure in "high genres" such as history, mythology or religion. On the other hand, design training was seen as a more suitable occupation for those women who needed to earn a living, and female students generally pursued a more 'genteel' occupation such as teaching or design.

However, the Schools of Design were generally seen as preparatory to go on to the schools of the Royal Academy, where women were also excluded from a complete training. But obstructing women's access to artistic training did not prevent them from seeking professional artistic careers. While fighting for their access into public institutions, women forged their way into the artistic arena. The nineteenth century witnessed Irish women receiving for the first time professional artistic training comparable to that of men. Many of them had to either focus on applied arts or continue their artistic career somewhere else. Those who could afford it, like Beatrice Glenavy, May Guinness or Mary Swanzy, escaped Ireland's social and artistic restrictions and travelled to the continent, which became the starting point of a new era. European academies were also closed to women, but the artistic bohemia in France encouraged the development of the ateliers (private studio instruction), considered an exemplary method of training. By 1880, Paris was the heart of the European artistic scene, and offered a more open-minded mentality for those women who wished to attend anatomy and life-drawing classes. Ateliers like Colarossi's or Julian's offered them the opportunity to be taken seriously, strengthened their skills and encouraged their interests. However, the enrolment fee was much higher for women than for men, and only well-off female artists could afford to attend them. The Irish artists trained in the continent became, according to Brian Fallon, "a very remarkable generation of women, all of whom were authentic personalities in their own right as well as influential and active in many fields. They were, in fact, Ireland's emancipated generation, independent-minded and sometimes vocally feminists – notable organisers and crusades for various causes, sometimes to the extent of becoming sheer busybodies and meddlers in almost everything around them".[82]

Female art education evolved throughout the century, from the middle-class "accomplishments" on applied arts, to the schools of design and, eventually, women's entrance into the fine art schools. In its search for a national identity, Irish art –focused on the past and the local context– had often manifested through a more formal and conservative style. Artistic training in the European ateliers offered Irish women the chance to learn the new trends and bring them to Ireland, in contrast to their male colleagues who mostly remained in Ireland and whose art tended to be more academic. However, even though some women were able to complete their education in one of the French ateliers or at the English private academies, their opportunities to show their work in Ireland were still very limited. Amateur artists were often charged in order to exhibit with professionals, and even those women artists who achieved professional careers were ostracised.[83] The exclusion of women from art schools and integral training became a major obstacle for those who wished to exhibit or pursue professional careers. According to Rozsika Parker and Griselda Pollock, this obstruction signified women's exclusion "from power to participate in and determine differently the production of the language of the arts, the meaning, ideologies, and views of the world and social relations of the dominant culture".[84]

The possibilities of earning a living out of art were scarce, especially for those women who did not belong to families of artists. Many artists who belonged to the working-class –often Catholics who could not afford private education nor travelling– focused on crafts such as engraving, pottery or embroidery. Since the early years of the Dublin Society, women had succeeded in the making of designs for printed and linen damask, as well as in their designs for porcelain. For many women, the choice of odd materials and techniques was simply an imaginative way to create within their limited possibilities, which had a great impact on applied arts through the foundation of artistic cooperatives characterised by a strong social conscience. The visibility of Irish artists in the twentieth century was also marked by inequalities and, although many women artists had then access to art schools, exhibitions and life classes, the reality is that academies and juries were dominated by men, and that art critics were mostly men as well. The Royal Hibernian Academy welcomed women into its annual exhibitions since its beginnings in 1826, and the number of female artists exhibiting increased as the nineteenth century went on. However, they were still excluded from an integral artistic training and full membership.

In 1922, Thomas MacGreevy criticised the lack of support women artists received in Ireland despite the fact that they were already very active in political and academic circles, and observed that some members of the Royal Hibernian Academy "can apparently only titter at the idea of a woman artist [...]. Yet we have several women artists of account [...] all of whom have to work with the knowledge that a man, no matter how inferior to theirs his work may be, stands a better chance of recognition (and of the increased orders that recognition brings) merely because he is a man".[85] The hegemonic and patriarchal structures of Irish society were also expressed in the reception of women's artwork by the press. There were some women art critics, like the first Anglo-Irish art historian Anna Jameson or the British author Lady Elizabeth Eastlake, but until the 1880s most of the critics were men and they reviewed female artwork condescendingly or ignored it for being infantile, amateur or untalented.[86] Some artists, mostly those who remained loyal to the Irish tradition, received favourable reviews occasionally,[87] but the reviews did not acknowledge the skills of the artists, and merely described the subject-matter of their paintings. All this only helped to maintain the inferior status of women in the artistic scene.

The arrival of the twentieth century in Ireland took longer than elsewhere. It was not until 1950s that the modern trends were accepted in Ireland, and those artists who embraced the European Avant-Garde had to face the rejection in their own homeland before becoming the catalysts of change and the leaders of modern art in their country. On the other hand, many of these women had financial means and did not have to compromise their art, as they came from comfortable backgrounds. They could allow themselves to experiment and explore new methods. The Free State favoured social realist works of the landscape of the West and depictions of the Irish peasantry, which dominated the Royal Hibernian Academy. Those female artists that were exposed to alternative artistic training during their time in the Continent, like Mainie Jellett, Evie Hone or Mary Swanzy, were less committed to established rules once they were back in Ireland. While they were fighting for the recognition of the avant-garde in their homeland through organisations like the Society of Dublin Painters in the 20s or the Irish Exhibition of Living Art in the 40s, others, such as Sarah Cecilia Harrison or Sarah Purser, focused on developing a deeper understanding of the visual arts in Ireland, and became involved in the most ambitious artistic adventure of the Irish Revival: the creation of the Hugh Lane Municipal Gallery of Modern Art. Its connection with the Revival was clear from the beginning, as the founder, Hugh Lane (1875–1915) was the nephew of Lady Gregory. In 1901, he had attended an exhibition of paintings by Nathaniel Hone and John Yeats organised by Sarah Purser, which became the beginning of Hugh Lane's campaign for a modern art gallery in Dublin. Impressed with Purser's exhibition, Hugh Lane commissioned John Butler Yeats to paint twenty-five portraits of important Irish people, including Lady Gregory and A.E. Russell. Drawn into the cultural life of Dublin, Lane began to focus on his idea for a modern art gallery, which he thought necessary –both for the Irish cultural life as well as for the public– if there was going to be a distinct school of painting in Ireland. The RHA exhibition changed every year, and contemporary Irish art was not easy to access to.

In his efforts to develop the Gallery, Lane purchased artworks that included paintings by Monet, Manet or Renoir, painters that were still not represented in the public galleries of Ireland. One of the main issues for Lane's project was the location of a permanent site for the Gallery, a problem that continued until 1924, the year Sarah Purser founded the Friends of the National Collection of Ireland. At their annual meeting in 1927, the Friends of the National Collection agreed to focus on finding a permanent location for the Gallery and, thanks to the efforts of Sarah Cecilia Harrison and Sarah Purser, a public inquiry was held in Dublin in 1928. Purser's appeals to president Cosgrave about the Georgian mansion Charlemont House in Parnell Square were successful and accepted by the Government early in 1929. Before leaving Dublin, W.B. Yeats visited one more time the Municipal Gallery and described to the Irish Academy of Letters how he "sat down, after a few minutes, overwhelmed with emotion […]. In those rooms of the Municipal Gallery I saw Ireland in spiritual freedom".[88]

According to Liz Sheridan, the foundation of the Gallery of Modern Art in Dublin would not have been possible without the efforts of women.[89] Not only Guinness, Purser or Harrison, but also Constance Markievicz, Clara Christian, Mrs. Ambrose McEvoy, Rose Barton, Estella Solomons, Mrs. Murray Robertson and Mildred Butler were also involved. They donated their paintings to the collection and organised subscription groups to buy works for Dublin from the Forbes collection of continental art. Constance Markievicz set up the Ladies' Committee that raised funds to purchase paintings. Lady Augusta Gregory proved to be essential in her nephew's dream to establish a gallery of modern art in Dublin that would dignify Ireland among the nations and serve as an inspiration for art students. She believed that the institution would "produce a school of painting equal in importance and in profit to any in the world".[90] When the Gallery opened in January 1908, the catalogue –the only one illustrated of the collection ever printed– was compiled by Sarah Cecilia Harrison. Ellen Duncan became the first curator of the Modern Art Gallery after Lane's designation as Director of the National Gallery of Ireland in 1913. Duncan was also the secretary of the Dublin United Arts Club, founded in 1905 to bring together people interested in art and to "crystallize the renaissance movement then going on in Dublin".[91] She was responsible for bringing to the Gallery the work of artists such as Cézanne, Gauguin, Van Gogh, Matisse or Pissarro, following Lane's ambition to improve the Irish cultural life, to give Irish artists the opportunity to see what was being done elsewhere and to provide Dublin with an outstanding gallery of Modern art.

The Municipal Gallery of Modern Art was only one of the many projects that proved the important contribution of women in the arts. Indeed, there have been many female artists and patrons in Ireland, although their presence has been silenced by academic literature, museums and public institutions. Their invisibility during the twentieth century was marked by contradictions and, while the number of women working in the arts increased, they became less and less quoted in the history books. This would not change until the 1970s, when feminist art historians began to explore the lives, experiences and careers of women. Between the Renaissance and the twentieth century, female artwork was considered by the critics either as an impressive exception, an example of "feminine sensibility", or an evidence of a woman's virtues over her skills as an artist.[92] Protestant or Catholic, rich or poor, Irish female artists were ostracised only because of their gender, but they challenged the opinion of many that women were not meant to create art. In 1889, Sarah Cecilia Harrison (1862–1941) reclaimed her creative capacity through her *Self-portrait* (fig. 3), painted in 1889. Like other female creators such as the Italians Sofonisba Anguissola (ca. 1532–1625) and Artemisia Gentileschi (1593–1656), or the Dutch Judith Leyster (1609–1660), Harrison portrayed herself as an artist who firmly holds her palette and her brush. Her canvas is not visible to the viewer as its importance lies on the woman herself and her career as a professional artist.

Fig. 3. Sarah Cecilia Harrison, ***Self-portrait***, 1889.
Oil on canvas, 61 x 51.4 cm. Collection Dublin City Gallery The Hugh Lane

Through her self-portrait, Harrison challenged the prejudices and condescension that every female artist named in this book had to face. Many remained single, and very few became mothers in order to pursue their wish to become teachers, artists and pioneers, and to reclaim their place in the Irish artistic scene. They pursued their own ambitions, stepped into the public arena as teachers, patrons and professional artists, and created their own cooperatives. They were also responsible for the founding of ground-breaking exhibitions such as the Society of Dublin Painters in 1920 (which showed the controversial *Decoration*, by Mainie Jellett), or the Irish Exhibition of Living Art. They brought modernism to Ireland, anticipated the creation of the Irish Free State and portrayed the cultural and political process that led to the Irish independence, while addressing gender issues through their work. By subverting, adopting and adapting the themes cultivated in the literary and artistic Revival, women artists created a whole new perspective of Irishness, nationalism and art itself. Their artwork challenged tradition and conservatism, and paved the way to the avant-garde in Ireland, becoming the pioneers of a new artistic era in the country. Not only they contributed in a very important way to the development of the visual arts in Ireland, but they also left a deep impression in the following generations. Many of them never described themselves as revolutionaries and, nevertheless, their artwork was essential in the development of the events that shook Ireland at the turn of the century and in the first decades of the twentieth century. Their art offers a new perspective of the Cultural Revival and Irish nationalism embroidered with personal stories.

# NOTES

1. Nicola Gordon Bowe, "Symbols of Ireland", in Government of Ireland, accessed on May 10th 2020, https://web.archive.org/web/20110614174614/http://www.gov.ie/en/essays/symbols.html
2. Gabriella Elgenius, *Symbols of Nations and Nationalism. Celebrating Nationhood* (Hampshire: Palgrave Macmillan, 2011), 1.
3. Declan Kiberd, "Irish Literature and Irish History", in *The Oxford Illustrated History of Ireland,* ed. Robert Fitzroy Foster (Oxford: Oxford University Press, 1989), 283.
4. Eavan Boland, *Object Lessons. The Life of the Woman and the Poet in Our Time* (New York: Norton, 1996), 66.
5. Elizabeth Grosz. *Jacques Lacan. A Feminist Introduction* (London: Routledge, 1990), 129.
6. John Turpin, "Visual Marianism and National Identity in Ireland: 1920–1960", in *Art, Nation and Gender. Ethnic Landscapes, Myths and Mother-Figures,* eds. Tricia Cusack and Síghle Bhreathnach Lynch (Burlington: Ashgate, 2003), 70.
7. Tricia Cusack, "Introduction: Art, Nation and Gender", *in Art, Nation and Gender. Ethnic Landscapes, Myths and Mother-Figures,* eds. Tricia Cusack and Síghle Bhreathnach-Lynch (Burlington: Ashgate, 2003), 9.
8. Clare Carroll, "The Construction of Gender and the Cultural and Political Order in *The Faerie Queene* 5 and *A View of the Present State of Ireland:* The Critics, the Context and the Case of Radigund", *Criticism,* vol. 32, no. 2 (1990): 163.
9. Mary Jean Corbet, *Allegories of Union in Irish and English Writing, 1790–1870: Politics, History and the Family from Edgeworth to Arnold* (Cambridge: Cambridge University Press, 2000), 16.
10. Jemma Tosh, "Rape me, I'm Irish: An Analysis of the Intersecting Discourses of Anti-Irish Racism and Sexual Violence", *Intersectionalities,* vol. 4, no. 1 (2015): 72.

11. See Sabina Sharkey, *Ireland and the Iconography of Rape: Colonisation, Constraint and Gender* (London: University of North London Press, 1994).
12. Anne Helmreich, "Domesticating Britannia: Representations of the Nation in Punch: 1870–1880", in *Art, Nation and Gender: Ethnic Landscapes, Myths and Motherfigures,* eds. Tricia Cusack and Síghle Bhreathnach-Lynch (Aldershot: Ashgate, 2003), 15–28.
13. Patrick Pearse, *Collected Works of Padraic H. Pearse. Political Writings and Speeches* (Dublin: The Éire-Gael Society, 2013), 160.
14. Marie Bourke, *West of Ireland Paintings at the National Gallery of Ireland from 1800 to 2000* (Dublin: National Gallery of Ireland, 2014), 26.
15. Rosende Pérez, "La Iconografía Femenina de Irlanda. Creación y Re/Construcción de una Nación en Femenino", *Lectora,* 14 (2008): 260.
16. Griselda Pollock, *Vision and Difference* (London and New York: Routledge, 2003), 160.
17. Richard Kearney, *Postnationalist Ireland: Politics, Culture, Philosophy* (London: Routledge, 1997), 118–119.
18. Niamh O'Sullivan, *Aloysius O'Kelly: Art, Nation, Empire,* (Dublin: Field Day, 2010), 99–100.
19. Mary E. L. Butler, "Womanhood and its Mission. Part II", *Dublin University Magazine,* vol. 53, no. 318, (May 1859): 696.
20. Éimear O'Conor, *Séan Keating. Art, Politics and Building the Irish Nation* (Newbridge: Irish Academic Press, 2013), 88–89.
21. Maev Kennedy, "Exhibition Reveals London's Admirable Irish", *The Guardian* (March 9th 2005), accessed on May 9th 2020, https://www.theguardian.com/uk/2005/mar/09/arts.artsnews
22. Sinéad McCoole, *Hazel: A Life of Lady Lavery, 1880–1935* (Dublin: Lilliput Press, 1996), 225.
23. Anne Cormican, "William Orpen (1878–1931): A Voice for Pluralism in the Long Nineteenth Century", in *Travelling Irishness in the Long Nineteenth Century. New Directions in Irish American Literature,* eds. Marguérite Corporaal and Christina Morin (New York: Palgrave MacMillan, 2017), 91.
24. Thomas M. Coffey. *Agony at Easter: The 1916 Irish Uprising* (Harmondsworth: PenguinBooks, 1976), 130.
25. Síghle Bhreathnach-Lynch. *Ireland's Art, Ireland's History: Representing Ireland 1845 to Present* (Omaha: Creighton University Press, 2007), 73.
26. Robert Upstone et al, *William Orpen: Politics, Sex and Death* (London: Philip Wilson, 2005), 73.
27. Paula Murphy, "Madonna and Maiden, Mistress and Mother: Woman as Symbol of Ireland and Spirit of the Nation", in *When Time Began to Rant and Rage. Figurative Painting from Twentieth-Century Ireland,* ed. James Christen Steward (Berkeley: Merrell Holberton), 94.
28. Brian Kennedy, "An Enduring View of Irish Identity: Paul Henry and the Realism of Fiction", *Irish Arts Review Yearbook,* vol. 15 (1999): 98–107.

29. Catherine Nash, “Remapping and Renaming: New Cartographies of Identity, Gender and Landscape in Ireland”, *Feminist Review,* no. 44, Nationalisms and National Identities (1993): 47.
30. Síghle Bhreathnach-Lynch, “Landscape, Space and Gender. Their Role in the Construction of Female Identity in Newly Independent Ireland”, in *Canadian Women Studies,* vol. 17, 3 (1997): 29.
31. Ruth Roach Pierson, “Nations: Gendered, Racialized, Crossed with Empire,” in *Gendered Nations: Nationalisms and Gender Order in the Long Nineteenth Century,* ed. Ida Blom et al. (London: Bloomsbury, 2000), 44.
32. Eavan Boland and Edna O’Brien are amongst those female writers who would later subvert the stereotype of Mother Ireland. See Pilar Villar-Argáiz, *The Poetry of Eavan Boland: A Postcolonial Reading* (Dublin: Academica Press, 2008), and Kathryn Laing et al., *Edna O’Brien: New Critical Perspectives* (Dublin: Carysfort Press, 2006). For information regarding Irish women’s fiction and gender, see Heather Ingman, *Twentieth-Century Fiction by Irish Women: Nation and Gender* (Hampshire: Ashgate, 2007).
33. Eavan Boland, “Outside History”, *The American Poetry Review,* vol. 19, no. 2 (March/April 1990): 33.
34. Sheehy, *The Rediscovery of Ireland’s Past,* 95.
35. David A. Ross, *Critical Companion to William Butler Yeats. A Literary Reference to His Life and Work* (New York: Facts on File, 2009), 432.
36. See Cyril Barrett. “Irish Nationalism and Art, II: 1900–1970”, *Studies: An Irish Quarterly Review,* vol. 91, no. 363 (2002): 223–238.
37. Arnold, *A Concise History of Irish Art,* 93.
38. Fintan Cullen, *A Shared Legacy: Essays on Irish and Scottish Art and Visual Culture* (London: Routledge, 2017), 80.
39. Myles Dillon, “George Petrie (1789–1866)”, *Studies: An Irish Quarterly Review,* vol. 56, no. 223 (1967): 226.
40. Sheehy, 17.
41. Sheehy, 45.
42. Síghle Breathnach Lynch, “Imagining the Past: The Marriage of Strongbow and Aoife”, *The Irish Review,* no. 29 (2002): 97.
43. Matthew C. Potter (ed.), *The Concept of the ‘Master’ in Art Education in Britain and Ireland. 1770 to the Present* (London: Ashgate, 2013), 15.
44. Nicola Figgis et al, *Art and Architecture of Ireland, vol. 2. Painting, 1600–1900* (London: Yale University Press, 2014), 126.
45. Quoted in Fintan Cullen, *Sources in Irish Art. A Reader* (Cork: Cork University Press: 2000), 70–73.
46. Fintan Cullen, “Politics and the Painter”, *The Irish Times* (May 1st, 2010), accessed on May 9th 2020, https://www.irishtimes.com/culture/books/politics-and-the-painter-1.659877
47. Claudia Kinmonth, *Irish Rural Interiors in Art* (London: Yale University Press, 2006), 184–185.
48. Michael Collins, *The Path to Freedom* (Dublin: Talbot Press, 1922), 119.

49. Bhreathnach-Lynch, "Landscape, Space and Gender", 29.
52. Fintan O'Toole. *Modern Ireland in 100 Artworks* (Dublin: Royal Irish Academy, 2016), 6.
51. Bhreathnach-Lynch, "Landscape, Space and Gender", 27.
52. Thomas MacGreevy, *Jack B. Yeats: An Appreciation and Interpretation* (Dublin: Victor Waddington, 1945), 19.
53. Kenneth McConkey, *A Free Spirit. Irish Art, 1860–1960* (London: Antique Collectors Club, 1990), 123.
54. Quoted in Karen E. Brown, "Thomas MacGreevy and Irish Modernism: Between Word and Image", in *Irish Modernism: Origins, Contexts, Publics* (New York: Bern, 2010), 101.
55. Brown, 101.
56. Gordon S. Armstrong, *W. B. Yeats and Jack Yeats. Images and Words* (London: Associated University Press, 1990), 224.
57. Thomas MacGreevy, "Three Historical Paintings by Jack B. Yeats", *Capuchin Annual* (1966), 396.
58. Quoted in Nicola Gordon Bowe, "Symbolism in Turn-of-the-Century Irish Art", *Irish Arts Review Yearbook* (1989/1990): 136.
59. George Russell, "On Behalf of Some Irishmen Not Followers of Tradition", in *Penguin Book of Irish Verse,* ed. Brendan Kennelly (Harmondsworth: Penguin, 1981), 314.
60. Diana Beale, "Time to give AE his due", *The Irish Times* (August 23rd, 2004), accessed on May 9th 2020, https://www.irishtimes.com/culture/time-to-give-ae-his-due-1.1154481
61. Quoted in Richard M. Kain and James O'Brien. *George Russell (AE)* (London: Bucknell University Press, 1976), 23.
62. Quoted in Karen E. Brown, *The Yeats Circle. Verbal and Visual Relations in Ireland, 1880–1939* (London: Routledge, 2011), 31.
63. Sheehy, *The Rediscovery of Ireland's Past,* 177.
64. See Nochlin, "Why have there been no great women artists?"
65. Nochlin, 159.
66. Henrietta L. Morre. *Antropología y Feminismo* (Valencia: Cátedra, 2009), 148.
67. Jeanne Sheehy, "The Training and Professional Life of Irish Women Artists Before the Twentieth Century", in *Irish Women Artists From the Eighteenth Century to the Present Day,* eds. Jenni Rogers et al. (Dublin: The National Gallery of Ireland and Douglas Hyde Gallery, 1987), 9.
68. E. Charles Nelson, "Irish Women Artists as Natural History Illustrators", in *Irish Women Artists from the Eighteenth Century to the Present Day,* eds. Jenni Rogers, Wanda Ryan-Smolin and Elizabeth Mayes (Dublin: The National Gallery of Ireland and Douglas Hyde Gallery, 1987), 28–29.
69. Sheehy, *The Rediscovery of Ireland's Past,* 7–11.
70. Delia Gaze, *Concise Dictionary of Women Artists* (New York and London: Routledge, 2001), 69.

71. Gaze, *Concise Dictionary of Women Artists,* 65.
72. Quoted in Shirley Armstrong Duffy, "The Role of Women in Irish Sketching Clubs in the Late Nineteenth Century", in *Irish Women Artists from the Eighteenth Century to the Present Day,* eds. Jenni Rogers et al. (Dublin: The National Gallery of Ireland and Douglas Hyde Gallery, 1987), 12.
73. Cyril Barrett and Jeanne Sheehy, "Visual Arts and Society, 1850–1900", *in A New History of Ireland. VI. Ireland Under the Union, 2. 1870–1921,* ed. William Edward Vaughan (Oxford: Oxford University Press, 1989), 449.
74. Armstrong Duffy, "The Role of Women in Irish Sketching Clubs", 13.
75. Geraldine Norman. *Nineteenth-Century Painters and Painting: A Dictionary* (Berkeley and Los Angeles: University of California Press, 1977), 27.
76. Maria Connolly and Paul Finucane. *Journeys Through Line and Colour: Forty Irish Women Artists of the Twentieth Century* (Limerick: University of Limerick, 2010), III.
77. Sheehy, *The Rediscovery of Ireland's Past,* 7–11.
78. Sara Gray, *Dictionary of British Women Artists* (London: The Lutterworth Press, 2009), 135.
79. Gaze, *Concise Dictionary of Women Artists,* 30.
80. Sheehy, 11.
81. Gaze, *Concise Dictionary of Women Artists,* 60.
82. Brian Fallon, *Irish Art, 1830–1990* (Dublin: Appletree Press, 1994), 108.
83. Gaze, *Concise Dictionary of Women Artists,* 65.
84. Griselda Pollock and Rozsika Parker, *Old Mistresses. Women, Art and Ideology* (London and New York: I.B. Tauris, 2013), 135.
85. Julian Campbell, "Art Students and Lady Travellers", in *Irish Women Artists from the Eighteenth Century to the Present Day,* eds. Jenni Rogers et al. (Dublin: The National Gallery of Ireland and Douglas Hyde Gallery, 1987), 20.
86. Gaze, *Concise Dictionary of Women Artists,* 69–70.
87. John O'Grady, "Sarah Purser HRHA (1848–1943)", in *Irish Women Artists, 1870–1970* (Dublin: Adam's, 2014), 18.
88. Speech delivered at the Banquet of the Irish Academy of Letters, August 17th 1937. Quoted in McConkey, *A Free Spirit,* 77.
89. Liz Sheridan, "Women and Dublin's Municipal Collection", in *Irish Women Artists from the Eighteenth Century to the Present Day,* eds. Jenni Rogers et al. (Dublin: The National Gallery of Ireland and Douglas Hyde Gallery, 1987), 15–16.
90. Quoted in Robert O'Byrne, "The Man Who Gave Us Modern Art", *The Irish Times* (January 19th 2008), accessed on May 19th 2020, https://www.irishtimes.com/news/the-man-who-gave-us-modern-art-1.930285
91. Kit Ó Céirin and Cyril Ó Céirin, *Women of Ireland: A Biographic Dictionary* (Galway: Tír Eolas, 1996), 237.
92. Pollock and Parker, *Old Mistresses,* 80.

# Part Three

# Presence I. Painters

# Images of the Nation

## Beatrice Elvery

Beatrice Moss Elvery (Dublin, 1883–1970) was the second of seven children born to Theresa Moss and the Dublin businessman William Elvery. Raised in a talented family, Beatrice was the sister of the well-known South-African portraitist Dorothy Kay, and the niece of the Edinburgh Arts and Crafts artist Phoebe Traquair, a significant figure in British art and one of the first women artists in Scotland to achieve professional recognition.[1] Aged only thirteen, Beatrice attended the Dublin Metropolitan School of Art, where her style became stimulated by Sir William Orpen. Teacher and pupil became lifelong friends, although in the later years Orpen was based in London while Beatrice worked in Dublin.[2] At the Dublin Metropolitan School of Art she also became a versatile sculptress under the tutelage of John Hughes, an Irish sculptor strongly influenced by the Italian Renaissance.

Elvery described herself as "the same sort of pagan as John Hughes",[3] which she addressed through the delicate Celtic touch of her artwork. She also absorbed her aunt's Pre-Raphaelite manner, displayed in paintings like *Affectionate Couple* (1902), an early pastel painted during her training at the School. It portrays a loving scene of a young Celtic woman holding her lover with her arms, wrapping his neck with her hair and bringing him closer. A work of notable beauty, the female character has been thought to be a self-portrait of the artist herself, whose long red hair was also highlighted in the canvas by other contemporary artists who portrayed her as a symbol of Ireland's Revival. Orpen painted her as the Irish icons Colleen and Brigid, and she was also sculpted by Oliver Sheppard as Roisín Dubh for the memorial to James Clarence Mangan. Patrick Pearse reported this sculpture as "the finest embodiment of the wonderful sweetness of Caithlin Ni Uallachain that has yet been carved in marble, or painted on canvas [...]. That face is an expression of the soul of Ireland if ever the soul of Ireland had been expressed in art [...]. Only in Ireland could such a fine face have been seen or imagined [...] the beautiful dream face".[4]

*Affectionate Couple* is only one of Elvery's many representations of amorous lovers who often appeared accompanied by fantastical figures of sea monsters and unicorns of classical flavour and modernist style. Orpen praised her "much temperament and great ability",[5] and always encouraged her to focus her artistic skills on painting. However, she also became Hughes' star pupil and a skilful sculptress who created works of great depth with clay, wood, stone and plaster. She exhibited with the Royal Hibernian Academy from 1902 onwards, and won the Queen's Prize for drawing in 1900 and the Taylor Art Scholarship of Sculpture three years in a row, from 1901 until 1903.[6] The first year, questioning that her modelled figure of a bather and the relief of a child's head had been worked without any sort of help, Elvery was asked to model a head from life in the presence of the judges.[7] The Taylor Art Scholarship gave her the opportunity to travel to Paris with her sister and her friends, the artists Estella Solomons and Cissie Beckett, in order to continue her training. Once back in Dublin, she spent her time teaching at the Dublin Metropolitan School of Art, illustrating children's books and drawing dissections for doctors and archaeological discoveries for the museums amongst other things. She moved freely between a great variety of media, from painting, sculpture or illustration, to furniture and decoration. Encouraged by Sarah Purser, she attended stained glass classes from Alfred E. Child and joined Purser's studio, An Túr Gloine, where she created windows for several churches throughout the country. Elvery went on to become a well-known artist thanks to her ability to capture the soul and deepest essence of her subjects. Her early work, dominated by an illustrative style, was influenced by the Arts and Crafts Movement and the work of her aunt Phoebe Traquair, who was a great admirer of Dante Gabriel Rossetti and Alexander Fisher.[8] Both aunt and niece participated in the 1904 Art and Crafts Exhibition in Ireland. Elvery showed ten items, including some terracotta works, a Christian stoup and a lectern in plaster that was later cast in bronze and praised by Paul Larmour as "a remarkable piece of organic art nouveau… There is nothing else like it in Ireland".[9]

Elvery's artwork often depicted the legends of ancient Ireland and developed new concepts of neo-Gaelic art, which led her soon to become a significant part of the cultural nationalist movement. In her autobiography, Elvery described how, through her involvement in the Revival, she developed an idealised view of Irish nationalism:

> From the time when I started going to the School of Art" –she explained– I had found it almost too easy to become romantic and emotional about Irish politics. I had been very impressed by Yeats's *Cathleen ni Houlihan*, and some early patriotic paintings by Jack Yeats. Irish patriotic songs and Irish patriotic poetry were very potent. It was difficult for a young, susceptible person not to be swept away in a flood of patriotism, but to be really involved to this movement it was necessary to have a great hate of England and everything English – I could never work myself up to that part of it.[10]

She designed the illustrations for several Revivalist volumes such as Katherine Frances Purdon's *Candle and Crib* (1914) or Patrick Pearse's Íosagán (1907), as well as for important Irish magazines like *The Irish Review* or *The Dublin Magazine*. She also produced calendars, Christmas cards and hand-coloured prints for Cuala Press, which were issued until after the Second World War, and designed illustrations for *Sinn Féin* magazine. She was the author of the original storyteller in the cover of *The Shanachie*, an Irish cultural magazine that published literary and artistic works of W. B. Yeats, Lady Gregory, Padraic Column or George Bernard Shaw.[11] Between 1907 and 1913, Elvery illustrated *Heroes of the Dawn* (1914) for Violet Russell, author and wife of A.E. Russell.[12] The book tells the story of Fionn MacCumhaill and his group of heroic warriors of the Ossianic Cycle which, along with the Mythological Cycle, the Ulster Cycle, and the Cycle of the Kings, conforms the four main categories of Irish mythology.

Versions of these myths and legends were created specifically for children during the Irish Revival, when authors and artists worked together in projects of theosophical background that aimed to recreate Irish heroes for the new generations.[13] Elvery's artwork for *Heroes of the Dawn* followed this concept, and her images are riddled with the characteristic visual symbols of Irish nationalism. A clear example is the illustration entitled *Where the Moonbeams Made a Path of the Grass, Finn Saw Two Fair Young Girls.* It portrays the mythical hero accompanied by an Irish wolfhound in the shadows of a natural Irish background, while two giant female figures from the Tuatha Dé Danaan stand in front of them dressed in white tunics. The Celtic atmosphere and adornments are present in many of Elvery's drawings, like *They Found Him Lying Peacefully Asleep on His Bed of Skins ad Rushes,* also from *Heroes of the Dawn.* Characteristic motifs of the La Tène Celtic culture such as zoomorphic figures, knots and spirals, are often included by Elvery in a descriptive style in black and white. However, some of her illustrations also contain delicate hues applied with coats of watercolour slightly layered, which gives her drawings a more ethereal look. These images served as an inspiration for other artists of the time like Letitia Hamilton or Maud Gonne and her illustrations for Ella Young's Celtic Wonder Tales (1910).

In 1907, Elvery created *Éire* (fig. 4), one of her most famous paintings and a symbol of Irish nationalism. The picture was created during her time in An Túr Gloine, where she spent six years executing windows several churches in Ireland. *Éire* was profoundly inspired by Yeats and Lady Gregory's *Cathleen Ni Houlihan*, a play previously mentioned in the first chapter of this book "Brief Overview of History, Art and the Role of Women in Ireland". The painting shows an allegorical Cathleen portrayed as a Madonna, and dressed in a green hooded cloak (a *cucullus*). The cape is closed by an ornament that, influenced by the antiquarian movement, recalls the Tara Brooch. Cathleen appears holding a child on her lap, a symbol of Young Ireland reaching his hands to the

Fig. 4. Beatrice Elvery, ***Éire***, 1907.
Oil on canvas, 91 x 71 cm. Collection of Lady Davis-Goff.

future.[14] The figure of Mother Ireland evokes the medieval images of Madonna Enthroned, with the difference that in *Éire* the female figure is seated on a Celtic cross, an upright high cross with the arms and shaft interlocked within a ring. These types of high crosses first appeared in Ireland during the eighth century and have been considered one of Ireland's greatest contributions to sculpture of the European Middle Ages, a period of cultural flourishing in Ireland also mentioned in the first chapter of this book. Along with the round tower and the Irish wolfhound, the high crosses became a symbol of the Revival thanks to the romanticisation of Ireland's past and especially after the publication in 1857 of Henry O'Neill's book *Illustrations of the Most Interesting of the Sculptured Crosses of Ancient Ireland*. Although there is nothing pure "Celtic" about these crosses, the Revival associated them with a flourishing "native" art of a time before Ireland was occupied by the British. They were also seen as an image of Irish ethnicity, especially once they were transported to America and they began to be associated with the Irish diaspora, a lost sense of community and a missed land.[15]

Elvery's enthroned Irish Madonna was also influenced by the Italian altarpieces of the Renaissance. She gives the impression of being illuminated from behind, a combination of light and shadow that has made the canvas to be read as a representation of the Second Coming, a symbol of the Irish fight for freedom.[16] Even though the iconography of the Madonna and the Child as a nationalist symbol was not new in the imagery of the Revival, Elvery's painting offers a darker and more surreal treatment of this subject-matter. The canvas shows the influence of Elvery's academic training and her knowledge of sculpture and stained glass, Byzantine mosaics and the Italian Quattrocento. At the same time, it embraces the Irish iconography by combining a Catholic theme with the emergent republic, although as Elvery stated, the painting was more a consequence of a nostalgic vision of Irish history than a desire for an independent Ireland. Nevertheless, the canvas was bought by Maud Gonne herself –who had played Cathleen in Yeats and Lady Gregory's play– and donated it to St. Enda's School, an institution created in 1908 by Patrick Pearse as an alternative to the Irish education system that, under British rule, prepared young boys "to be good Englishmen or obedient Irishmen".[17] *Éire* addressed Pearse's vision of the connection between the past and the future of Ireland, and he even used the painting as a cover for the 1907 Christmas edition of *An Claidheamh Soluis*. He interpreted the canvas as the triad of the "Past, Present and Future – Memories, Disappointments, Hope", with the present conceived as a purgatory time that needs to be overcome by the connection between Ireland's heroic past and a hopeful future.[18] The painting portrayed the link between the national and the religious through the subject-matter of the Madonna with the Child, a representation of the redeemed and the damned in Christian iconography. The figures behind the Madonna are warriors, saints, scholars and martyrs of the heroic Irish past, while the naked figures portrayed under the cloak represent the new generation of Ireland sheltered by *Éire*. The Child, stretching out his hands, personifies the future of the nation.

Elvery's canvas became a landmark painting in promoting the idea of a free Ireland, but it also insisted on the idea of a passive role for women in the struggle for independence and in the public sphere. Elvery thought her work of little interest to Irish nationalist although it had all the elements of Irish nationalism, from the red hair of the Irish Madonna to the High Cross and the Celtic clothing of the figures and, of course, the symbolism. When, some years later, a past-pupil approached Elvery and remarked that *Éire* had "inspired him to die for Ireland", the artist was "shocked" at the thought that her "rather banal and sentimental picture might, like Helen's face, launch ships and burn towers".[19]

Like the Gaelic League, St. Enda's School also wished to conserve and develop the Gaelic language through modern Gaelic literature. Pearse published several translations of traditional Irish tales, poems and plays often illustrated by Beatrice Elvery. As she did not know Irish, Pearse used to come to her studio in An Túr Gloine to translate the stories of his books, as the artist recalls in her autobiography:

> While I was in the Stained Glass Works I had illustrated a child's book for Patrick Pearse, one of the leaders of the Rising who had been court-martialled and shot. He was a rather bulky, pale, shy young man whose black clothes made him look as if he belonged to some religious order. As his book was in Irish and I did not understand the language, he used to come to my studio to translate the bits that he wanted me to make drawings for.[20]

The book Elvery refers to was Íosagán agus Scéalta Eile, written by Patrick Pearse and published in 1907. It comprised four stories set in the Irish speaking area of Connemara, and was accompanied by a frontispiece in black and white and four illustrations in colour with bold, linear and descriptive figures set in a rural Irish landscape. Like in Pearse's writing, art also held a key place in the life of St. Enda's School, which was adorned with works by A.E. Russell, Jack B. Yeats or Sarah Purser. Inside the school entrance, a painting by Edwin Morrow showed the young Cú Chulainn taking arms for the first time. He appeared surrounded by the words from the Irish saga *Táin Bó Cúailnge*, aiming to inspire the students: "I care not though I were to live but one day and one night provided my fame and my deeds live after me".[21] The hero knows that by taking arms he will be eternal, but he will also die young.

The School was home to another artwork by Beatrice Elvery, Íosagán (1907), a representation of Christ as a child with his arms open in the form of a cross and set in a rural landscape somewhere around Dublin. The artworks displayed in the school were integral to Patrick Pearse's vision of educational excellence. The fusion carried out through the visual arts in St. Enda's has been described as the "heart of Irish identity" for establishing an analogy between religion and nationalism, and for summarising, at the same time, the ideology of St. Enda's School through the visual arts.[22] Like *Éire*, Íosagán addresses the connection between the nation and the religious, and it was requested by Pearse himself. The painting displays a quote from St. Luke in Irish: "and the Child grew, and waxed strong, full of wisdom and the Grace of God was in Him". The depiction of the boy with his arms wide open has been read by some authors as an image of the crucifixion,[23] addressing the idea of Christ as a child close to his death. The use of the Irish word *macaomh* (boy-warrior) in the quote is not accidental either, as Pearse was involved in the process of the painting and *An Macaomh* was also the title of St. Enda's journal. The idea of a boy-warrior connects the image of Christ as a child and martyrdom with the sagas of Cú Chulainn. It symbolises sacrifice for a common good and the afterlife salvation, the idea of a collective "redemption" also embraced by *Éire*. In 1913, Pearse described this identification with his own words:

> The story of Cú Chulainn symbolizes the redemption of man by a sinless God. The curse of primal sin lies upon a people; new and personal sin brings doom to their doors; they are powerless to save themselves; a youth free from the curse, akin with them through his mother but through his father divine, redeems them by his valour; and his own death comes from it. I do not mean that the Táin is a conscious allegory: but there is the story in its essence, and it is like a retelling (or is it a foretelling) of the story of Calvary.[24]

Elvery's personifications of Mother Ireland and her representation of Celtic motifs alternated with her interest in early Christian imagery. Pagan and sacred themes are combined in her painting, sculpture and crafts. The artist carried out several works exploring the theme of the mother and child, like the pastel entitled *The Irish Madonna* (1907–1910) or her painting *Woman and Child* (n.d.), which portrays a classical seated Madonna embracing a kneeled child with her arms. In the background, one can see a landscape of fantasy with a monster and a boat on the water, a castle on the top of a hill and two giant figures dressed in Celtic clothes, recalling Elvery's illustrations of the Tuathá de Danann for *Heroes of the Dawn*. *The Irish Madonna* was also praised by critics at the 1904 exhibition of the Arts and Crafts Society of Ireland for its "naiveté and grace".[25] Her stained glass artworks and her cards for Cuala Press showing a caring Virgin Mary bathing her child or ironing beside the window became sacred scenes illustrated through the daily life of the Irish peasantry. The theme of the mother and child was also explored by the artist in sculpture, in works like *Glendalough* (1904). Made out of pipe clay, this is one of Elvery's most symbolic creations, and a rare example of her early sculpture, little of which has survived. It was conceived after Elvery had spent a night at the ancient monastic site of Glendalough, in Co Wicklow, founded by St. Kevin in the late sixth or early seven centuries as a place of retreat. Elvery claimed to have experienced there "the extraordinary sense of something brooding over".[26] The sculpture shows the legacy of Auguste Rodin and the influence of Oliver Shepperd's *Róisín Dubh* (1906) in her portrayal of a woman grieving for her children. The female head of Elvery's artwork was conceived as a personification of the upper lake of Glendalough, and it shelters in her hair seven small naked figures symbolising the Seven Churches. The sculpture became a symbol of the aspirations of Irish nationalism.[27] Unfortunately, Elvery often could not afford to get her work cast in bronze, and *Glendalough* remained in plaster.[28]

In 1910, and subsidised by a family member, she left for the Slade School of Art where she studied under Wilson Steer, who tried to discourage her from continuing her studies, and under Henry Tonks, who found her work very basic: "The speed, the slickness, the skill. It is horrible!".[29] Orpen differed, and in his autobiography he remarked:

> One [young artist in Ireland] who stood out alone – Beatrice Elvery, a young lady with many gifts, much temperament, and great ability. Her only fault was that the transmission of her thoughts from her brain to paper or canvas, clay or stained glass, became so easy to her that all was said in a few hours. Nothing on earth could make her go on and try to improve on her first translation of her thought.[30]

Back in Dublin, Elvery ran a studio, taught in the Metropolitan School of Art for a while and painted portraits for a living before her marriage to Charles Campbell, the second Baron Glenavy, in 1912. The couple spent eight years in London, where she quickly became familiar with the Bloomsbury Group and the writers D. H. Lawrence, S. S. Koteliansky and Katherine Mansfield. The Campbells returned to Dublin in 1918, when Beatrice ceased working so broadly and focused on raising their three children. She continued to exhibit fantasy paintings at the RHA, and some of her graphic work, like her illustrations for *Heroes of the Dawn*, was published. It was a politically turbulent period in Ireland and, when Campbell was appointed secretary of the new Department of Industry and Commerce in 1922, the couple became targets for anti-treaty violence.[31] Their house in Clonard, Terenure, was burnt down by anti-treatyites that very same year, destroying much of her work. They lived at several different addresses until they settled in Kimmage, Co. Dublin. Elvery was by then an important member of the Dublin's artistic scene. She helped to establish the Dublin Drama League, and collaborated with the Dublin actress and director Shelah Richards, who was in fact Elvery's goddaughter. The artist assisted Richards in the production of two plays in 1936, and also created theatrical designs for plays like Kikuchi Kwan's *The Housetop Madam* in the Abbey Theatre. She continued illustrating, mostly for Lily and Elizabeth Yeats's guild, the Cuala Press. Her folk and faery scenes became unique in the iconography of the Revival, influenced by the work of her friend Jack B. Yeats.

During the 1930s, Elvery returned to painting almost exclusively, and her artwork made her one of the artists who contributed to the introduction of Modernism into the Irish cultural scene. She was appointed an associate of the

RHA in 1932, joined the more radical Dublin Painters' Society and held a solo show at their premises in Stephen's Green in 1935. She never exhibited with the Irish Exhibition of Living Art, despite her modernist style. Her later work shows enigmatic paintings of pastoral landscapes and symbolic figures, influenced by the art of Venice that the artist visited in 1932. *Rival Musicians* or *Unicorn* (c. 1950) are examples of Elvery's finest style of warm harmonies of colours, theatrical scenes and a combination between reality and illusion that gives the canvas a sense of suspended action. Paintings like *World War I* (n.d.) proved how women were not confined to producing sentimental images of children, flowers or landscapes. *The Intruder* (1932) was painted the same year she was elected an honorary member of the Royal Hibernian Academy, and has been regarded one of the artist's greatest works. Described as "a sort of Thessalian allegory of desire",[32] it portrays a surreal picnic in a dream-like Arcadian forest scene where a female centaur tries to attract a young man into the woods. When it was first exhibited in Dublin, the Irish press and public appeared confused. As Elvery recalled in her autobiography, the committee of the Haverty Trust considered it "obscene", and *Punch* magazine published a caricature of the painting by George Morrow under the title *The Home Wrecker.*[33] However, the *Irish Times* described it as a "reminiscent of an eighteenth century French theme, in which a golden-haired female centaur startles a picnic and bathing party beneath formalized foliage".[34] The *Irish Independent* defined it as a "sylvan and classical painting of a fanciful nature" and "rather novel, with its strange whimsical figures".[35] The painting was acclaimed at the 1933 exhibition of the Royal Academy of London and praised as a recall of Pisanello. Its poetic vision was the centre of her first solo exhibition held in 1935 with the progressive Dublin Painters' Society. *The Intruder* was one of the few paintings that she praised in her autobiography despite the contemporary hostility to the work.[36]

Because of paintings like *The Intruder*, she has been regarded as the first Irish artist to go surrealist, although she never thought of her art or herself in this way.[37] As a response to the critics who said that she painted from photographs, Elvery created *Motherhood (or Birth Control)* in 1932, where she portrayed two women burying a baby; however, still-life paintings were what she enjoyed the most. According to W. B. Yeats, she was an artist that belonged with her aunt Phoebe Traquair in the company of the "last romantics", those who "chose for theme traditional sanctity and loveliness".[38] Scarcely remembered today especially due to the fact that her work dwells on the fantastical, Elvery developed a unique artwork within the iconography of the Irish Revival by combining mythology, realism, modernism and religion. She exhibited at the Leinster Lecture Hall, Ritchie Hendriks Gallery, Leicester Galleries in London, the Royal Academy and the Royal Scottish Academy. In 1955 she held a solo show in the Victor Waddington Gallery, which was described as a "remote and gentle world [...] a static world, views through a sort of kindly, nostalgic haze in which the initial action or emotion were frozen", in a "welcome escape from the facile high-pressure clichés of so many contemporary painters".[39] From 1902 onwards she exhibited with the Young Irish Artists, sharing room with Mary Swanzy, Eva Hamilton, or Estella Solomons, and becoming a member of the "new age of Irish Women's Suffrage".[40] Hailed as "one of the rising school of modern Irish workers",[41] Elvery was elected an Academician of the Royal Hibernian Academy in 1934, after exhibiting at the institution for over thirty years.

## Margaret Clarke

Although Beatrice Elvery's surreal and mythological scenes seem to contrast with Margaret Clarke's more academic portraits, both artists had more in common than it seems at first sight. Despite coming from different backgrounds, both artists studied at the Metropolitan School of Art, were deeply influenced by the work of William Orpen, became Academicians of the Royal Hibernian Academy in the first decades of the twentieth century and, through their work, they discussed the idea of womanhood and the nationalist rhetoric.

Née Crilley, Margaret Clarke (Co. Down, 1884–Dublin, 1961) was born to a Catholic, working-class and nationalist family much given to learning.[42] Her father was a hackler in the linen trade who encouraged his daughter to pursue a career in the arts. Margaret believed in the importance of art in education, and attended night classes at the Newry Municipal Technical College with the aim of becoming a teacher. She belongs to the earliest generations of Catholic women who benefited from the educational reforms gained by more progressive nuns. Her success in the South Kensington Board of Education exams granted her a scholarship for the Dublin Metropolitan School of Art. While attending the School, Clarke continued working for the Art Teacher's Certificate and, at the same time, mixed with a group of artists that included Séan Keating, Kathleen Fox, Beatrice Elvery and the stained-glass and graphic artist Harry Clarke. As a sort of premonition, Orpen described this group of students as a "promising youth",[43] and all the members went on to play a significant role in Irish art before and after the foundation of the Free State.

Margaret Clarke became one of Orpen's star pupils, won several medals and awards, and was appointed Orpen's teaching assistant after finishing her studies in 1911. Between 1913 and 1915, the students spent the summers painting in the Aran Islands, where Clarke produced detailed studies of ancient ruins, landscape and the peasantry.[44] She was designated in Orpen's stead when he ceased teaching at the school in 1914, and Clarke took over as a teacher in the life room until 1919. Orpen's work left a deep mark on Clarke's style of detailed features and plain interiors. Her manner combined the Irish academic tradition with a modern-like free use of the brush, strong line and an imaginative use of bright colours. She experimented with decorative patterns and stood out for her skills at figure drawing and her ability to capture light, shadow and movement on the canvas. Her academic training and draughtsmanship had already been proved in early paintings and drawings like *Girl's Head* (1909), which showed promise of a deeper exploration of portraiture later in her career. Her support of the ideas of the Revival was apparent in portraits such as *The Gael* (n.d.), a painting of her son-in-law John Damien Bourke portrayed as a modern man. However, Clarke never felt tempted to join Cumann na mBan – as many of her contemporary artists did–[45] and she focused on painting instead. In her 1914 *Self-Portrait* she portrayed herself as a professional artist beside a canvas, holding a palette and wearing a brilliant blue cardigan and a white blouse, hardly a suitable attire for painting. Looking directly to the viewer, she appears confident and honest against a neutral background that contrasts with the bright colours of her clothing. Although better known for her portraits, she also painted landscapes, still lives and genre painting, as well as religious and literary themes often represented in a highly symbolic manner. Margaret was well aware that the personification of Ireland as a woman/mother played a central role in Irish nationalism, and she was also familiar with the discourse of Irishness and identity addressed by the Revival. Her paintings became the way to question concepts of race, whiteness and gendered identities in a subversive and allegorical manner. [46]

Margaret married Harry Clarke in 1914 and, like many other women artists of the time, continued to pursue a career in the arts while working in Harry's stained-glass studio, running a household, raising three children and also looking after her husband, who suffered from tuberculosis. She spent long periods in sanatoriums as Harry's health deteriorated. Following his death in 1931, Margaret became the director of the studio, upholding her husband's artistic reputation and protecting his legacy.[47] Genre paintings became a luxury, as the money was little and they did not sell well. Despite her busy life, she kept on working on portraits, which were a better source of income than her symbolic paintings.[48] During her early career she had found assignments thanks to the support of Thomas Bodkin, which led to regular commissions for important works like the portraits of Dermod O'Brien RHA, the Archbishop McQuaid or the dramatist Lennox Robinson. She also designed posters for the Empire Marketing Board in 1930, after the insistence of the High Commissioner for the Irish Free State that Irish artists, and not British, should be involved in the promotion of the nation.[49] One of her most important commissions was a portrait of Éamon De Valera in 1928, whom she portrayed in a unique, informal and relaxed manner that combined informality and status. Probably required by the commissioner, this treatment of the sitter was seen as a way of helping to banish the memories of De Valera's more controversial past.[50] Clarke had been recommended for the task by the then president of the Royal Hibernian Academy, Dermod O'Brien, who was a great admirer of her portraiture: "What I like about her work is her sincerity and insight and characterization. She does not content herself with getting a surface likeness but seems to search into the character of the sitter and get at the soul of him or her".[51]

The Irish-Canadian John J. Shelly, who commissioned the portrait of De Valera, also acquired another painting by Clarke, entitled *Mary and Brigid* (fig. 5) and painted in 1917. When the canvas was rediscovered in Canada in 1996 by the curator Ingrid Jenker, curators and art historians insisted on the idea that the painting was no more than a double family portrait of Clarke's sister and niece, with no political significance.[52] The motto "the personal is political" was never more accurate, and Jenker offered an alternative read of *Mary and Brigid*

Fig. 5. Margaret Clarke, ***Mary and Brigid***, 1917.
Oil on canvas, 107 x 83 cm.
Collection Mount Saint Vincent University. Gift of John Shelly, 1967.

as a visual allegory of nationalism that combined a double portrait of Clarke's family with a symbol of an independent Ireland.[53] She was well acquainted with nationalist leaders such as Constance Markievicz, and her career and her artwork were with no doubt affected by the Cultural Revival and the political context of her time. However, Clarke was no "radical" nationalist and, as her granddaughter Sara Burke recalled, "[her attitude was] more an artisan one of 'they are destroying our beautiful city' than encouragement for the fighting. They would best have been described as armchair republicans, and would have opposed partition".[54]

Although the composition of the painting and its frontality are based on the medieval icons of the Virgin and Child, Clarke's treatment of the subject-matter stands far from this traditional Christian imagery and proposes further readings that combine the themes of the Madonna, Mother Ireland and Irish nationalism.[55] The artist has placed the two figures in the landscape of the Aran Islands –a symbol of the Irish struggle– and she has portrayed the two Dublin-born characters wearing peasant costumes, traditional of the West of Ireland. The elements of the canvas are based on her studies of a thorn tree branch and her sketches of the holy well of St. Ghobnait's Church on Inis Oírr. These motifs, along with the contemporary treatment of a traditional subject-matter, show the influence of Revivalism in Clarke's manner while offering a new perspective of female experiences. The artist has established a dialogue between Brigid, the Irish patron Saint and a symbol of Ireland's pre-colonial culture, with the figure of the Virgin Mary as a personification of the Catholic Church.[56] St. Brigid is a figure of legend, surrounded by the same literary exaggeration as the stories of other Irish mythological women. The evidence tells that the cult to this saint comes from a pagan goddess, but by the ninth century she was the most well-known Irish saint outside Ireland and another major example of the combination of legend and history so common the Irish tradition. In pre-Christian Ireland, Brigid was a deity of healing, poetry and smithcraft, and was associated to the Tuatha Dé Danann. As protector and muse of the poets, and linked to agricultural fertility and healing, the pagan Brigid matches with the Christian figure of St. Brigid. She was also said to be able to control the weather, to return life to the dead, to move rivers, to speak with animals and to prophesy.[57] According to Lady Augusta Gregory in her *Book of Saints and Wonders* (1906), "everything she put her hand to used to increase [...] she bettered the sheep and she satisfied the birds and she fed the poor".[58] The daughter of a slave and a member of the warrior class, Brigid formed the first community of nuns in Ireland and travelled around the country starting religious communities. According to the eleventh century *Liber Hymnorum*, she was granted some land by the king of Leinster in Kildare, where she founded the first monastery in Ireland. By the end of the fifth century, nuns and monks worked side by side in the abbey, and Kildare grew into one of the most prestigious monasteries of the island and was well-known throughout Christian Europe.

Brigid became one of the most powerful women in her country and an unusual figure within the male-dominated early Christian church in Ireland. Thus, Clarke's painting explores the complex relationship between Irish women and the Church, an institution that deprived women of the powers they held during the pre-Christian era, but also provided them with a native Irish identity that eventually became the means to confront British colonialism.[59] Through this subject-matter, Clarke recalls a past when women played an active role in their society, and compares it with her own context, a time when the new leaders of the nationalist movement, hand by hand with the Catholic Church, demanded women to return to the place where they "naturally belonged": the home, a domain that had been emptied during the war when women had to take up roles in the public sphere and fight shoulder to shoulder with their male counterpart. The authorities claimed that women's return to the household duties was essential to the stability of the family, the nation and the Catholic society. Clarke's representation of motherhood, however, challenged this discourse and stood far from the passive women portrayed by many other artists and writers of the time. Jenker has suggested that the painting was "a prophecy of the emergence of the Irish Republic" in which actual women would play a significant and active role.[60] The strength and determination of Clarke's characters confront the viewer. They question the moral and passive maternity demanded by the Church and the State, and offer a new perspective of a civil and an active motherhood in a new Ireland.[61] In a time when women had been called to cooperate with men in the fight for Irish independence, Clarke chose Saint Brigid as the main subject of her painting, a female patron saint of Ireland well-known for her dedication to the poor and her fight against oppressor forces, including religious leaders. Through the reference to Brigid and Bríg in her canvas, Clarke reclaims a new place for women in a modern Ireland.

Margaret Clarke placed great importance on this painting. It was exhibited in the Royal Hibernian Academy in 1917, and in her 1924 solo exhibition at the St. Stephen's Green Gallery in Dublin, where it won a medal in the genre class and it was one of the highest priced works.[62] The canvas and two other portraits were condescendingly reviewed in 1924 in *The Irish Statesman*: "One always has the feeling of clever handling and, for no reason whatever, the impression that, if nothing else, these pictures were made in their sitters' image [...]. There is life about them, and if only art meant similitude Mrs. Clarke would be no less than a genius".[63] However, *Mary and Brigid* proved Clarke's talent, not only for portraiture, but also for more complex visual narratives and allegories that challenged traditional gender stereotypes. This painting gained ideological significance when it was exhibited at the Royal Hibernian Academy after the Easter Rising, when the Exhibition Gallery was destroyed by fire. Clarke was well aware that Irish nationalism had made a priority to redefine the role of women during the first decades of the twentieth century, and that the idea of womanhood had become central to how the State defined itself as a virtuous and moral Catholic nation.

Fionna Barber has raised awareness about the importance that Margaret's studio had regarding this matter.[64] Her workspace was situated at the top of the family house in Dublin, where the family lived from 1922 onwards. Margaret always presented herself as an artist in full control of her studio, her domain, in a time when women's rights within the public sphere were going backwards and women's citizenship was identified with the home and motherhood. Many of her works were carried out within the family home, a domestic space that Clarke manipulated, subverted and acknowledged as a transformative agent that shaped the identity of its occupants.[65] According to Fionna Barber, the fact that the artist established a professional space in the family home had an effect on her subject-matters. She often painted portraits of her children, as well as domestic themes with Julia O'Brien –Clarke's housekeeper and childminder– as her main model. Although Clarke, a middle-class mother of three children, did not have the opportunity to travel to Paris like some other artists of her time, she read and collected books of art history and contemporary art. Her work shows the influence of the Old Masters such as Caravaggio, whose *Judith Beheading Holofernes* (1599) shows a remarkable resemblance to Clarke's *The Wife/The Haircut* (1926–1927). The tumultuous sky and the expressive figures of *Mary Magdalen* (1927, also known as *The Ascension*) draw from El Greco's unique style as well.[66] Clarke's representation of religious iconography is, as we have seen in *Mary and Brigid*, genuine and different. Unlike the traditional representation of the Magdalene as a repentant, Clarke portrays this biblical character in a sort of ecstasy that recalls Bernini's *Saint Teresa* (1647–1652), challenging once more the normative expectations of women. *Mary Magdalen* has also been linked to the history of the Magdalene Laundries in the twentieth century.[67] These so-called "rehabilitation" centres for "fallen women" operated from the eighteenth century up until the end of the twentieth century; they were first run by the Protestant Church and later by the Catholic Church. They were also supported economically by the Irish government in exchange for laundry services. Initially set up to reduce prostitution, they eventually received inmates from psychiatric institutions and jails, victims of rape, women with special needs and pregnant young girls. Over 11,000 women were incarcerated since the foundation of the Irish Free State. Many spent years in the laundries –if not their whole life–, living in brutal conditions, working for free and often being forced to give up their children for adoption.[68] The last one closed its doors in 1996, three years after the scandal following the discovery of a mass grave in the land of the Sisters of Our Lady Charity in Donnybrook, Dublin, where 155 unmarked tombs appeared.

The red dress worn by Julia O'Brien in *Mary Magdalen* also appears in *Bathtime at the Crèche* (ca. 1925), modelled again by O'Brien. The painting, inspired by a family holiday in Laytown, Co. Meath, represents a domestic scene of great symbolism where two women are portrayed looking after a group of children. The kids were modelled by Clarke's sons Michael and David, her daughter Ann and her nephew, Terry, who appears seated on the floor at the forefront. Julia O'Brien was the model for the two adult figures. One of them is at the back, dressed in blue contemporary clothes, holding the hand of a kid and carrying a towel. The other woman, seated beside Terry, stands out for her bright-coloured dress. She is holding a black baby on her lap, which may have been influenced by a carved head of a baby that the Clarkes had in their possession. According to Fionna Barber, the black baby contrasts all the other white figures creating an enigmatic feeling in the painting and questioning concepts of race in a nationalist Ireland, given that most of the characters portrayed by Irish artists of the time were characterised by their whiteness.[69] Clarke's portrayal of a fragile and uneasy relationship between woman and child has also been read as a personification of Ireland's social issues.[70] The red-dressed woman in this painting seems emotionally cut off from the child, and the same feeling can be found in a study for this painting entitled *The Foundling* (1925). The idea of an abandoned, illegitimate black child and an unmarried pregnant woman in the 1920s recalls once again the experiences lived by women in the Magdalene Laundries. In her painting of social significance, Clarke offered a peculiar vision of the mother and child motif, creating a new representation of a nationalist subject-matter, and giving a more realist outlook about women's reality in twentieth-century Ireland.

The changes of the 1920s are also allegorically embodied in paintings like *The Dressmaker* (1924), an intimate scene of two women –dresser and client– shortening a dress, or *The Nuns' Hour* (1929), which portrays a group of religious women on a Wicklow beach. *The Wife/The Haircut* (1926–1927) is a rich and contemporary interpretation of the story of Samson and Delilah, while *Ophelia* (1926) stands far from the dramatic Pre-Raphaelite depictions of the Shakespearian character drowned in the water and surrounded by flowers. Now, a contemplative woman dressed in black is sitting in the woods beside a cluster of ivy. Instead of portraying her as an eternal victim, Clarke offers in her painting an alternative reading of this well-known character from Shakespeare's *Hamlet. Strindbergian* (1927) is another reinterpretation of a dramatic theme, and probably Clarke's largest painting. Enigmatic and theatrical, it was influenced by the work of Gauguin and the Symbolists. The painting is based on Strindberg's *Ghost Sonata*, an introspective reflection about human tragedy staged in 1935 by the Dublin Drama League.[71] Julia O'Brien and Ms. Gavin, the cleaner of the workshop, appear amongst the characters in the painting. Along with *Bathtime at the Crèche*, *Strindbergian* is one of Clarke's main explorations of "sadness, suffering and isolation" in a narrative style, influenced by Orpen's allegorical work.[72]

Many of Clarke's complex paintings remained unsold during her lifetime. She often felt frustrated and limited by her academic training, although her personal and genuine style combined her conservative manner with a modernist flavour that evokes the Fauvist movement and painters like Matisse, Gauguin or Franz Marc.[73] She was also influenced by her husband, famous for his modernist stained-glass designs and book illustrations such as Edgar Allan Poe's *Tales of Mystery and Imagination* (1923).[74] As an alternative to commissioned portraits, Margaret Clarke explored new trends, techniques and styles in the portraits of her own children, which are much more consistent with the depth and symbolism of her genre paintings. However, the frustration of not being able to turn to a thoroughly modern style, along with her busy life and the lack of time, made her stop painting in the early 1950s.[75] Overshadowed by her colleagues, she became one of the less familiar artists of her generation in the years following her death in 1961. Thomas Bodkin, director of the National Gallery of Ireland between 1927 and 1935, referred to her as "Mrs. Clarke, the wife of Mr. Harry Clarke [...], one of the most brilliant of that remarkable group of students which Sir William Orpen fostered". Clarke wrote back to Bodkin: "I hope I shall be able to attract your appreciation of my individual efforts as a painter, rather than the fact that I am the wife of one artist and the pupil of another".[76] Despite all the discrimination and prejudices, Margaret Clarke was one of the greatest Irish portraitists of her time, and was highly regarded by her colleagues and by leading figures in Irish culture including William Orpen or Thomas MacGreevy.

Along with Beatrice Elvery or Grace Gifford, Clarke belongs to the new age of Irish women's suffrage and in 1927 she became the second woman artist –after Sarah Purser– to become elected a full Academician of the Royal Hibernian Academy after a hundred years of the institution's existence. Her recognition proved that she was indeed considered an exceptional artist, although some authors have highlighted the fact that Margaret Clarke was accepted as a full member of the RHA immediately after the independence was gained in the South. The exhibition of paintings such as *Mary and Brigid* in nationalist venues may have been one of the reasons for her success in the official institutions of the newly Free State.[77] Clarke exhibited regularly at the Royal Hibernian Academy from 1913, held two solo shows (in 1924 and 1939) and participated in various group exhibitions, both in Ireland and abroad. In 1932 she was one of the very few artists invited to paint St. Patrick in honour of the Eucharistic year, for which she painted *St. Patrick Climbs Croagh Patrick.* She was also involved in independent artists' organisations and liberal artists' groups such as the Radical Painters' Club and the Dublin Painters' Society, and was a founding member of the Irish Exhibition of Living Art, where she showed the bold and colourful portrait of her daughter *Ann with Cat* (1930–1931). She proved herself a very capable business woman who also challenged academic conventions, gender stereotypes and concepts of race, nation and identity. Her legacy has recently begun to be rehabilitated, and she is now being considered a significant figure in the history of early twentieth century Irish art.[78]

# Landscape and Rural Life

### Lilian Lucy Davidson

Like many of her contemporaries, Lilian Lucy Davidson (Bray, 1879–Dublin, 1954) also insisted on the representation of the Irish landscape and its inhabitants through her artwork. She, however, had a different approach to this subject-matter due to her humble background, which led her to portray the hard-working people of the Gaelic speaking areas of Ireland, the Gaeltacht.[79] Davidson was the sixth child of Edward Ellice Davidson and Lucy Rising Davidson (née Doe), and was educated privately before attending the Dublin Metropolitan School of Art at the age of sixteen. She won several prizes in 1895 and 1896, and was also awarded a scholarship and free studentship at the Royal Dublin Society in 1897, the very same year her father died. Having completed her studies, she taught illustration in her studio in Earlsfort Terrace in Dublin, and in several schools in the city. She successfully prepared her students for the annual examinations of the Royal Drawing Society of London, the Taylor Scholarship and the Royal Drawing Society's Teacher/Artist Diploma examinations.[80] As well as a painter and teacher, she also became a prolific author of poetry, short stories and plays for the Gate and Torch theatres often under the pseudonym of Ulick Burke.[81] Her most famous play, *Bride*– set in the West of Ireland – was staged at the Gate Theatre in 1931, directed by Hilton Edwards and designed by Michael MacLiammoir. Davidson began her exhibiting career at the Irish Watercolour Society with *The Bonfire* in 1912, and was elected a member of the committee in 1934. She also established herself as a regular Royal Hibernian Academy exhibitor since 1914 until her death. Following her exhibitions in 1926, 1936 and 1940, the *Irish Times* praised her strong individuality and stated that she had "vision, and crude and rude, as some of her subjects may be, out of every human sympathy with the humblest she composes scenes of life and interest".[82] She was appointed an Associate of the Academy in 1940.

Davidson's landscape painting was shaped by European ethnography and the ethnographic art popularised in Paris, especially in the Académie des Beaux-Arts by the hand of the etcher and lithographer Théodore Valerio (1819–

1879), who depicted the inhabitants of Eastern Europe, their culture and their customs. One of the first ethnographic painters was Jean-Léon Gérôme (1824–1904), who was also the master and one of the main influences of Aloysius O'Kelly.[83] Like O'Kelly, Davidson became attracted by the West of Ireland as an uncontaminated land which still offered a traditional lifestyle, the remains of a vanishing era. Paintings like *The Harbour, St. Ives* (1916) or *The Flax Pullers* (1921) display the bright palette, strong impasto and illumination contrasts that she maintained throughout her career. Jack B. Yeats's early representational work left a mark in Davidson's style, and she as well absorbed the different artistic trends she became familiar with through her travels around Cornwall and Sussex, France, Belgium and Switzerland. Her economic circumstances were not good enough to keep her abroad for too long, and her artwork did not become that influenced by European modernism.[84] She, however, got to explore the work of the post-impressionists, Honore Daumier and Jean-François Millet, and she portrayed the same prototype of humanity in her representations of the Irish peasantry, their daily life and their surroundings in paintings like *The Holy Well* (n.d.), a pioneer artwork in Irish naturalism. This painting is set in a landscape of the West of Ireland, with a rough ground, a cloudy sky and mountains in the distance. The scene shows a peasant couple praying beside a holy well. The man, dressed in dark clothes and kneeled, holds his hands together and bends his head, lost in his prayers. The old woman is standing, dressed in the typical costume of the islanders with her head and shoulders covered with a shawl. She looks directly to the viewer. The painting recalls Jean-François Millet's evocative *The Angelus* (1857–1859), a scene of a man and woman who have stopped digging potatoes and are portrayed reciting the Angelus.

The sense of solitude that we find in *The Holy Well* surrounds many of Davidson's paintings, like *No More to Sea* (n.d.), a scene of a lonely, hunched sailor seated on his boat stranded in the sand, with thick, white clouds in the background. In their pamphlet *Irish Plays* (1906), W. B. Yeats and Lady Gregory described how "the Irish peasantry of the hills and coast speak an exuberant language and have a primitive grace and wildness due to the wild country they live in, which gives their most ordinary life a vividness and colour unknown in more civilised places".[85] Following this idea, Davidson's early paintings represented the sense of a rapidly vanishing world and illustrated the traditions more associated to the past, to a pre-Christian era. Throughout her career, she returned to the subject of fairs and markets (e.g. *Fair Day, Westport, n.d.*), and scenes of hard-working Irish peasants, encapsulating the idea of the West as symbol of the essence and soul of Ireland.[86] Especially during the 1920s and 1930s, she travelled to Donegal, Achill and Connemara, whose landscape served as the scenery for many of her paintings like the group of people harvesting seaweed in *Gathering Kelp* (n.d.), or working the fields in *The Turf Cart* (n.d.) and *Bringing Home the Turf (n.d.)*. The busy shop portrayed in *Fair Day in Miss O'Dowd's* (n.d.) is also placed in Roundstone, Connemara, and its design reveals the effect that Davidson's involvement in theatre had on her work. She empathised with the struggle and hard life of the peasants, although she was not one of them, and included self-portraits in several of her paintings like *The Country Races* (n.d.),[87] where she appears seated and looking towards the viewer. Her landscapes are populated by white thatched cottages, green fields and stone walls, which shaped her views of an idyllic, pastoral country that matched the political lines of Irish nationalism. Her paintings often show a high horizon and a rough ground painted with an earthy palette. Her use of colour distributed in flat areas evidences a strong sense of design and proves the influence of Naturalism and French Impressionism which she was exposed to while in France in the 1910s. Her best works are the ones that portray theatrical night scenes of the West such as *Cottages – Keel, Achill* (1928), *Night in Claddagh* (1933) or *Night* (n.d.), often inhabited by lonely peasant women lost in their thoughts. In Davidson's sceneries women are not portrayed as passive figures but as characters that evoke an emotional response in the viewer. The influence of Jack B. Yeats is evident, but her representations of the peasantry and the landscape is darker than his, only brightened up by the contrasts between the darkness of her palette and the light coming from the windows of the traditional cottages. In a unique atmosphere enhanced by strong contrasts of colour and tone, Davidson explored the concept of Irishness and contributed to develop a national genre in a Post-Impressionist manner.

A recurrent character in Davidson's landscapes was the peasant woman, a central element in her compositions. The painting *Fair day in Miss O'Dowd's* shows women dressed in typical shawls and petticoats gathering provisions, drinking, and enjoying themselves. Outside the door a group of men is chatting. The viewer, placed inside the scene, meant to enjoy the atmosphere of informality and warmth inside the shop. *Going to the Fair* (n.d.) also focuses on the life of peasant women by portraying two female figures over one of Davidson's characteristic rough hills of the West. In the background there are thatched cottages of white walls and straw roofs, and, above them, the cloudy and changeable sky of Ireland. The woman on the left, younger and dark-haired, is wearing a brown shawl, while the figure on the right represents an old woman of white hair whose head is covered with a red hood. Her yellow shawl shows dramatic contrasts of light and shadow, common in Davidson's artwork. Both women wear black shoes and the typical red skirt of the rural areas of Ireland, and they seem to have stopped their chores and to be enjoying a chat before going to the fair, one of Davidson's favourite subject-matters. *Fashions at the Fair* (c. 1940) also illustrates a scene of a busy market day, in which animals and peasants seem to happily share the space. Davidson used colour to highlight certain elements in her paintings and, in *Fashions at the Fair*, while men appear dressed in dark clothes, women are easily discernible through their coloured shawls and bright red skirts. Even though many of her compositions illustrate women enjoying some time off in markets and fairs, Davidson's female characters also appear engaging in farming activities, like in *The Turf Cart* (n.d.), where a woman is depicted working with her husband beside a cart and a horse, with a mountain and a dark sky in the background. In *The Turf Stack* (n.d.), another old white-haired woman has rolled up her sleeves and appears lifting heavy stacks of turf. The background is covered in wood and turf piled up, painted in Davidson's characteristic blue and purple hues inspired by the Irish dusk.

Davidson's work was mainly centred on the representation of the Irish speaking areas of the country, but she was also well known for her portraits and genre paintings like *The Old Curiosity Shop* (n.d.), *The Tinker's Breakfast (n.d.)* or *A Warm Hearth* (n.d.).[88] *The Golden Shawl* (n.d.) is an impressive self-portrait of the artist with short dark hair, and wearing a golden shawl of beautiful tones over her shoulders. Her right arm is placed on the armchair, while the left arm rests on her lap giving the artist a relaxed, confident and determined look. *Here Is the News* (n.d.) illustrates the daily life in the towns of Ireland by depicting a group of men gathered outside the *Irish Times*, chatting and reading the news. It is interesting to examine their clothing and its fabric, the detailed chequered patterns and the jackets in homespun material. As well as the everyday nature, Davidson also illustrated events of the Irish history like *Gorta* (fig. 6), a late work that deserves a special mention for being an unusual painting at the time and unique within Davidson's artistic career. Painted in 1946, *Gorta* (the Irish

Fig. 6. Lilian Lucy Davidson, ***Gorta***, 1946. Oil on canvas, 70 x 90 cm Courtesy of Ireland's Great Hunger Museum, Quinnipiac University, Hamden, CT. © The Estate of Lilian Lucy Davidson.

word for "hunger") has been considered the first modern example of the main style of Famine commemoration.[89] The narrative sense has been eliminated and there is no recognisable place or time, but the subject-matter is unquestionable: the painting represents a family digging a grave for their son in unconsecrated ground. The figure in the centre is digging the grave just as if he was still digging potatoes, and looking straight at the viewer. On the left, the mother is holding the baby waiting for the grave to be finished. On the right side, the father is sitting on the ground grabbing the beads of his rosary. This symbolist painting of the human drama was profoundly inspired by Picasso's blue period and the Expressionist movement, both in form and in colour. The peasant characters are portrayed as blue skinned skeletons dressed in rags, inhabitants of Ireland's coffin ships ready to bury their child. Davidson's manner echoes the elegant and dark palette of Beatrice Elvery, and recalls Davidson's heavy moonlight scenes in *Night at Claddagh* (ca. 1933) or *The New Moon* (n.d.). Like Mainie Jellett, the artist made use of a symbolic blue colour, which draws from Christian iconography and is particularly associated to mourning. However, *Gorta* has lost the heroic atmosphere inherent to Irish nationalist art, and makes way instead to a portrayal of injustice and poverty, and the most terrible consequences faced by ordinary people. It recalls another painting by Davidson entitled *The Potato Harvest* (1931), which is a more positive perspective of the reliance of the Irish peasantry on the potato. *Gorta*, previously known as *Burying the Child,* is a representation of the deepest pain of the poor and the darkest side of humanity during a tumultuous period.[90] A portrayal of loss, anger and reality, it has been regarded as one of the most painful illustrations of the Great Famine.

Unlike many of her well-off women colleagues, Davidson depended on her work for a living. She became one of the few working-class artists who got to make a place for themselves in the Irish artistic arena and, like the painter Estella Solomons, she also portrayed many of the leaders of the nationalist movement such as the architect Joseph Holloway –who redesigned the Abbey Theatre for its opening in 1904–, A.E. Russell, Sarah Purser or Jack B. Yeats. She earned her income through teaching and writing, as well as through private commissions and the sale of her exhibited works.[91] Her work was exhibited not only in Ireland but also in Chicago, Amsterdam, London and at the Salon de la Societé Nationale in Paris. She was also one of the founding members of the Torch Theatre in Dublin, where she designed sets and contributed with literary works.[92] She contributed to the Royal Hibernian Academy with more than 130 paintings since she started exhibiting there in 1914, and became an associate member of the institution in 1940. Davidson remained attached to Irish naturalism, and did not embrace the more avant-garde trends explored by fellow colleagues and friends like Mainie Jellett, although her involvement with the Dublin Painters' Society shows her interest in modern trends. Far from Paul Henry's image of the heroic peasant, Davidson empathises with her subjects and their struggle, and illustrated it in the most honest manner. She remained unmarried for the rest of her life, and broke the mould both through her artistic style and as a single woman of humble background who worked hard to be recognised as a professional artist. After her death in 1954, the writer Winifred M. Letts lamented that her obituary, despite praising Davidson's career in painting and teaching, did not make any reference to her writing:

> Sir. In the recent obituary notice of Lilian Davidson ARHA, whose loss seems irreparable to so many, there was no mention of her gifts in literature. As well as being a keen critic of drama, she had written plays. Her play 'Bride' was produced by a London theatre. She wrote as Ulick Burke. I do not know her poems –to me poetry was implicit in her pictures– but she was a poet on paper as well as on canvas.[93]

## Letitia Marion Hamilton and Grace Henry

Davidson's view of the West of Ireland and its people was shared with two other landscape artists: Letitia Marion Hamilton (Meath, 1878–Dublin, 1964) and Grace Henry (Aberdeen, 1868–Dublin 1953). Letitia Hamilton was born to an artistic family of Anglo-Irish background.[94] She was the second daughter of the landowner and JP for Meath Charles Robert Hamilton and his wife Louisa Caroline. She was also the cousin of the leading watercolourist Rose Barton, and the grand-granddaughter of the satirical artist and watercolourist Marianne-Caroline Hamilton (née Tighe), who spent her youth in London taking lessons from the printmaker John Spilsbury and his daughter Maria. A skilled artist, Caroline Hamilton created illustrations of the Irish society satirising subjects like education, religion or even the dominant classes. Letitia's sister, Eva Hamilton, also went on to become a portrait painter. Both sisters studied at the Alexandra College and at the Dublin Metropolitan School of Art, where they attended drawing and painting classes under William Orpen. Eva also studied at the Slade School of Art under Henry Tonks, and she went on to become a skilled portraitist. However, with the coming of the Irish Free State, the demand of portraits declined and Eva focused on landscape painting following the path of her sister. At the Metropolitan School of Art, Letitia also attended enamelling classes under the British-born enameller and metalworker Oswald Reeves. Her early enamelwork of Celtic influence entitled *Inspiration* won a silver medal at the Board of Education's National Competition in the enamelling section in 1912, and was also exhibited in Dresden where it received favourable reviews. Hamilton's Art Nouveau manner in enamelwork foresaw her modernist style and her interest in the exploration of colour and form through painting later in life.[95] She continued her studies at the Slade School of Art in London, also in Belgium under Frank Brangwyn and in France under Anne St. John Partridge, where she came under the influence of Impressionism.[96] Less inspired by Orpen than her sister Eva, Letitia's paintings of hunting and of Irish and European landscapes engaged with the avant-garde of the continent.

Eva was the first of the two sisters to exhibit, showing her work in 1898 with the watercolour Society of Ireland, although she later focused on portraiture. Letitia's earliest watercolours representing the gardens at Hamwood where she had been born were exhibited at the Watercolour Society of Ireland in 1902 under the name "May Hamilton". The 1920s also witnessed Letitia's more mature artwork and, in this time, she changed her signature from MH (May Hamilton) to LMH (Letitia Marion Hamilton). She travelled, often with her sister, to France, Italy and Yugoslavia, which increased her interest in the effects of light and colour while portraying the everyday life (e.g. *The Village Pump,* n.d; or *The Window,* n.d.).[97] In Venice she rented a gondola studio from her friend, the art historian and antiquarian Ada Longfield. In Italy Letitia explored the effects of the light and the water, and changed her palette to pastel tones, which she would later apply to her Irish landscapes of spontaneous manner, fluid colours and loose brushwork. Her Italian experience was combined with the influence of Van Gogh, whom she greatly admired, and the French Impressionists. She created small sketches in oil that she later developed into larger, finished paintings. She made a great use of impasto, which she applied with the palette knife in thick, white tones offering a brighter perspective of the Irish landscape compared to Davidson's night scenes in blue and purple hues. Letitia's personal style resulted in paintings that gave the impression of a sculpted relief on the canvas.[98]

Because Letitia's father was only able to provide a dowry for one of his six daughters –Lily–, both Eva and Letitia remained unmarried and provided the main income through their art, in which they put their efforts.[99] Letitia exhibited at the Paris Salon, Goupil Gallery, as well as at the Royal Society of British Artists and with the Scottish Society of Women Artists in Edinburgh. She held a solo show at the Victor Waddington Galleries in Dublin in 1945, and another one in 1948, the same year she won a bronze medal at the Olympic Games in London for her painting *Meat Hunt Point to Point Races,* the only Irish medal that year.[100] From 1939 onwards, Letitia turned her gaze to Cork and Connemara. She portrayed towns like Glengarriff or Roundstone (e.g. *Roundstone Harbour, Connemara, n.d.)* and the everyday of the peasants in *Bringing in the Turf, West of Ireland* (n.d.) or *Cottages in the West (Dooagh, Achill Island)* (n.d.) with even more impasto than before. Equestrian scenes like *Meat Hunt* or *The Kildare Hounds at Maynooth* (n.d.) became also more common to the artist, who was raised in a family with great interest in horses. Her painting *A Fair Day, Clifden* (n.d.) was included in the exhibition entitled "The Birth of Modernism in Irish Art" in Dublin Castle and, in 1939, her work was also chosen by Victor Waddington to promote Irish art in the United States. In the late 1950s, Hamilton became the president of the Dublin Painters Society. She had exhibited at the Royal Hibernian Academy from 1909, being elected a member of the Academy in 1944 and showing over 200 paintings at the venue.

In her later years, she collected the work of fellow modern Irish artists such as Evie Hone, Louis Le Brocquy and Jack B. Yeats.

In the 1920s, Letitia Hamilton took part in the founding of the Society of Dublin Painters that would change the course of Irish art. Another founder member of the Society was Emily Grace who, like Hamilton, centred her artwork on the portrayal of the inhabitants of the West coast of Ireland, primarily the island of Achill in County Mayo. Grace Henry (née Mitchell) had been born in Aberdeen (Scotland), the second youngest of ten children of the Reverend John Mitchell of the Church of Scotland and his wife Jane.[101] Raised in a well-off family, Grace was educated at home and studied art in London, later in Brussels under Ernest Blanc-Garrins, and then in Paris at the Academie Delécluse,[102] and by 1900 she had already exhibited at the Aberdeen Artists Society. During her time in Paris she met the Irish painter Paul Henry, whom she married in 1903. The couple spent seven years in England, where they went on to become particularly influenced by the post-impressionist movement. Grace's early self-portrait *The Girl in White* (1910–1912) already shows the influence of Manet on her artwork, and a skilful use of colour that she would explore during her time in County Mayo. Grace and Paul moved to Achill Island around the time when this work was painted, and they spent eight years there. Gracy's style became profoundly inspired by the isolated and wild landscape of the West.[103] Although the couple illustrated similar subject-matters, the approach of each artist was very different. Like Davidson, most of Grace's paintings portrayed traditional cottages and nocturnal scenes illuminated by the moonlight in grey, purple and blue hues. One of the best examples of her artistic audacity is *The Long Grey Road of Destiny* (1913–1914), a nocturnal illustration of a little village with expressive mountains and landscapes in the background. Her interest in the Fauvist and Expressionist movements provided the base for a very personal artistic manner that seemed abstract at times. Through her bold use of sombre tones –influence of May Guinness–, and rapid brushstrokes, Grace created sculptural shapes by reducing the forms to the basics. She focused on achieving a sense of atmosphere and depth of colour in her search for the soul of humanity and the essence of the islanders.[104] Her sombre landscapes were substituted in the late 1910s by brighter scenes of the Irish daylight. *The Top of the Hill* (ca. 1920) is one of Grace's illustrative artworks, a scene of three women chatting on a rough ground with a cloudy sky and the sea in the distance. The painting recalls Davidson's aforementioned painting *Going to the Fair*, as Grace's characters have also put their duties aside and are portrayed enjoying their conversation and a moment of rest on the hills.

Grace and Paul Henry separated in the late 1920s, although they never divorced. She spent most of the 1930s abroad, but continued exhibiting in Ireland, where she returned after the Second World War. She showed at the Royal Academy in London, the Leicester Galleries, the Fine Art Society and the Victor Waddington Galleries. In 1922, five of her works were shown at the Irish Exhibition in Paris. On the advice of Mainie Jellett, the artist also spent some time in France studying under André Lhote.[105] However, Cubism was never a great inspiration to Grace, who was more interested in the new ideas of the Fauves and the Expressionists and in developing her own personal style. One of her paintings, exhibited at the Dublin Painters Society in 1923, was described in *The Irish Times* as "perhaps the best picture in the exhibition. This bold painting is not quite Mrs. Henry's usual style. Is far more 'modern' than most of her work; but it does not suffer from that".[106] She was appointed Honorary Member of the Royal Hibernian Society in 1949 and died in 1953, overshadowed by her husband. Many of her works were labelled as "Grace Henry (Mrs. Paul Henry)" until the 1970s.

Davidson, Hamilton and Henry's artwork proposed a different vision and a new interpretation of the Irish countryside. Far from the more traditional portrayal of the peasants as heroes of the nation, they illustrated contemporary scenes of the daily life in the Gaeltacht, the hard work of Irish women, brief moments of conversation between the inhabitants, or peasants lost in their own thoughts. Their recurrent portrayal of female peasants dressed in traditional clothes is not a coincidence: Lilian Davidson, as well as Letitia Hamilton and Grace Henry, were well aware that the red skirts and the shawls of their characters emblematised rural Irishness and were associated to a tradition that gave women a very specific role within the nation. Their paintings illustrated the debate developed during the Irish Revival about the importance of clothing within the nationalist movement, in a time when Irish traditions were being portrayed as fragile and threatened by external influences, while the national identity was characterised by the idea of an Irish "race" with emphasis on exclusion of otherness and on sameness.[107] In the context of a nationalist and Catholic society in which women were expected only to play a biological role, the clothing of peasant women was considered a symbol of rejection of the modern English fashion that dispossessed women from their reproductive functions.[108] The emphasis on the dresses in the portrayal of the peasantry corresponds to the importance of clothing as a marker of national identity. Through their clothing, women became associated to the rural landscape and to a very specific way of life. Far from accidental, this image played a central role in the colonial and romantic discourses of the nineteenth century and after. Peasant women were often portrayed as pretty girls with dark or red hair, dressed in the same clothes that Davidson used for her gatherers, shepherdesses, farmers. They usually appear with their heads covered by a shawl, and often barefoot as a symbol of their connection to the land, and the lack of urban sophistication. It became as well an indication of the clash between countryside and cityscape.

The image of the peasant woman, unlike other allegorical personifications of Ireland such as the Motherland, Hibernia or the Virgin Mary, was a figure *embedded* in the country, and it thus became a very powerful symbol of what Irishness meant. The icon of the female peasant was primarily associated with rural life and chastity, matching the national discourse about femininity: a woman's duty was to look after her household and her family, and hence to guarantee the continuity of the nation. However, the dual association of Irish women to motherhood and the Irish wilderness developed an image of a *wild* and fertile woman that clashed with the Catholic notions of womanhood and with the socioeconomic system that aimed to control female sexuality. According to Linda Nochlin, "at the same time that the peasant woman is represented as naturally nurturing and pious, her very naturalness, her proximity to instinct and animality could make the image of the female peasant serve as the very embodiment of untrammeled, unartificed sexuality".[109]

With the foundation of the Free State, the depiction of the young female was replaced by an old and rustic woman who was more easily represented according to the demands of motherhood within the State. As the postcolonial theorist Catherine Nash described, the West of Ireland stood "at the centre of a web of discourses of racial and cultural identity, femininity, sexuality and landscape which were being used in attempts to secure cultural identity and political freedom".[110] Focusing on the Irish peasantry as her main subject, Lilian Lucy Davidson was one of the many artists who contributed to a complex cultural discourse determined by the crucial economic and socio-political necessities of the time. The icon of the young, beautiful red-haired peasant girl remained with very little changes within the popular imagery, and was even addressed throughout the twentieth century in films like John Ford's *The Quiet Man* (1952). This symbol became so powerful that it was not until the late 1970s that it began to be deconstructed. The symbol of the female peasant reinforced the idea that women were biologically determined to perform certain roles within the nation, confining them solely to the domestic sphere until very recently. However, despite the nationalist imagery that depicted women as passive mothers, house makers and nurturers of the Irish 'race', women made major contributions to the Irish land movement on a daily basis during the last decades of the nineteenth century. The movement involved not only upper and middle-class urban leaders of the Ladies Land League, but also, and more importantly, women who belonged to the peasantry and were motivated by economic necessities and not –or not only – by nationalist aims.[111] In the magazine *Bean na hÉireann*, the members of Inghinidhe na hÉireann protested against the idealisation of poverty and the harsh lifestyle of "pretty barefooted, red-petticoated cailin", because women were actually being forced to emigrate due to their "bleak and colourless life of endless drudgery".[112] Their hard work, although often overlooked, was recognised in the paintings of artists like Lilian Davidson, Letitia Hamilton and Grace Henry.

## Mary Swanzy

Like Davidson, the style of Mary Swanzy (Dublin, 1882–London, 1978) also became more allegorical after the war, with complex scenes of intricate imagery and deep symbolism. Swanzy was born in Dublin, into a well-off family of Anglo-Irish background, as her father, Henry Swanzy, was a renowned ophthalmic surgeon. She was educated privately in drawing and fine art painting, attended the Alexandra College and then continued her education in Versailles and Freiburg (Germany), becoming fluent both in French and German.[113] Once back in Dublin, she attended May Manning's art classes with John Butler Yeats as a visitor teacher. Swanzy also enrolled in the evening program at the Dublin Metropolitan School of Art, where she studied modelling under John Hughes, and received painting tuition at the Royal Hibernian Academy mentored by Nathaniel Hone and Walter Osborne. Her family encouraged her to follow the conventional path for an Irish female artist, which meant focusing on portraiture and becoming a teacher. Indeed, her first works exhibited at the Royal Hibernian Academy were portraits and, at the age of twenty-three, Swanzy's mastering of the academic style was proved in the portrait of her father *Sir Henry Swanzy* (1905), which was described by Nathaniel Hone as "the best picture painted in Dublin for thirty years".[114]

However, Swanzy had another plan in mind and, focusing on landscape and genre painting, she developed her own unique style far for everything that was being done in Ireland at the time. She painted outside the conventions, moved freely between different artistic manners and explored numerous trends throughout her life. She continued her artistic training in Paris, where she studied at the Acadèmie de la Grande Chaumière and Colarossi's, and attended the salon of Gertrude Stein, one of the most important patrons of modern art. There she became acquainted with the work of Matisse, Picasso, Cézanne, Gauguin and Daumier. Her early paintings, like *Stormy Day in the West of Ireland* (n.d.), combined the modern influences of her travels and her appreciation of the artists of the Renaissance with a more academic training.[115] Like Grace Henry, Swanzy also explored the Fauvist style during her time in Paris. Once back in Ireland in her early twenties she became, according to Thomas MacGreevy, the artist that brought Cézanne's influence to Ireland for the first time.[116]

Her efforts to open a teaching atelier, however, failed, as well as her attempt to pursue a career as a portrait painter. As a critique to the patrons and the gender stereotypes of the time, she claimed that "men wanted to be painted by men, and women were to be expected to paint pussie-wussies and doggie woggies".[117] From the 1920s onwards she decided to travel extensively as a form of a self-imposed exile, especially following her cousin's death in 1921.[118] The Inspector Oswald Swanzy had been involved in the murder of the Sinn Féin Lord Mayor of Cork in 1920, and was shot by the IRA one year later in a reprisal attack that led to three days of rioting in which twenty-two deaths were recorded. After the event, Swanzy would avoid national politics for the rest of her life.[119] She had never showed any devotion for a national Irish art despite the fact that her main subject-matter was the landscape, a historically loaded theme in Irish art as we have already seen. Instead, she focused on developing her own particular style influenced by modern trends without the weight of Irish nationalist ideas, although her artistic development makes sense in the context of the social, political and artistic changes of the time.[120] She always retained an interest in Irish art and maintained her links with Ireland, a country whose landscape she often portrayed in paintings like *Fishermen, Kilkeel, County Down* (n.d.), which shows a talented treatment of the water reflections through colour, or *Cottage Garden* (n.d.) and *View towards the Dingle peninsula from Dooks* (ca. 1917), where the line loses strength making way to areas of colour through spontaneous and rapid brushstrokes. However, women painters like Lilian Lucy Davidson or Mary Swanzy rejected the nationalist treatment of the West of Ireland led by artists such as Séan Keating and Maurice McGonigal. Instead, they turned their gaze to the Continent, partly as a reaction to the political situation in their country.

In the 1910s Swanzy's artwork lost its Irish centre and became increasingly cosmopolitan, although she never lost sight of her Irish connection. The changes in her style are already discernible in *Miss Muriel Swanzy* (1906), a portrait of her sister exhibited at the Royal Hibernian Academy in 1907 which already shows a post-impressionist influence in Swanzy and the hatching style that she would develop throughout the decade. While the features of the sitter displays Swanzy's mastering of academicism, the background and the clothing are defined by thick lines of contour and painted in rapid but controlled brushworks that Swanzy experimented with under the influence of Vorticism and Futurism, two contemporary movements that explored the motion of the modern life.[121] Vorticism was a short-lived trend created in the 1910s in England by a British avant-garde group that rejected landscape and nudes and favoured a geometric style in order to express the dynamism of the urban environment and the machine. This idea was shared by the Futurists, a movement developed few years earlier in Italy which also emphasised the power of the machine and the changes of the modern world.[122] Swanzy adopted the Vorticists' bold use of the line and dramatic colours and addressed the ideas of the Futurists' urban scenes in her own rural and exotic landscapes. During the 1910s she began to frequently exhibit her work at the Salon des Beaux-Arts in Paris, and in 1920 she became a member of the organising committee of the Salon des Indépendants.

The 1910s also witnessed the development of Orphism, a short-lived but influential style created in France by Robert and Sonia Delaunay around 1912. Inspired by Cubism and Fauvism, Orphists reduced their compositions to geometric fragmentations where colour was an essential aesthetic element. This idea remained a major influence in Swanzy who, familiar with the theories of André Lhote and Albert Gleizes, adopted many Cubist principles only to break them afterwards in her own manner.[123] Her paintings often included a narrative discourse that separated her from those contemporary artists who centred their work on the search of pure abstraction. Even though she spent most of her time abroad, Swanzy has been considered one of the first Irish artists to adopt

Cubism, along with Mainie Jellett.[124] Swanzy broke up colour into forms, and her objects were depicted from several different perspectives in time and space simultaneously. Her Cubist knowledge was combined in her marine and harbour scenes (e.g. *Moored Boats*, n.d.) with Sonia Delaunay's Orphism, Paul Cézanne's Post-Impressionism, Symbolism and Surrealism. In her creative process, Swanzy first fragmented the forms, and then combined them with layering patterns to simulate motion, in a rich palette of colours that she utilised to emphasise the shapes in landscapes like *The Storm* (n.d.) This painting recalls one of Swanzy's earlier works entitled *A View of Semur-en-Auxois* (n.d.), a composition of the architecture of the medieval French town that the artist probably visited in the late 1910s. The sense of motion achieved through the vortexes and the swirling patterns of *The Storm* was probably an influence of the Italian Futurism the artist became familiar with during her time in Italy before the First World War. However, unlike movements like Cubism or Futurism, Swanzy included two small figures in the bottom of her composition as a sort of preview of her late more symbolic artwork.[125] This can also be seen in *Young Woman with a White Bonnet* (ca. 1920), an earlier work –and probably a self-portrait– influenced by the Italian futurist Giacomo Balla that already makes use of fragmentation, spirals and interplays of shadow and light in order to create a sense of motion. For her use of light and her dynamic style that combined curved and angular forms, Swanzy was described as "Cubo-futurist" as well as a "surrealist working in a Cubist convention".[126]

The 1920s became a very busy decade for Swanzy, who continued travelling and sending paintings to major exhibitions in Dublin, Paris and London. A woman in her forties, she spent the interwar time travelling the world freely; she went to Eastern Europe, the Far East and Yugoslavia and assisted with post-war work in Czechoslovakia with Lady Muriel Paget's Mission. She travelled to Hawaii, where her uncle was a well-known sugar merchant, and where she portrayed scenes of his house in paintings like *La Maison Blanche with Figures on the Lawn* (ca. 1923–24). Between 1924 and 1925 Swanzy visited Honolulu and Samoa, where she stayed with an aunt and illustrated the exotic landscape of the islands as well as its inhabitants, and found herself amazed by the colours of the flora, stunned "at how many greens there are in the world".[127] Her paintings have been often compared to the Tahitian scenes that Paul Gauguin had carried out thirty years earlier.[128] However, Swanzy's portrayal of the islanders stood far from the depictions of Paul Gauguin, who described the Tahitian inhabitants as "noble savages" in need the help of white men in order to keep some sort of control in their societies.[129] Paul Gauguin's colonial perspective led him to avoid male representation in his paintings and to focus instead on naked and lethargic women for the pleasure of male, Western, privileged viewers. Swanzy did not follow his discourse and, from a feminist and liberal perspective, she portrayed both men and women dressed, working and contently engaged in their daily activities.[130] In 1924, her aunt's house served as the venue for

Fig. 7. Mary Swanzy, ***Samoan Scene***, 1923.
Oil on canvas, 152 x 92 cm.
Collection Crawford Art Gallery, Cork. © The Artist's Estate.

Swanzy's small exhibition of her Czechoslovakian and Hawaiian paintings. Her time in Samoa was particularly productive, leading to an iconic body of work within the Irish artistic scene. Her several works of Samoa were also exhibited in Honolulu and California that very same year and in 1925 she submitted several Samoan scenes to the Royal Hibernian Academy and to the Galerie Bernheim-Jeune in Paris. *Preparing the Meal, Samoa* (ca. 1923) summarises Swanzy's portrayal of the people of the South Pacific. Three female figures are represented in the canvas: two are chatting in the background, while in the centre of the composition there is a monumental figure, seated on the floor and concentrated on preparing a meal. In *Samoan Scene* (1924) Swanzy also focuses the composition on the figure of a female figure with a naked torso. She, as well, seems relaxed and calm, as a natural part of the local colourful landscape. The combination of light and shadows embraces the other human figures in the background, who are portrayed working, chatting and sitting at the shadows of the trees. Another painting also entitled *Samoan scene* (fig. 7) and created in 1923 illustrates a similar scene of a woman, in this case with her back towards the viewer, observing two women and a child bathing in the river. Even though these paintings focused their narratives on women, the natives –especially the girls– were not so keen to pose, and human figures are quite rare in Swanzy's Samoan works.[131] Most of her compositions of this period show landscapes, tropical plants, flowers or buildings in scenes characterised by the contrasts of the sunlight and the shadows of the trees in the forests.

Back in Ireland, Swanzy found herself trapped between the consequences of the war, the violence in her own homeland, and the new, strongly Catholic, Irish Free State in which she probably did not feel quite comfortable. In 1926, after her parents' death and thanks to her inheritance, she travelled to England and stayed with her sister, Clair Swanzy. Her exhibitions in Ireland were the way to remain in contact with Irish artists and trends while living abroad. Although some of her works were rejected by the Royal Hibernian Academy, and some of her exhibitions received a negative response from the conservative Irish public, she remained loyal to her style partly thanks to her well-off background which allowed her not to depend on her income for a living.[132] Her palette became darker throughout the 1930s and especially after the Second World War, when she began to create paintings at times disturbing. Like Davidson, a more symbolic and surrealist dimension was evident in Swanzy's late artwork.[133] She sought primordial truths, and her work adopted a dark and allegorical tone that was accentuated in the 1960s, when she started to combine her personal narratives and her interest in world religions with the art of the Renaissance and ancient cultures. Despite the fact that she remained unattached to Irish politics, she did mingle with some of the leaders of the Cultural Revival like Sarah Purser, whose portrait by Swanzy is a record of a lifelong friendship. Purser also reviewed Swanzy's first important solo exhibition in Dublin in 1919, which she described as particularly relevant for its modernity.[134] Like Davidson and

Hamilton, she also contributed to the complex discourse of Irishness in her own way. These artists focused their artwork on the landscape, a subject matter loaded with nationalist symbolism at the time. Swanzy became one of the first Irish painters that worked with Abstraction; she criticised the colonial system through her artwork and was one of the first artists that brought modern art to Ireland. She portrayed the life of the humble and the peasantry in late works like *The Harvesters* (1943) or *Beggarman* (n.d.). Her depiction of a desperate mother and her daughter in *Irish Potato Famine* (ca. 1940) or the sorrowful women in *This is Our Gift, Our Portion Apart* (1942) show the impact of Ireland's turbulent times on women's lives. Swanzy was conscious of the way in which her gender had impacted on her career: "if I had been born Henry instead of Mary, my life would have been very different".[135]

She became a member of the Society of Dublin Painters along with Paul and Grace Henry, Jack B. Yeats and Letitia Marion Hamilton. This forum offered its members the opportunity to hold group exhibitions as well as a solo show once a year in a time when the opportunities to exhibit were not that accessible. The Society included some artists who regularly exhibited at the Royal Hibernian Academy, but it represented the breakaway from the British academic canon that still prevailed and the opening to modern movements and European trends, encouraging experimentation and the development of new ideas. However, despite the fact that these adventure welcomed artists who embraced the avant-garde tendencies usually disregarded by the Royal Hibernian Academy, Swanzy's work was greeted with incredulity when she first exhibited at the venue: a writer in the *Irish Times* in 1921 described how he had failed to "recognise the shape or colour of nature" in her paintings.[136] She did not exhibit her Cubist works in her homeland until 1932, when her friend Sarah Purser invited her to show her work at Mespil House. This was nearly ten years after Jellett's *Decoration* was shown in Dublin. Like Swanzy, many members of the Society of Dublin Painters were not particularly concerned with nationalism or with a distinctively Irish school of art, and often felt "an uncomfortable feeling of strain and a self-consciousness at what "being Irish" meant".[137] However, she became an integral part to the modernist movement in Irish art and a link between the European avant-garde and the national artistic scene. She first exhibited at the Royal Hibernian Academy in 1905, and continued to do so until 1951 and then again in the 1970s. She was elected Honorary Member of the Royal Hibernian Academy in 1949. Her retrospective show at the Dublin Municipal Gallery of Modern Art in 1968 was a turning point in her recognition and rediscovery.

# Painters of the Revolution

## Constance Markievicz

Unlike Beatrice Elvery, Margaret Clarke, Lilian Davidson and Mary Swanzy, Constance Markievicz (Sligo, 1868–Dublin, 1927) openly participated in the revolutionary movement. A politician, revolutionary, feminist and social reformer, Markievicz became one of the leading figures of Irish nationalism and the first female Member of Parliament elected to Westminster. Better known for her involvement in the struggle for Irish freedom, she was also a talented artist who made herself a name as a landscapist before focusing her efforts on the nationalist cause.[138]

Constance Georgina Gore-Booth was born into an Anglo-Irish family in London. She was the first of the five children of Georgina and Henry Gore-Booth, Baronet of Sligo. As a daughter of an upper-class family, Markievicz participated in the London and Dublin social seasons, and was presented to Queen Victoria in 1887.[139] However, she had a different future in mind and, instead of finding a husband and settling down as expected of a well-educated young lady, in 1893 she persuaded her father to rent a studio for her in London, where Markievicz attended the Slade School of Art. By this time, Alphonse Legros had retired, and Markievicz studied under Alphonse Frederick Brown (1851–1941), who was a member of the New English Art Club influenced by French Impressionism. She also received lessons from the Swedish painter and draughtswoman Anna Nordgren (1847–1916), who was friends with Sarah Purser, and both Nordgren and Markievicz exhibited together at the Society of Women Artists in London.[140] She continued her studies in Paris, in the Académie Julian. It was in the French capital that she met Casimir Dunin de Markievicz –later Count of Markievicz– an artist born to a wealthy Polish family and whom Constance married in 1900.[141] In 1901 the couple had a daughter who was called Maeve after the legendary Irish queen whose grave is supposed to be in Knocknarea, Co. Sligo.[142] In 1903, the family visited the Markievicz estate in Ukraine, where Constance painted "the most dramatic picture of her artistic career".[143] *The Conscript* (1903) depicts a young peasant sitting at a table in a cottage, accompanied by his family.

He is having his last meal, for a long journey awaits: he has been conscripted into the Russian Army. The painting was based on a real story of the hardworking Ukrainian peasants that Constance saw during her visit in Zywotowka, and exhibits a sharp social critique of contemporary issues. The boy never came back, as he was killed in the Russian-Japanese war of 1905.[144]

The marriage of Constance and Casimir did not last, and the couple separated amicably in 1909. Once back in Ireland, she came into contact with the vibrant intellectual, artistic, suffragist and nationalist society of the moment, in which she took part actively. Markievicz continued painting and gained reputation as a landscape painter. However, she was better known for her portraiture. She depicted some of the nationalist figures of her time, including Mary Kelly – member of the Irish Citizen Army and part of the garrison of the Easter Rising– or James Connolly in a watercolour that she created after his execution in 1916. Constance exhibited regularly with A.E. Russell at the Leister Lecture Hall, and also collaborated in his play *Deirdre*, staged at the Abbey Theatre in 1907.[145] In 1905, along with other influential artists including Sarah Purser, John Butler Yeats, Walter Osborne and Nathaniel Hone, she helped founding the United Arts Club, set up to bring together the Dublin artistic and literary community. There she met some of the leaders of the nationalist movement including Douglas Hyde, Michael Davitt, John O'Leary and Maud Gonne. In 1908 she joined the newly created Sinn Féin, and publicly supported the Irish cause. W. B. Yeats's response to her political activities was initially patronising and hostile, although it was to soften with the time: "Women, because the main event in their lives has been giving themselves and giving birth, give all to an opinion as if it were some terrible stone doll".[146]

Markievicz's activism continued and she founded Na Fianna Éireann, the youth branch of the Irish Republican Brotherhood. The movement, named after Fionn MacCumhaill's legendary group of warriors, was created with the aim of preparing young Catholic, nationalist boys for marching, applying first aid and using weapons. This very same year Markievicz also joined Inghinidhe na hÉireann, where she was to become one of the most committed members. She often contributed to the organisation's publication, *Bean na hÉireann* (The Woman of Ireland), created in 1908 and described as the "women's magazine that men buy".[147] Markievicz designed the masthead for the magazine's issue of December 1910 (fig. 8), for which she illustrated a woman dressed in a tunic of Celtic flavour and with a cloak over her shoulders adorned with the Tara Brooch. The figure holds a banner with the name of the publication in Celtic calligraphy. Behind her there is a round tower and the sunburst, an image linked to early Irish nationalism. The sunburst flag, first thought to have been used in the mid-nineteenth century by the Irish Republican Brotherhood, was inspired by the tales about Fionn Mac Cumhail and the Fianna of the Irish mythology, and it became the symbol of the Na Fianna Éireann as a promise of a new day and a better future for Ireland. This image also appeared in Markievicz's writing

·bean·na·h-Eireann·
(THE WOMAN OF IRELAND)

VOL. II, NO. 22.] Mí na Nodlag (DECEMBER.) 1910. [PRICE ONE PENNY.

O'NEILL'S
For GRAMAPHONES,
PHONOGRAPHS
and RECORDS,
— also —
LUCANIA CYCLES
(IRISH MANUFACTURE)
EASY PAYMENTS ARRANGED.
SOUTH KING ST., DUBLIN.
Telephone, 2041.

The Dublin
Woodworkers,
17 WELLINGTON QUAY.
For Chairs, Tables, Cabinets, Bedroom
Suites, Picture Frames,
Mirrors and Overmantels, carved, gilt,
and polished.
And Everything in Woodwork.
All Made in Ireland by Irishmen
Artistic Work and Reasonable Prices.

A' dTuigeann Tu?

The nicest Costume I ever got, and the best fitting is the one I am now wearing, of Irish material.

IRISH ART COMPANIONS. 28 Clare St.

Fig. 8. Constance Markievicz, Front cover (vol. II, no. 22)
from ***Bean Na hÉireann***, 1910.
BMH-CD-005-3-09. Bureau of Military History. Courtesy of Military Archives.

for *Bean na hÉireann*, where she published a monthly column of allegories of the Irish resistance entitled "Woman with a Garden", which ran from February 1909 until March 1910. In her writings Markievicz used the concept of the garden as a metaphor of the political struggles in relation to women and the nation. Her images of the "tender plants" and "poor wee bulbs" referred to the youthful militancy, while the more mature blossoms recalled those martyrs who had died for Ireland. Autumn blossoms were emblematised as the vibrant sunburst that Markievicz had included in her illustration for *Bean na hÉireann*. Her innovative columns have been described by Karen Steele as a way to "reclaim the garden's political potential for both women and nationalists by composing features that allegorically described how readers could resist domesticity and imperialism through that most visible icon of the Ascendancy class: the garden".[148]

Through her involvement in Inghinidhe na hÉireann, Markievicz became more and more radical and influenced by other nationalists such as Helena Molony, editor of *Bean na hÉireann*, Patrick Pearse and the trade union leader James Larkin. She helped Maud Gonne and Hanna Sheehy Skeffington in the committee that distributed food to the children of the poorest areas of Dublin, some of which joined Markievicz's Fianna Éireann. She also attended the strikes and helped in the soup kitchens of the Irish Transport and General Workers' Union at Liberty Hall set up during the Great Lock-Out in 1913 in order to help starving families. James Connolly became a significant influence in Markievicz's political career and, in an article written for *The Nation* in 1927, she described how when Connolly "began to organise the Irish Citizen Army, he brought me along, teaching me as he got to know me, as a comrade, giving me any work that I could do, and quite ignoring the conventional attitude towards the work of women".[149] She became an officer in the Irish Citizen Army, took part in the planning of the 1916 rebellion and, when the Rising began in Dublin, she was second-in-command to Michael Mallin in the garrisons at St. Stephen's Green.[150] Although sixteen nationalist leaders were executed after the surrender, the death penalty for Markievicz was commuted due to her sex, and substituted by a life sentence. While in jail, her sister and poet Eva Gore-Booth managed to smuggle art material that Markievicz used to draw sketches and create watercolours. She illustrated two books for her sister entitled *The One and the Many* (1904) and *The Death of Fionavar* (1916). The first one, illustrated with pencil, ink and watercolour, shows Markievicz's diverse influences that go from the romantic paintings of William Turner or the Aesthetic illustrator Aubrey Beardsley to Japanese art, French Symbolism and, especially, the Pre-Raphaelites.[151] The manner of Markievicz is intimately connected to other artists of the Irish Revival such as Kathleen Fox or A.E. Russell.[152] The poems of *The One and the Many* are, like Markievicz's illustrations, filled with symbolic references to Classical antiquity and Christian mysticism.[153] The second book, *The Death of Fionavar,* is a short play that tells the story of Queen Maeve, a metaphor of the fight of the human mind against the forces of domination and pity, a symbol of peace and war.[154] Published in 1916, the book was a response to the events of the Easter Rising addressed through Irish folklore, and it was dedicated "to the Memory of the Dead, the Many who died for Freedom and the One who died for Peace",[155] making a special reference to the pacifist and nationalist writer Francis Sheehy-Skeffington, executed in 1916. Constance's illustrations follow the tone of the text, and the pages are riddled with winged horses flying freely, and flowers and landscapes with Celtic and Gothic motifs embraced by an atmosphere of symbolism and mysticism.

Markievicz's time in prison turned out to be very productive creatively, but this was not unusual among artists. According to Casey A. Jarrin, some of the most important literary works of the emergent Irish nation by John Mitchel, Michael Davitt or Oscar Wilde were born out of the experiences of incarceration, and art was not oblivious to this cultural productivity behind bars.[156] Prison became, for many Irish nationalists, a subversive milieu for contemplation and for artistic production, and it witnessed the creation of countless murals, graffiti, letters, sketches and watercolours. A well-known example of this artistic resistance was Grace Gifford, a nationalist woman of Protestant background who also attended the Metropolitan School of Art and the Slade School of Art before becoming involved in politics and the nationalist cultural movement by the hand of Constance Markievicz.[157] Grace joined both Inghinidhe na hÉireann and Sinn Féin, where she became a member of the executive committee after the Rising. Opposed to the Treaty, she put her artistic skills at the service of the party through banners and posters, and she even published her satirical cartoons in three different collections.[158] For her participation in the Women's Prisoners' Defence League (WPDL), she was incarcerated in 1923 along with other women such as Kathleen Lynn and Mary MacSwiney. There, she kept herself busy with painting the walls of her cell. One of her most notable works was a painting of the Virgin with Child painted in 1923 and known as the *Kilmainham Madonna*.[159]

Like Gifford, Markievicz used her time in prison to write, draw and paint. Thanks to Eva, during her incarceration in the Aylesbury and Holloway jails, Markievicz was able to create sketches, watercolours and drawings illustrating both her life in prison and her political ideals. Many of her watercolours represent patriotic allegories with the Fianna warriors or Irish mythological goddesses ornamented with Celtic motifs. She also illustrated the daily life of the peasantry through the depiction of young girls surrounded by geese or driving sheep in a landscape set in the West of Ireland, of by portraying sturdy men and women engaged in farming activities such as burning kelp. The quiet life of the elderly peasants was also addressed in several sketches set in the interior of traditional cottages, where old women appear sitting beside a smoking woodfire or looking after the youngest children. One particularly unusual sketch is a nocturnal raid on an elderly couple in bed, but the fact is that Markievicz's artwork in jail was not exempt from criticism. A sketchbook entitled by the artist as *Scenes in Prison* narrates her life in jail through sketches of her cell or the prison chapel, and also contains caricatures of the ministers of the Irish Free State such as Blythe, O'Higgins, Cosgrave or Collins.[160] She also created a watercolour illuminated page of the Proclamation of the Republic in calligraphy, with two creatures, influenced by the motifs of the Book of Kells, devouring the Union Jack.

Markievicz was released from prison in 1917 following the general amnesty grated by the government in London. However, she was jailed again the year after over an alleged 'German plot'. Other nationalist leaders were also arrested, including Éamon de Valera, Arthur Griffith or William Cosgrave. Markievicz was sent to Holloway Jail, in London, where she was held alongside Hannah Sheehy-Skeffington, Kathleen Clarke and Maud Gonne, whom she portrayed in a watercolour entitled *Mrs. Gonne MacBride* seated in a cell and wearing a mourning dress after her husband John MacBride's execution following the Easter Rising. On December 28th 1918, while in jail, she became the first woman elected MP to the British House of Commons, although she did not take her seat, and took part in the formation of the first Dáil instead.

Around the time of the Civil War, Markievicz also produced propaganda cartoons where she criticised the Treaty and its supporters. Between 1922 and 1923 these sketches featured in several clandestine newspapers, including *Poblacht na hÉireann* and *The Republican War Bulletin*.[161] Cartoons like *Free Staters in Action* addressed the brutality of the Free State Forces, and the well-known series entitled *Free State Freaks* caricatured the politicians who had supported the Treaty. The series denounced the supposedly new-found wealth and status of these public figures, a criticism that clashed with Markievicz's own privileged background. Through her cartoons, she drew attention to the fact that government ministers were overpaid and out of touch with ordinary people.[162] Even Michael Collins, despite –or maybe partly because of– his respected revolutionary record, became one of Markievicz's main targets, and was often depicted in her cartoons as a puppet of the British government (e.g. *Churchill's Puppets*) or as a traitor to the cause holding a gun to Hibernia's head.[163] However, her sketches not only were a sharp criticism of the Free State, but they also became a depiction of the life of republican women during the Civil War. Despite her beliefs in gender equality, Markievicz's female characters were sometimes relegated to conventional gender roles for nationalist reasons.[164] Traditional stereotypes helped to emphasise the apparent brutality of the Free State Forces, and Markievicz did not hesitate to use them as political propaganda. Some of her characters were wives and mothers who had been forgotten by the Free State and found themselves alone and defenceless during the war. *At a Republican Home* (n.d.) portrays a child that kisses goodbye to his father before he goes to war while the mother says: "kiss Daddy goodbye, darling, he's going to fight for the Republic".[165] *Republican Dependents Fund* (ca. 1922)[166] shows a mother sitting with a child on her lap and two other children beside her. They all look fearfully at the head of Piaras Béaslái, chief of the press censorship department during the Civil War. The caption of the cartoon asks: "Will you allow the wives and children of dead and imprisoned republicans to starve because the Free State censor Pierce Béaslái has suppressed the appeal sent to the Daily Papers". Markievicz also drew some women subjected to violence and intimidation during the war, such as Sinéad de Valera – Irish author and wife of Éamon de Valera – portrayed surrounded by her children and being held at gunpoint by soldiers in the illustration *Midnight Assassins. Raid on Mrs. Éamon de Valera* (ca. 1922).

There were, however, exceptions in Markievicz's gendered characters, and she depicted some female leaders of the nationalist movement as active figures and in a non-victimising way. The activists Charlotte Despard and Maud Gonne were represented in a cartoon of the attack on a meeting in O'Connell Street in 1922.[167] Also, in *The Bodyguard of the Republic* (ca. 1922) Markievicz portrayed Hibernia in front of an Irish flag with one arm around a female republican fighter in military uniform. At her feet there is a man carrying a gun, and behind her a background of flames and smoke. Markievicz's illustration shows Ireland being defended by both male and female republican fighters, which was also addressed in *The Dead: Stand Firm, Fear Not, Be True. Victory Will Be to Those Who Can Endure Most.* Here, Hibernia appears flanked by the living and the dead, a representation of the leaders executed after the Rising –Con Colberton and Sean Heuston– and a symbol of the Irish Republican Army, the Fianna and the women of Cumann na mBan.

In 1918, Constance Markievicz became the first female elected to the House of Commons as a Member of the Parliament. However, on her release from Holloway Jail in March 1919, she refused to take her seat, following Sinn Féin's policy of abstentionism.[168] She joined the Dáil as Minister for Labour of the first Irish rebel parliament, the only woman serving in De Valera's cabinet.[169] In 1926 she abandoned Sinn Féin and, along with Kathleen Clarke, supported De Valera in the creation of the party Fianna Fáil, abandoning Cumann na mBan to do so. She died in June the following year. The numerous portraits of her late years portrayed her as a revolutionary, fierce woman, which contrast with the early portraits that presented her according to her privileged backgrounds and the conventions placed on a woman of her class. Markievicz had soon acknowledged the potential of portraiture for political expression and propaganda; she took control of her photography portraits and shaped her public identity through this medium. According to Donal Maguire, curator of the exhibition *Markievicz: Portraits and Propaganda* (National Gallery of Ireland, 2018/2019):

> All of the key figures involved in that period were having their photographs portraits taken, usually in the same studios: you'll see the likes of Michael Collins against the same backdrop as Markievicz's portraits. However, [the men's] photographs tend to be more statesman-like, where they'll be in suits, sitting at a desk and writing, whereas she presents herself as a military figure, a woman of action.[170]

Just like her artwork, the portraits of Markievicz as a feminist republican dressed in the uniform of the Irish Citizen Army became a shout to the women of Ireland to take up arms and join her in the fight. This is also the way Kathleen Fox portrayed Markievicz in one of the most remarkable paintings: *The Arrest* (1916).

## Kathleen Fox

The daughter of Captain Henry Charles Fox of the King's Dragoon Guards and Mary Rebecca Colclough, Kathleen Fox (London, 1880–Dublin, 1963) was born to an Irish Catholic upper-middle class family with a British Army tradition.[171] Her Republican sympathies and her connection with the British Army often caused dilemmas and difficulties in the artist –Fox herself married a British official in 1917, Lieutenant Cyril Pym, who died in the war one year later–, although this situation was not uncommon in Ireland at the turn of the century.[172] Probably against her family's wishes she attended the Dublin Metropolitan School of Art from 1903, with fellow students Willie Pearse (the younger brother of Patrick Pearse), Grace Gifford, Mrs. Joseph Plunkett, Albert Power and Constance Markievicz. During her artistic training, Fox became first interested in the Arts and Crafts movement and often worked with metalwork and enamelling –for which she won a gold medal in the National Competition of 1908 under the guidance of Oswald Reeves– as well as carver wood, stained glass, silver or costume design. Her interest in painting was encouraged by William Orpen, who became a significant influence in Fox's realist manner (e.g. *China and Japan*, 1902). She was Orpen's most gifted protégés at the Dublin Metropolitan School of Art, and eventually became his assistant in 1910, until Margaret Clarke started teaching part time. That very same year, she attended the Royal Hibernian Academy life school, and in 1911 she exhibited at the Academy for the first time with her painting *Science and Power*, a portrayal of her good friend the sculptor Albert Power at work in his studio. She continued her training in Paris and Bruges, and returned to Dublin before the Easter Rising. During the World War I she kept a studio in London before moving to Nice, and exhibited there as well as in France and in Dublin.

The year 1916 changed everything. The events following the Rising led her to become more and more interested in politics, as well as more patriotically inclined, something her family did not approve. Fox was working as an assistant to Orpen at the Dublin Metropolitan School of Art when she heard that there was a "rising" and went to St. Stephen's Green to see what was happening.[173] She drew some sketches of the scene, and then finished the work secretly over the next weeks, hiring models and making studies for a painting in a large canvas whose dimensions accentuated the monumentality of the events. The result was *The Arrest* (1916) (fig. 9), a depiction of the surrender of the Irish

Fig. 9. Kathleen Fox, ***The Arrest***, 1916.
Oil on canvas, 182 x 140 cm. The Niland Collection.
Image courtesy of The Model, home of The Niland Collection. © The Artist's Estate / IVARO, Dublin (2020)

Citizen Army volunteers in front of the College of Surgeons. In her painting, Fox's use of the perspective enlarges the dimensions of the British army, whose well turned-out uniformed British soldiers contrast with the portrayal of the Irish Volunteers. Constance Markievicz is portrayed wearing the uniform of the Irish Citizen Army, which she joined following the 1913 Dublin lockout, and stands firm beside Major Michael Mallin. She allegedly kissed her gun before handing it in to a British official, which became one of the iconic moments of Irish nationalist mythology. Her gesture was criticised by the press as "unfeminine", although this did not shock Markievicz, who had already been ridiculed in the press for being too masculine.[174] *The Arrest* is an example of how women's political activism challenged the imagery of the male-soldiers as protectors of the motherland. Through her painting Fox highlighted the fact that neither Markievicz nor Mallin had actually surrendered. In her discussion of the events with Nora Niland, –founder of the Sligo Municipal Art Collection that currently holds the painting–, Fox stated: "If you notice, I've never used defeated. They did not surrender. They asked for a truce and if you notice in my picture, you see the little white flag up beside the tricolour, but when that little flag went up the British Army came along and the Citizen marched out of the college".[175] Kathleen Fox also painted a group of spectators turning their gaze to Markievicz. She stands out in the painting, not only because she is a woman in the uniform of the Irish Citizen Army and surrounded by men, but also because she was recognised by the mostly working-class crowd thanks to her work for the poor. Fox included a self-portrait of her within the mass, a woman under the sole tree that looks directly to the viewer which, according to Bhreathnach-Lynch, proves Fox's subjective disposition to the painting.[176] Under an apparent objectivity, Fox's self-portrait draws the viewer into the event, encouraging them to participate or empathise with those who were arrested during the insurrection. This perspective has been compared by Deirdre Kelly with Van Eyck's *The Arnolfini Portrait*,[177] a painting that includes the signature of the artist above the mirror: "Jan Van Eyck was here". In their paintings, Fox and Van Eyck become witnesses of the scene they represented and, by taking part in the action, the authors can no longer remain objective.

When the horror of the executions came out, Fox secretly finished the canvas and sent it to New York, fearing the British reinforcements that had instructions to suppress any expression of Irish independence. The painting remained in New York thirty years until it was re-discovered and sent to the Sligo County Museum in 1962.[178] Painted directly from a first-hand witness, *The Arrest* holds a great historical importance for being an immediate artistic response to contemporary Irish events, but this was not the only painting that Fox executed during these turbulent times. *Ruins of the Four Courts* (1922) was painted only a few years after *The Arrest*, and it illustrates an apparently tranquil viewpoint across the Liffey River. The calm atmosphere is, however, disturbed in the background, where the buildings are being destroyed in one of the attacks at the beginning of the Civil War. Another painting of the building, *View of the Four Courts* (n.d.), was created by the artist before the destruction of the building,[179] but the academicism and the precision of this previous painting clash with the darker atmosphere in *Ruins of the Four Courts*. The building was bombed by the government in an attempt to evict the members of the IRA that opposed the Treaty and had occupied the building. Those who were portrayed together in 1916 were now divided. In *Ruins of the Four Courts* the dome of the building is missing, and the heavy clouds melt with the black smoke that emanates from the ruins as a warning of what is to come.

Fox's husband, the lieutenant Cyril Pym whom she married in 1917, was killed in action in 1918. Fox returned to Ireland with her daughter in the early twenties, and focused on oil painting. Between 1911 and 1957 she showed 82 works at the Royal Hibernian Academy, most of them still life and interiors, but also portraits and figure compositions. She also exhibited at the Royal Scottish Academy, the Royal Academy, the New English Art Club, the National Portrait Society and the Society of Women Artists. She made herself a name as a portraitist thanks to paintings like *The Most Rev. Dr. Mannix, Archbishop of Melbourne* (1937), a portrait of the Archbishop Daniel Mannix which bears a great resemblance to Velazquez's *Portrait of Innocent X* (1650), especially in his arms resting on the chair and in the background draperies. The work of the Spanish painter seems to have influenced Fox's manner greatly in more paintings like her *Self-Portrait* (ca. 1920), where the interior, the many canvasses and the visual ambiguity recalls *Las Meninas* (1656). In this self-portrait Fox depicts herself as an artist with a brush and a palette in her hand. She is standing in a room that evidences the upper-middle class Fox was born to. Like in Sarah Cecilia Harrison's self-portrait, we cannot see what is happening on the canvas, as the subject-matter of the mysterious painting is not important. By hiding the canvas, Fox states that she *is*, first and foremost, an artist. One can, however, guess that she is painting a self-portrait and, therefore, looking herself in a mirror situated in the same place as the viewer. Fox's style was shaped by Orpen's realism, but also inspired by the Symbolist and pre-Raphaelite movements, and Art Nouveau. The depiction of a gypsy woman in *The Fortune Teller* (1922) stands out within the iconography of the nationalist Revival that built the Irish identity as opposed to cultural pluralism or multiple identities. Despite her symbolic portraits and her depictions of contemporary events in Irish history, Fox remained better known for her late paintings of flowers, on which she focused during the 1940s and 1950s. However, her life and her career proved that Irish women artists were not content with painting just flowers and landscapes. Kathleen Fox walked along the most dangerous places of Dublin to illustrate the spirit of the Rising while carrying messages between the leaders, for which she was known as "the artist of the Rising" or "the little rebel".[180] Markievicz, for her fight for the poor and Irish independence, gained the title of "the rebel countess". Both rebels, Fox and Markievicz, surpassed the limits imposed to women. They conquered the streets, enriched the Irish artistic scene and narrated first-hand the troubled events of their times.

## Estella Frances Solomons

While Kathleen Fox was the artist of the Rising and Constance Markievicz narrated her own revolutionary experiences, Estella Frances Solomons (Dublin, 1882–1968) became the portraitist of the leaders of the Irish struggle.[181] Born into a cultured and eminent Jewish family, Solomons was the second of four children of the well-known optician Maurice E. Solomons and the talented musician and poet, Rosa Jane Solomons of Hull. Her sister Sophie went on to become an opera singer while her brother Bethel, involved in the Dublin cultural movement, worked as a doctor. Solomons attended Miss Wade's select school for young ladies and the Alexandra College before taking classes with William Orpen at the Metropolitan school of Art at the age of sixteen. At the School, the artwork of the seventeenth-century Old Masters inspired her interest in etching and in the possibilities of the chiaroscuro. At the Royal Hibernian Academy, she studied life drawing under Walter Osborne, whose depiction of Dublin's harsh life left a mark in Solomon's career and inspired her rural and urban landscapes in etching. Wishing a more independent life far from the Jewish suburbs of Dublin, Solomons studied at the Chelsea School of Art in London and the Academie Colarossi in Paris, where she attended life-drawing classes along with Cissy Beckett and Dorothy and Beatrice Elvery. The most important moment of her artistic training was her visit to the Rembrandt Tercentenary in Amsterdam in 1916, which became the main influence for her spontaneous portraits, far from the manners of Sarah Cecilia Harrison or Sarah Purser (e.g. *Dutch Girl*). This exhibition encouraged even more her interest in etching, and led Solomons to take up printmaking in the 1900s. She, however, did not stick to the Academician style based on her traditional artistic education or the Old Masters manner, although her style, technique and the media she worked with were without a doubt influenced by them. Many artists portrayed Solomons throughout her life. One of them was her cousin and friend Louise Jacobs, an artist and a suffragette member of the Suffrage Atelier, which promoted women's rights to vote through artistic propaganda. Solomons and Jacobs went on a painting trip to Holland in 1911, and exhibited together in the Arlington Gallery (London) in 1935, along with Solomons' good friend Mary Duncan, receiving favourable reviews. A remarkable portrait of Estella Solomons was executed by Frances (Cissie) Beckett, with whom she had exhibited at the Leinster Hall in Dublin in 1903. The painting probably dates from the early years of the 1900s, when Beckett and Solomon travelled together to Paris, and it belonged to Solomons' friend and benefactor Kathleen Goodfellow. Cissie Beckett (1880–1951), the aunt of the author Samuel Beckett, also attended the Dublin Metropolitan School of Art and exhibited at the Royal Hibernian Academy between 1897 and 1908, until her marriage with the antique dealer William Sinclair and the duties of motherhood forced her to put her artistic career aside. Her painting of Solomons illustrates the artist seated comfortably on a chair and turning her gaze to the viewer against a neutral background. She appears dressed in a bright dress with her shoulders covered by a transparent shawl and holding a fan with her left hand while the right arm rests on the chair. This portrayal of Solomons encapsulates the gipsy-like expression that the artist herself also highlighted in her own self portraits.[182]

Upon Solomons' return to Dublin, aged 24 and unmarried, she began to participate in the Irish cultural nationalist circles. With Dorothy and Beatrice Elvery and Frances Beckett, she had exhibited at the Leinster Hall in Dublin in 1903, and two years later she began exhibiting at the Royal Hibernian Academy, where she showed over 250 paintings throughout her life. In 1910 Solomons opened her own studio in Pearse Street, Dublin, where she also installed an etching print. There, she carried out portraits of the leaders of the cultural Revival such as the poet Joseph Campbell, the clergyman and scholar Padraig de Brún, Alice Milligan, or Frank Aiken, the IRA Chief of

Staff in 1923. She was a witness of the suppression of the Irish republicans by the British government and, while sketching the life and the poorest neighbourhoods of Dublin, she was banned by the Royal Irish Constabulary from drawing in public places. Her unsentimental etchings portrayed the streets of the city that had not changed with the arrival of modern times, which gained her a good reputation as a talented etcher. She was one of the very few artists in Dublin who specialised in this medium, and took part in the small, but talented and influential, etching movement in Ireland during the turn of the century and up until the foundation of the Graphic Studio in Dublin in 1960.[183] The Etching Revival had begun in France in the 1850s, when important artists such as Edgar Degas, Camille Pisarro or Mary Cassatt explored the medium. Artists like James Abbott McNeil Whistler popularised it in Britain in the following decade, and Ireland took over in the 1880s with artists like Sarah Cecilia Harrison (e.g. *Study of a Man's Head,* 1880), who was also a collector of prints, and then donated her selection to the Municipal Gallery of Art in Dublin when it opened its doors in 1908.[184] The Irish Myra Hughes was one of the very few women who became a member of the Royal Society of Painters-Etchers in London, also holding a solo exhibition in Dublin in 1910. Her plain-air studies of nature and the city inspired the work of Solomons, who illustrated the old neighbourhoods of the city, the untouched and the traditional in the same way that Irish painters portrayed the landscape of the West of Ireland. Influenced by Rembrandt and Whistler, Solomons's etchings captured the essence of a vanishing time while remaining distant from the inhabitants. Her particular visions of the soul of Dublin in the first years of the twentieth century inspired the artist Mary Duncan to take up etching, and both artists exhibited in a joint show at the Mills Hall in Dublin in 1919. Solomons illustrated several books such as Padraic Colum's *The Road Round Ireland* (1926) and D. L. Kelleher's *The Glamour of Dublin* (1928), which published eight etchings of Dublin back streets and alleyways inspired by Rembrandt's dark portraits and his chiaroscuro. Solomons' etching of *A Georgian Doorway* was published in *Leabhar Ultáin* (1920), by Katherine MacCormack, who also worked in the Dun Emer Guild. *Leabhar Ultáin* (The Book of St. Ultan) was a collection of poems, drawings and pictures by Irish artists such as Harry Clarke, A.E. Russell, Beatrice Elvery, Grace Henry, Maud Gonne or Jack B. Yeats, and authors like Douglas Hyde Alice Milligan and Susan Mitchell.[185] While favouring the employment of women, the book was sold to raise funds for St. Ultan's children's hospital in Dublin, which was founded by two important members of Cumann na mBan: Madeleine ffrench-Mullen and Kathleen Lynn. In the early 1920s, Solomons also began teaching etching at the Dublin Municipal Technical Schools. Described as a woman of "unyielding patriotism and lifelong devotion to all things Irish",[186] she resigned when, with the creation of the Irish Free State, the Dublin Technical School asked her to take the Oath of Allegiance to the British Crown.

Solomons joined Cumann na mBan in 1916 under Phyllis Ryan, later the wife of President Sean T. O'Kelly. She was joined by two other Jewish women: Fanny and Molly Goldberg. As a Cumann na mBan member, Solomons studied signalling and first aid, and was taught to use a revolver by a member of Sinn Féin known as "the Butterman", because he was officially working as a milkman. Shortly after, Solomons carried out a painting of his wife entitled *The Butterwoman* (n.d.), where she portrayed her as a peasant woman against a neutral background. Solomons was a devoted republican supporting her comrades during the Easter Rising and War of Independence. She took the anti-Treaty side during the Irish Civil War, and smuggled weapons in the vegetable garden of her parents, who welcomed with surprise their daughter's sudden interest in gardening.[187] Her studio in Pearse Street ended up becoming a safe house for the leaders of the Dublin's cultural and political movement, hosting figures such as Arthur Griffith or Horace Plunkett. Séamus O'Sullivan, who married Solomons in 1926, described her workshop as "not only a centre of artistic activity and goodly conversation, but [...] also a centre of quiet, of calm; a place of refuge for many whose political and national activities had brought them a very undesirable amount of notice in 'the bad times'".[188] Through her passion for painting, Solomons became very good friends with Ernie O'Malley, a young IRA officer from Co. Mayo and future member of the Irish Academy of letters. During his imprisonment between 1922 and 1923, O'Malley and Solomons stayed in touch by mail, and she often sent him literary and artistic publications at his request.

Solomons' portraits display a particular academicism that she never disturbed in the manner that Mainie Jellett, Mary Swanzy and Evie Hone did. However, her style was characterised by its strong line and composition and stood far from sentimentalism. The formality of her early paintings was substituted by a unique spontaneity present both in her landscapes and in her many portraits. Solomons sheltered many men on the run, both in her studio and in her family home, and also painted them during their stay. The rapid brushstrokes, often necessary due to the particularity of the sitters on the run, gave her portraits an impressionist touch. Her interest for the detail and everything around her was evident from the beginning of her artistic career, in her self-portraits and her sketches of the Dublin people, streets and alleys, architecture and docks. She managed to obtain official passes during Ireland's troubled times in order to sketch in some military precincts.[189] Thanks to her meticulousness and to the intimate atmosphere and unique manner of the paintings, her portraits went on to become Solomons's best work. However, and with the constant raids taking part in her studio, she decided to burn the portraits of those who took refuge there as they could be used as potential evidences against her. *On Parole* (1920) is one of the very few surviving paintings that show one of the men on the run. It is a dark portrait of a man of determined expression and sharp features whose identity remains unknown. Solomons's spontaneity seems to clash with her skilled draughtsmanship, a result of the particular and dangerous situation of the sitters hiding in her workshop. She also portrayed leaders of the Cultural Revival like Ella Young, a painting of rapid brush-stroke where the poet and founding member of Cumann na mBan appears against one of Solomons's characteristic neutral backgrounds. Ella Young was one of the authors involved in the Literary Revival along with Maud Gonne and W. B. Yeats. She decided to learn Irish, and travelled to Achill Island in order to collect folklore for her collaborations with A.E. Russell. In 1912 she joined Sinn Féin and was incarcerated for her opposition to the Treaty. After her release, Young spent the rest of her life in California, where she lectured in Irish myth at the University and published several books. Another anti-Treaty sitter portrayed by Solomons with great dignity was Erskine Childers, a writer born in London who became a supporter of Irish republicanism. From 1919 he was involved in Sinn Féin propaganda, was arrested in 1922 and executed few weeks later. His son was the fourth President of Ireland between 1973 and 1974.

In 1914, Erskine Childers smuggled weapons from Germany to Howth, Co. Dublin, in his yacht with the help of another sitter of Solomons's, Darrell Figgis. Figgis was a poet and journalist who moved home to Ireland from Ceylonn in 1910. He was portrayed by Solomons wearing a brown jacket against a dark blue neutral background, and turning his gaze to the viewer. Figgis had also become involved in politics and joined the Irish Volunteers and, although he did not take part in the Easter Rising, he was nevertheless arrested and incarcerated in Reading Gaol, Berkshire, England. Highly regarded and trusted by Arthur Griffith, Figgis supported the Treaty and was elected to the Sinn Féin executive in 1922 and took part in the draft of the Constitution of the Free State. The journalist Frank Gallagher, who was a very good friend of Erskine Childers's was as well portrayed by Solomons in the group portrait entitled *The Morrow Family and Frank Gallagher* (n.d.).The artist Jack Morrow also took part in the nationalist movement and held in his studio several meetings where the planning of the Rising took place, while Gallagher joined the Irish Volunteers, participated in the Irish Bulletin and was also imprisoned for opposing the Treaty. The Irish Volunteer Seán Milroy was another sitter of Solomons'; he was portrayed seated, wearing a black coat, and with his hands interlaced, in a relaxed posture against a bright white background. A volunteer in the Rising, Milroy was arrested and incarcerated in England following the insurrection. After his release, he became Sinn Féin's director of elections in 1918, and was elected to the Dáil and also the Northern Irish Parliament, although he did not take his seat in the North and resigned from the Dáil in 1924. Along with Séan McGarry and Éamon de Valera, Seán Milroy was involved in one of the most famous prison escapes in the Irish revolution, when in 1919 the three men broke out of Lincoln Jail in England with a key hidden in a cake.[190]

Solomons portrayed many other important characters of the time such as James Stephens, A.E. Russell, Thomas Bodkin, Padraic Colum or Jack B.

Yeats. However, one of her most beloved sitters was her lifelong friend and revolutionary companion Kathleen Goodfellow. The two women met while fighting in the Rising and joined Cumann na mBan together. Born into a Quaker family, Goodfellow attended the Alexandra College, obtained a degree in Arts at Trinity College and became a writer who published poems and books such as *Three Tales of the Times* (1921) under the pseudonym Michael Scot. Solomons carried out several portraits of Goodfellow. One of them is entitled *Woman in Riding Habit* (n.d.), a darker-coloured painting where the sitter is portrayed as an androgynous figure dressed in her riding uniform, with her hair hidden under a hat and holding a whip. *Portrait of a Woman* (n.d.) is a more intimate and brighter portrait of Goodfellow sitting in a house interior with a book on the table. Although the composition is more detailed than most of Solomons' portraits, she still displays her vivacious manner and characteristic interplay of light and shade. More focused on the person than on the surroundings, *Portrait of Kathleen Goodfellow* (c. 1923) offers a half length portrait of Solomons' friend in which the artist returns to a neutral background only disturbed by a painting on the wall. Dressed in a blue coat and shirt and with a classic 1920s short hairstyle, this portrait of Goodfellow highlights the sitter's facial expression of strength and determination that matches her involvement in the political struggle.

In 1926 Solomons married James Starkey (Séamus O'Sullivan), following the death of her parents who opposed to the wedding of her daughter and a Methodist. O'Sullivan, who had become a very important part of Solomons's life from the 1910s onwards, was a prolific author, deeply influenced by the Irish Revival, who published several books of poems such as *The Twilight People* (1905), *Verses, Sacred and Profane* (1908), *The Earth-Lover and Other Verses* (1909), or *Twenty-five Lyrics* (1933), with a preface by George Russell. His *Mud and Purple: Pages from the Diary of a Dublin Man* (1917) was also illustrated by Estella Solomons. O'Sullivan was an admirer of Arthur Griffith and those who took part in the Easter Rising and fought for an independent Ireland, whom he praised in his book *The Rosses* and Other Poems (1918).[191] While sheltering republicans on the run in their home in Rathfarnham, both O'Sullivan and Solomons published *The Dublin Magazine*, a literary journal founded by the former in 1923. Solomons's friend Katherine Goodfellow, was the main patron of the magazine, and collaborated with the project financially and by offering editorial assistance. A Quaker, a Jewish and a Methodist, the three friends became very well known within the Dublin cultural arena. The turbulent years of the War of Independence and the Civil War divided families, friends and also artists. The artistic world was deeply affected, and the Literary Revival lost many of its leaders following the execution of Thomas MacDonagh, Joseph Mary Plunkett, Erskine Childers and Patrick Pearse. Authors like O'Sullivan and artists like Solomons became disillusioned, a sentiment that was addressed by O'Sullivan in one of his editorials for *The Dublin Magazine*:

> Painfully and rather wistfully, we are stretching out in search of some living organism to which we feel we belong and have a right to attach ourselves for the preservation of our vitality. For we are today in the somewhat troubled position of trying to assert a national entity that has not yet fully declared itself, we feel deeply the need to knit ourselves with those elements in our past that will best help us to its disclosure.[192]

Through their publication, O'Sullivan, Solomons and Goodfellow addressed the consequences of the war in the artistic scene, the concept of Irishness and the issue of the reconstruction of the nation after 1922. *The Dublin Magazine* became a very important literary publication featuring drama, poetry and fiction by authors such as Padraic Colum, George Russell, Samuel Beckett or Austin Clarke. The beautiful cover of the first issue was designed by the artist Harry Clarke, husband of Margaret Clarke and Ireland's greatest stained glass artist, and it portrayed a gentleman and a lady with two dogs over a silhouette of Dublin city with its characteristic Nelson's Pillar.[193] Solomon and Goodfellow proved to be essential to the long-life of the publication especially in sourcing advertising, a difficult task in the early years of the Free State. The magazine ran for over thirty years, and played a significant role in the artistic and literary scene until O'Sullivan's death in 1958.

Solomons became inspired by modernist trends, had an Academic training and admired the Old Masters, but never stuck to any trend nor did she follow any convention.[194] Although she was praised for her fine dark-toned portraiture and the unsentimental treatment of her sitters, she was also a talented plain-air painter of Irish landscape. She carried out many small-sized, spontaneous and elegant landscapes influenced by the wind, the waves, the fields and the freedom of the West of Ireland in the manner of Eva Hamilton or Lilian Lucy Davidson. Like A.E. Russell, she had a deep affection for Donegal, although from the 1930s she turned her gaze to Kerry, its changing colours and the atmosphere of the south-west of Ireland. Many of her landscapes were exhibited at the Royal Hibernian Academy for over sixty years, and Seamus was often portrayed reading or walking with a pipe in her mouth in landscape paintings such as *Seamus Reading in the Sand Dunes (n.d.), Seamus O'Sullivan on the Strand, County Kerry* (n.d.) or *The Green Hollows* (n.d.). Like most of Solomon's characters, Seamus was included in her paintings as part of the natural scenery and never as an intruder. She barely worked with watercolour when executing her landscapes, which was rather unusual for an artist at the time, but she created few portraits of Seamus in this medium. She always showed preference for oil, a medium she also used to portray the daily life of the Irish peasantry and the changeable weather of the West in paintings of recurrent subject-matters such as *Bringing Home the Turf* (n.d.) or *Hayfield Near Rush* (n.d.).

After the Civil War, Solomons became disenchanted and hopeless. She abandoned her political activities and focused her efforts on the promotion of

Irish culture. Her artistic activities became a celebration of Irish nationalism, and a tribute to those who fought for the independence. Throughout her life, she held two solo exhibitions, something quite rare at the time among Irish female artists. The first one was held in her studio in 1926 and was entitled *Sketches*. The second took place in the Dublin Painters Gallery in 1931, and was also dominated by landscapes. In her participation in major group exhibitions she often showed portraits. She took part in Hugh Lane's project for a gallery of modern art, was elected an associate member of the Royal Hibernian Academy in 1936, and had to wait another thirty years to become an honorary member. In the political and social arena, she organised a coal fund around her studio in Pearse Street and assisted the wounded soldiers of World War I and the republicans in 1916 in addition to her own fight in the struggle. She organised an Aeridheacht in support of the National Aid association, to which many of her artist friends contributed. Although most of her portraits are lost, the remaining paintings have become a record of the generation of artists and revolutionaries who shaped the new Ireland. Solomons herself, as an Irish female nationalist who never lost touch with her Jewish background, became an example of Irish diversity within the Revival and the nationalist movement.

# Modernism and Tradition

## Mainie Jellett

Mary Harriet Jellett (Dublin, 1897–1944) was born to a middle-class Anglo-Irish family. Her father, William Morgan Jellett, was a barrister and a Unionist member of the British Parliament, while her mother Janet McKenzie Stokes was not hostile to the idea of a free Ireland.[195] Encouraged by her mother –who was also a musician– Jellett became an accomplished pianist although she was determined to pursue a career in Fine Arts.[196] She had her first painting lesson at the age of only eleven, and studied drawing under Elizabeth Yeats, the daughter of the artist John Butler Yeats and sister of W. B. and Jack B. She was also trained by May Manning and Sarah Cecilia Harrison before taking classes in France from the age of fourteen.[197] In 1904, she was admitted into the Dublin Metropolitan School of Art where she studied under William Orpen, who inspired Jellett's early style in her bright large nudes and realist portraits. She, however, was inclined to take a more Impressionist road that would eventually lead her to external, innovative influences.[198]

Jellett's interest in the Impressionist movement was supported by the British painter and printmaker Walter Sickert (1860–1942). He was one of the leaders of the avant-garde in England, who taught Jellett at the Westminster School of Art in London between 1917 and 1919 and encouraged her to develop her skills in drawing and composition through the work of the Old Masters and the French Impressionists. Jellett adopted Sickert's free use of the brush and his impressionist palette in outstanding drawings of precise lines such as *Crows Amongst the Barley Stooks* (1919) or *Betty on the Rocks* (1919). Her skilled draughtsmanship was displayed in impressive nudes in oil like *Seated Female Nude* (ca. 1919), a depiction of a contemplative lady who crosses her hands modestly against a dark background of visible, thick brushstrokes. "For the first time drawing and composition came alive to me" –wrote Jellett –, "and with Sickert's help I began to understand the work of the Old Masters".[199] This period was a turning point in Jellett's style, and was identified by the artist in her essay entitled "An Approach to Painting" (*The Irish Art Handbook*, 1942) as the first of the three revolutions that divided her artistic career.[200]

It was during her time at the Westminster School of Art that Jellett met Evie Hone (1894–1955), a fellow artist who was to become her soul mate and lifelong friend. Jellett had already established herself as a professional artist in Ireland after winning the Taylor Prize and Scholarship in 1920;[201] however, both Hone and Jellett were eager to avoid the conservative Irish artistic scene of the time. The two friends decided to move to Paris in 1921 to study under André Lhote (1885–1962), who brought about the second revolution in Jellett's art. While Sickert had encouraged her to explore the expression of her soul through the artistic practice, Jellett had not found any spiritual challenge during her training in London. This was about to change in France, where Jellett was introduced for the first time to Cubism by the hand of Lhote, who also became her second approach to the work of the Old Masters, the Renaissance art and the manner of Rubens. A passionate of the history of painting, Lhote considered art a craft to be mastered only through patience and study. He worked tirelessly throughout his life to comprehend the permanent nature in the great achievements of the Old Masters. The basis of his teaching was the tension between nature and painting, a strain that had been present through the whole history of representational art.[202] The more Jellett explored Abstraction, the more her appreciation for the Old Masters progressed, a process she described as a "revelation":[203] "[Lhote] opened our minds to the vast realm of research and riches in the Old Masters, and showed us clearly how his reaching and ideals followed logically the living tradition based on permanent truths which are the heritage of all great art, but which seek re-expression in each new cycle of art movement".[204]

In the course of her training with Lhote, Jellett studied the work of the Italian Primitives as well as the European tradition and Celtic art, which encouraged her interest in colour and shape. She began to use natural forms as a starting point towards the creation of form for its own sake. Lhote's influence in Jellett's artwork can be seen in its angular forms, the harmonies of colour and in the contrasts between straight and curved lines. Her style was now far from the softer and more conventional work she had done in Dublin and London under Sickert's guidance. However, Lhote's method of re-interpreting a landscape, a figure or any other representational subject through geometrical shapes did not seem abstract enough for Jellett. She defined his teaching as somewhere halfway between "the extreme Cubism of Gleizes and official academic teaching and impressionist ideals".[205] She was decided to search for "extreme Cubism", which she addressed in a very particular way by combining it with Christian art and the Irish tradition.[206]

After a year under the tutelage of Lhote, Jellett, along with Evie Hone, decided to take one step further and started a new exploration of non-representational art under Albert Gleizes (1881–1953), who marked Jellett's third revolution. Gleizes was an academic and theorist amongst the Cubists that had published, along with Jean Metzinger, the first history of the movement in *Du Cubisme* (1912).[207] Jellett praised his style as "the purest and most austere form of non-representational work".[208] Gleizes's method of *translation* and *rotation* was developed while he was working with Jellett and Hone, and explained in his book *Painting and its Laws*, written in 1922 and published in 1923. The method was radically different from Lhote's, and consisted on starting with nothing but geometrical shapes which echoed the ones of the canvas (*translation*), and then rotating the basic forms in order to create a dynamic composition which would introduce the concepts of time and movement into the painting. The notions of translation and rotation are borrowed from physics, where *translation* describes the "movement of an object in relation to other objects in space", while *rotation* refers to the "movement of an object in relation to itself".[209] The object Gleizes refers to is no other than the canvas itself, the form of the area to be covered with paint. The canvas is the starting point of the artist's act. This was a crucial point for Jellett, as she described:

I went right back to the beginning [with Gleizes], and was put to the severest type of exercise in pure form and colour, evolved on a certain system of composition. I now felt I had come to essentials, and though the type of work I had embarked upon would mean years of misunderstanding and walks of prejudice to break through, yet I felt I was on the right track.[210]

To Gleizes, the act of *translation* depended on balance, proportion and harmony, all those characteristics inherent to Classical painting. The idea of *rotation*, however, consisted in disturbing them, in making the eye engaging in the activity of turning round and within the canvas in an organised manner: the *rhythm*.[211] The idea of the eye as an active observer in society and in the world itself was associated to the concept of *contemplation*, "the inner activity of the soul".[212] The painting should therefore correspond to the reality of human nature, not to the perfection of the machine. According to Gleizes, the rhythmic nature of art had been forgotten since the Renaissance, but it had been well understood by the "primitive" work of the Celts and Western Christianity, and by the art of the great religious ages.[213] Gleizes' work became not only an effort to find God, but also an attempt to find the human faith. His religious beliefs were the result of his dissatisfaction with the old system, with obsolete principles that in a post-war world were no longer valid. His work addressed his rational confrontation of three problems: collective order, individual differences and his role as a painter.[214] He proposed a union between theology and popular art with a benefit in society, and the search of God and faith –which was the main subject of his art–was focused on inner principles. To him, painting was a "song for the eye which touches the heart and captures the mind",[215] and thus he established an essential identity between divine love and nature, in which God was discernable.

Jellett followed the ideas of her master in her artistic expression of spirituality and the Irish tradition. Through her collaboration with Gleizes, she went on to develop a deeply spiritual and intellectually complex artwork comparable to the masterpieces of Celtic and Christian art. Jellett also explored nationalist subject-matters and portrayed the wild west of Ireland in paintings like *Achill horses*, but she avoided stereotyped ideas and nationalist sentimentalism as she focused on biblical themes of abstract flavour that she often entitled *Composition*.[216] These works, built from a central eye or *heart* that spread in arcs of colour, contained figurative elements depicted in a symbolic and non-representational manner. They displayed the new visual language that Jellett was developing and that addressed Ireland's Celtic tradition as well as Christian themes.

Jellett returned to Ireland in 1921, and began to make a living out of painting, lecturing and teaching. She never taught non-representational art unless specifically requested, but she did work to convert the Irish public to the modern trends through education and understanding.[217] However, introducing abstract art into the Irish scene was not an easy task, and the artist received many critics of those who opposed to any type of painting that was not submitted to the *establishment*. In 1923, along with Paul and Grace Henry, Letitia Hamilton, Harry Clarke and others, both Jellett and Hone showed their early Cubist works at the Society of Dublin Painters. Jellett's *Decoration* (1923) (fig. 10), one of the paintings exhibited at the venue, was to become a turning point in Irish art, although it also caused great controversy. A.E. Russell, who was editor of the *Irish Statesman* at the time, wrote an article praising Harry Clarke's contribution to the exhibition while harshly criticising Jellett's *Decoration*:

Fig. 10. Mainie Jellett, ***Decoration***, 1923. Tempera on Wood panel. NGI.1326. Photo © National Gallery of Ireland.

> We turn from Clarke's pictures and find Miss Jellett a late victim to Cubism in some sub-section of this artistic malaria. She seems as heartily as any of the Cubists to have adopted as motto Fuseli's famous outburst, 'Damn nature. She always puts me out.' The real defect in this form of art is that the convention is so simple that nothing can be said in it. It is as impossible to be subtle in this convention as it would be to write poetry if the poet was limited to use fifty words, the same words, no matter how many poems he wrote or what moods he wanted to express. In fact, what

> Miss Jellett says in one of her decorations she says in the other, and that is nothing [...]. The sorcery of Harry Clarke and Miss Jellett's incautious exposure of herself have occupied all the space a stern editor will allot to a reverie over art [...]. The exhibition is well worth seeing, and we hope the visitors will not be led away, as we were, by the super humanities of Harry Clarke or the sub-human art of Miss Jellett.[218]

For its part, *The Irish Times* published a review under the title "TWO FREAK PICTURES" in which the writer confessed himself confused by Jellett's paintings that were "in squares, cubes, odd shapes and clashing colours [...]. They may, to the man who understands the most up-to-date modern art, mean something; but to me they presented an insoluble puzzle".[219] Indeed, Jellett's *Decoration* was linked to the Irish tradition and addressed religious themes, but the fact that these references were lost even in the strong Catholic Irish society proved the degree to which abstract art was seen as dark and unintelligible by the public. For Bruce Arnold, *Decoration* marked the start of modernism in Ireland and, although some modernist paintings had been seen in Ireland already, Jellett's painting brought the issue of modern art into public focus.[220] Thomas MacGreevy was one of the few critics that gave *Decoration* a positive reception and, in his article to *The Klaxon,* he compared Jellett's style with Byzantine art and the illuminations of the Book of Kells while describing the painting as a "combination of Modernism, religion and a search for national identity".[221] MacGreevy criticised the conservative taste of Ireland's artistic establishment as well as its lack of knowledge and willingness to engage with modern art. Through his writings he became an advocate of modernism and a supporter of Irish female artists in time when the predominant discourse was patriarchal and associated to art academies: "That the freedom from subject [matter], from painted psychology, from symbolism, has heightened the aesthetic value of her work is not, I think, to be doubted by anyone who has seen the pictures she has exhibited during the past four or five years", wrote MacGreevy about Mainie Jellett.[222]

The public reaction to *Decoration* was a perfect example of the Irish resistance to European modernism. The painting depicted, in fact, a very personal view of the subject of the Madonna with Child. Jellett had abandoned the traditional perspective in art and portrayed the figures through abstract forms framed within a pentagonal shape, reminiscent of an altar piece. Jellett was well aware of the importance of art as a vehicle of expression of the deepest human spirituality. Like Gleizes, she considered representational painting to be a materialist attitude in a world more concerned in copying the external appearances of things than in focusing on nature and soul. Realism and perspective had distorted what they were supposed to represent, and the concepts of rhythm and movement were not compatible with the ideals of representational art.[223] Hence, Jellett encouraged observing and understanding nature through Abstract art, a movement that was more interested in spirituality and in comprehending universal truths rather than in appearances: "A picture should be a miniature universe, with all its forms interdependent, as the organisation of the universe itself. It should have a centre and unlimiting point of interest like the sun in the solar system [...].A picture should be as complete as the human body so that the removal of any of its members would upset the equilibrium of the whole".[224]

This concept of form in non-representational art was connected to the non-materialistic ideal of the Middle Ages of France and Italy. It was also linked to the beliefs of the Celtic culture, something that Irish artists of the day, above all painters in Europe, should have recognised. By combining the values of ancient Ireland with the ideology of the Free State, Jellett gave a nationalist feeling to her artwork, which she used to find the connection between the past and the present, figuration and abstraction. *Decoration* stands out as one of the works that best exemplified the connection between Modernism and Irish ancient art, and created a sense of pride in Ireland's heritage. Jellett herself declared that "if a Celtic artist of the eighth or ninth century were to meet a present day Cubist or non-representational painter, they would understand each other".[225] Both Celtic art and Cubism developed forms enclosed within the limits of their outside shape and interlaced in a rhythmically organised movement. Form was considered in pure relation of one shape to another and, in the manner of the Celtic artist-sculptor that followed the shape and contour of the stone to engrave spirals, squares and triangles, Jellett worked with the canvas to exteriorise her struggle finding a balance between her spiritual beliefs and the modern world. By combining Celtic art with Abstraction Jellett aimed to return the significance of pre-Christian culture to Ireland, which would offer spiritual health to a troubled country:

> I will try to point out the similarity of ideals between the art of the modern movement (headquarters Paris) and the ideals inspiring Celtic art, and try and show that if we could only open our eyes to the truth behind Celtic art and the treasure house we have in this country in what it has left us, we might then become conscious of a reality that would give our art a national character.[226]

However, in her campaign for new principles in art, she opposed to any naive creation of neo-Celtic language. Ireland had produced, between the fifth and the twelfth centuries, one of the greatest and most powerful expressions of Celtic art in Europe, and she aimed to translate the greatness of that era into the modernist language. Jellett firmly criticised the fact that Irish art had become nothing more than an extension of the English school, and insisted on the importance of reaching to France and other European countries where art was involved with politics and society in order to explore the real nature of Irishness.[227] Inspired by the Arts and Crafts movement, she challenged the superficiality of traditional academicism and firmly believed that the artist was no more than a crafts person who had a social role to play, and that art should be politically and socially involved.

Jellett has been described as a "Christian feminist"[228] who discussed her own spirituality in feminine terms, especially through her many abstractions of the Virgin Mary, "the most popular female emblem of religious and political identity in Ireland".[229] The cult of the Virgin was related, within Irish culture, to the Christian manifestation of ancient goddesses revered in Celtic societies. In Jellett's painting this subject matter became the bridge that linked Modern art to the Catholic public of the Free State. It was addressed in some of Jellett's most important works such as *The Virgin of Éire* (1943) *or Homage to Fra Angelico* (1928), a painting that –only five years after *Decoration*– was warmly embraced by the public and the critics in the *Irish Times* and the *Irish Statesman*. It is not strange that Jellett paid tribute to Fra Angelico and his *Coronation of the Virgin* (ca. 1435), as her style was deeply influenced by this Renaissance artist both in the flat patterning and in the colours. The symbolism of the gold leaf, blue and red were very much appreciated by the Great Masters of the fifteenth century as well as in Byzantine art.[230] Jellett herself believed in the spiritual power and essence of colours, which she always chose with great precision. Through the symbolism of her paintings she aimed to address her deepest thoughts about religion and identity. In her emotive and serene *Homage to Fra Angelico* Jellett had already moved from an extreme abstraction to more recognisable figures, searching for a way to communicate with the Irish public. The theme of the canvas is the coronation of the Virgin as Queen of Heaven, a common subject matter in Gothic art and the Early Renaissance, when art played an essential part in popular devotion.[231] Thomas MacGreevy wrote that Jellett's *Homage to Fra Angelico* had lost none of the "humble devotional yet gravely dignified temper that gives Fra Angelico's work its universal and enduring appeal".[232] She transformed a fifteenth-century piece into a modern expression of spirituality, which gained her the respect of her contemporaries and convinced the public of the importance of modern art in society. However, although her style developed into a more intelligible language for the public, she later addressed more complex abstractions. *The Virgin of Éire* summarised Jellett's new language and illustrated her concept of a national spirit. Alongside Evie Hone's stained-glass, Jellett portrayed the most artistically advanced Marian images of the time, which the art critic James White described as containing a "depth of feeling which is strangely moving" that suggests peace and suffering without puerile sentimentalism.[233]

The artist was aware that good international press reviews were essential in order to silence the critical reactionaries in Ireland. Thus, apart from her exhibitions in her homeland, she also showed her work in Paris, Versailles, London, Brussels and Amsterdam during the 1920s. In 1927, the *Irish Times* described her as "the only serious exponent in this country of the ultra-modernist school of painting"[234] and, at the Irish Art Exhibition in Brussels in 1930, Thomas Bodkin declared that "Irish art of whatever persuasion was animated by a single lyrical spirit".[235] She exhibited at the Royal Hibernian Academy between 1930 and 1937, and with the Watercolour Society of Ireland from 1931–1937. During the Second World War, she attended many weekends painting at Sutton House or at Collinstown House with other artists such as Nano Reid, Eva and Letitia Hamilton, Harriet Kirkwood, Ruth Jameson or Norah McGuinness. George Furling, director of the National Gallery of Ireland between 1935 and 1950, described those days as "informal, but hard-working weekends, often with Mainie Jellett as the ringleader".[236] She played a leading role in the Irish artistic arena as a non-representational painter and as a member of the Society of Dublin Painters that sponsored the modern movement in Ireland during first half of the twentieth century. She also became a central figure to the establishment of The Irish Exhibition of Living Art in 1943 and, alongside Séan Keating, Jellett represented Ireland in the 1939 World's Fair in New York, an exhibition that illustrated the great diversity of Irish art. Regarding this fair, Ciarán Benson has pointed out the difference between "revolution" and "rebellion" in comparing Jellett's modernist art with the nationalist academicism of other artists, like Séan Keating, who were more concerned about embodying the virtues of the new State.[237] Jellett, however, regarded modernism as an attempt to create a national identity for itself. She worked relentlessly to find support in her homeland, whose local artistic scene, longing for peace after years of violence and instability, remained attached to a highly conservative aesthetic.[238] A patriotic artist, she wished for Ireland to flourish both in the arts and in prosperity, and hence, she was critical of the power of the Catholic Church in Ireland and with De Valera's politics regarding health, education, welfare and the control over marriage and sexuality. However, she turned this to her advantage and, through her art and lectures, spoke out about the nature of Irishness, the urge of a cultural identity and the needs of the country. Jellett's combination of Abstraction and Irish heritage opened the doors to revolutionary trends in Ireland. Her art went on to become the vehicle to address her beliefs, her spirituality and her experiences regarding nationalism and violence. As the artist recalled years later, this was not easy: "My voyage of discovery from student to professional painter was stormy and varied. At least three times I have gone through major revolutions in my work, style and ideas and more or less started afresh".[239] According to Bruce Arnold, her career turned into the greatest force for artistic change in the inter-war period in Ireland.[240]

## May Guinness

Mainie Jellett, however, would probably not have taken the path she did without the influence of May Guinness, whom she admired.[241] Guinness (Dublin, 1863–1955) was born to a well-off family in Rathfarnham, Dublin. She was the third of the seven children of Mary Davis and the landowner and solicitor Thomas Hosea Guinness, descendant of the brewer Arthur Guinness.[242] She was educated at her family home in the rural area of Tibradden by German and French governesses, and later attended Miss Power's school. Although she wished to pursue a career in the arts, she had to assist in the education of her younger siblings and had a late start in art. She did have an early and long association with the Watercolour Society of Ireland from 1892, and took art lessons under May Manning. However, she did not begin to study art seriously until the death of her father in 1888. In 1894, along with her cousin the watercolourist Mildred Anne Butler, Guinness travelled to Newlyn (Cornwall) to take lessons under the supervision of the Limerick-born artist Norman Garstin. This trip became Guinness's first encounter with *plein-air* naturalist painting. She executed landscapes and genre paintings and, once back in Dublin, she also explored other media such as embroidery, fresco and glass painting, and woodcut at the Cuala Industries.[243] She travelled to Italy in 1902, where she studied the work of the Old Masters. Around 1905 she went to France and spent three years studying at different academies.[244] Her time in Paris marked the beginning of her artistic development. There, she became familiar with Fauvism and the manner of Matisse, one of the main influences of her work. Early paintings of Guinness display an Art Nouveau flavour inspired by Matisse, but she also embraced the modernist art of the Catalan painter Hermenegildo Anglada Camarasa and the vibrant palette of the Dutch Fauvist Kees van Dongen.

Like Aloysius O'Kelly, Guinness also went to Brittany in order to learn to paint from nature. At that time, Post-Impressionism and academic Realism were the dominant trends in Ireland with the exception of artists such as Jack B. Yeats, Mary Swanzy and May Guinness herself, who had already begun to explore international modernism through their work.[245] Guinness's style reflects a Fauvist use of colour inspired by Matisse, and Raoul Duffy's rapid brushstrokes, which she saw at the Salon d'Automne in Paris. Fauvism left a long-lasting mark on Guinness, who developed a bold use of colour and line, despite the fact that the movement itself did not last. It began in France around 1904 and the artists held their first exhibition at the Salon d'Automne in 1905. The movement only held three shows, and lasted until 1908, although its influence continued beyond 1910. After witnessing the garish and aggressive colours employed by the artists at the Salon d'Automne, the art critic Louis Vauxcelles labelled them as "fauves", which means "the wild beasts". Even though the term was used by Vauxcelles as a derogatory adjective, it was soon assumed by the public and adopted by the history of art without any negative connotation. Amongst the members of the movements were Maurice de Vlaminck, André Derain, Henri Manguin, Albert Marquet, Emile Otón Friesz and Jean Puy and, in 1906, they were joined by Raoul Dufy and George Braque. The group was organised around the figure of Henry Matisse (1869–1954), whose expressive colours and forms had a deep effect on the work of May Guinness. She also spent some time working in the studio of Kees van Dongen, one of the leading Fauvists in France who was also influenced by the work of Henri Matisse. Van Dongen exhibited with the German Expressionist group Die Brücke (The Bridge) in 1908, but he never abandoned his Fauvist manner. This became the high point of Guinness's artistic career.[246] Guinness's early works such as her small studies of Paris (e.g. *Tug Boat on the Seine, Paris,* n.d.) recall the colour and the free but controlled brushstrokes of the Fauves. *Portrait of a Woman* (ca. 1922) was painted when Guinness was already familiarised with the work of Matisse and, even though it shows the artist's knowledge of fresco painting, the influence of the Fauves is also undeniable. Guinness employs direct and vigorous brushstrokes without mixing the colours, and her depiction of the woman is flat and outlined with thick black lines of contour. She synthesised her figures in her search of essential forms, and ignored the traditional concepts of perspective and volume. One of the earliest modernist paintings in Irish art history is *The Infant* (1905), a portrayal of a woman reading to a child inspired by Pablo Picasso and Georges Braque's use of blocks of colours.

Her artistic training was interrupted by the First World War, a break in her studies that she decided to use by serving as a military nurse in the French armed forces.[247] For her bravery she received the Croix de Guerre and the Medáille de la Reconnaissance Française. Once the war was over, she focused her attention on painting and attended classes at the studio of André Lhote, where she became friends with Evie Hone and Mainie Jellett. The popularity of Lhote's studio amongst Irish women artists was such that in Dublin his pupils were jokingly labelled as "Lhote's wives".[248] However, while Jellett and Hone abandoned Lhote in 1921 to study under the most purist Albert Gleizes, Guinness favoured Lhote and kept attending his studio. She became a skilful portraitist, exemplified in the marvellous painting *Two Irish Girls*. This portrait of Mainie Jellett and Evie Hone was carried out around 1922 and combined the European avant-garde with an Irish subject-matter. Painted in the Cubist style, it portrays two girls with a traditional Irish cottage in the background. The forms are geometrical and flat, and Guinness chose a rather pale range of colours for the canvas. The heads of the figures show Guinness's knowledge of Classical painting which she reworks through areas of colour. The figure on the right is seated with her hands interlaced and turning the gaze to her right. The woman on the left, holding her head on her hand, looks directly to the viewer. The background features Guinness's interpretation of the Irish countryside through basic geometrical forms and a range of colours that evokes Lilian Lucy Davidson's nocturnal scenes of the Claddagh. *Woman with Red Hair* was also painted in the 1920s, and can be compared to *Two Irish Girls*. However, the figure appears more hieratic, and the limited palette draws from the Fauvist painter Albert Marquet.[249] As Matisse remarked in 1925, "Marquet did not have enough money for colours [...]. Perhaps this economic condition favoured his style".[250] *Woman with Red Hair* abandons any notion of perspective in favour of flattened forms, geometric shapes and bold sculptural outlines. The general rigidity of the portrait is skilfully combined with the lyrical curvature of the woman's neck. According to Séan Kissane, this could be "the most Cubist"[251] of Guinness's paintings, an image that goes beyond portraiture to become a symbol.

May Guinness fell for France, a country she visited many times throughout her life. Scenes of French towns and inhabitants became common in her artwork, and she even held two solo exhibitions in the French capital, in 1925 and 1930. Like Mary Swanzy and many other artists of her time, she never dated her works, although they can be classified according to their style. *Still Life* (1930), held in the Hugh Lane Gallery, is an example of André Lhote's effect on her work, which during the 1920s became more Cubist and stylised in her scenes of day-to-day life. The canvas illustrates simplified objects of the everyday life (a dresser with plates, an ewer, a table with a vase of flowers and a book) in a combination of vertical, horizontal and diagonal lines, and strong contrasts of light and shades through a flatter pattern of colour. Like the Fauves, Guinness maintained a thick, black line of contour for her objects, which in her artwork are still recognisable. However, she never adhered only to one method, and instead she adopted elements of every different trend she was exposed to and adapted them to her own manner. This amalgam of artistic forces distinguished Guinness from Mainie Jellett, who spent her career exploring her masters' philosophies and methods in order to get a better understanding of their teachings. According to Hilary Pyle, Guinness was –like Mainie Jellett and Evie Hone– deeply spiritual.[252] However, each woman chose their own path in their depictions of spirituality. While Jellett and Hone opted for Celtic Christianity, Guinness preferred to portray "her love of humanity and everyday life".[253] Depictions of still lifes and mundane scenes became, in the hands of May Guinness, representations of the deepest human essence. In a very enigmatic style and inspired by the principles of Abstraction, Guinness illustrated scenes of the places she visited, such as Brittany or Belgium (e.g. *Golden Wedding in Belgium*, n.d.).

Guinness explored Fauvism and Cubism, and in the late 1920s she also moved to a more expressive style in paintings like *Umbrella Pine in a French Landscape* (1928), one of the many works that she based on early sketches. Her depiction of the landscape was genuine and original, different to what was happening in the Irish academic circles of the time. It combined an Impressionist use of the brush with a more Fauvist influence in colour and form. In 1920 she held a solo show at the Eldar Gallery in London, an avant-garde venue. The exhibition was entitled *Decorative Paintings and Drawings* and in the catalogue, Guinness declared that her paintings did not aim to represent, but "to decorate".[254] According to Hilary Pyle, this emphasis on the concept of decoration was a statement of her adhesion to the Abstract movement –as we have seen, Mainie Jellett had given one of her paintings the title of *Decoration*–. Along with Swanzy, Guinness was unique amongst the group of female artists that embraced modernism, as they both belonged to a previous generation. Guinness exhibited with the Society of Dublin Painters and at the Irish Exhibition of Living Art, where she showed some of her early works. In

1925 she held a solo show at Victor Waddington Galleries, a pioneering venue in selling modern Irish art, as well as British and continental works, years before the Irish Exhibition of Living Art was founded. She later travelled Palestine, Sicily, Greece and Spain portraying the landscape and daily life of every country she visited. By 1943, aged eighty, she had become the eldest member of the Dublin Painters Society. Her work had changed very little from the 1920s, except for a more Cubist flavour in the simplification of forms in paintings like *A Religious Procession in Brittany* (n.d.).[255] In her late years, Guinness tended to spend most of her time at her house in Tibradden, where she continued working on her art. Aged seventy-two, tired of the limits of Cubism, she returned to her "flat rhythmic arrangements of line and colour".[256] Her late work still evoked the work of the Cubist Marie Laurencin, the Fauvist Raoul Dufy and, of course, Matisse. Her last shows were held at the Victor Waddington Galleries in 1946 and at the Leicester Galleries in London in 1949. She also exhibited at the Royal Hibernian Academy from 1897 until 1911, when she refused to keep showing her works there following an unspecified dispute.[257]

In 1956, a year after her death, a retrospective exhibition was held at Dawson Hall, in Dublin. There, she was described by James White as "the first of her race to paint her way into the heart and spirit of the new movement of the twentieth century".[258] Even though she attended the same ateliers than her colleagues, the artistic approach of each one of these artists was completely different. They also belonged to different generations. While Jellett and Hone were in their early twenties when they attended Lhote's studio, Guinness –who was a contemporary of Lavery ad Orpen– was already sixty.[259] Because of her early experiments with the modernist trends, she was considered by James White a "courageous innovator" whose gentler manner, her knowledge of Cubist principles and her elegant sense of lyricism "gave her work a freedom from formal organisation, and the necessary tenderness to make it personal and unique".[260] Her manner, her travels and her early explorations of the European modern trends became a major influence in the artwork of painters like Mainie Jellett or Evie Hone, who were encouraged to investigate the infinite possibilities of colour and form.

## The Arrival of Modernism

Swanzy, Jellett and Guinness were, according to Marianne Hartigan, "the catalysts for the introduction of modernism into Irish art".[261] As female artists of well-off Protestant background, they had the means to escape the conservatism of the Irish schools and, without having to depend on their artwork for a living, they could allow themselves to surpass the limits of their academic training and to explore new possibilities in art. They studied and worked abroad, and brought their experiences and their knowledge of the European avant-garde to Ireland when they came back. These women developed as the alternative to the male dominated Royal Hibernian Academy that followed the lines marked by De Valera and the new Irish Government. Despite the rejection, the mockery and the disregard, they followed the path they considered right, searching for a way of addressing their experiences within nationalist Ireland and the tumultuous twentieth century in Europe. Jellett, as well as Guinness and Swanzy, never married and remained childless, which at the time allowed women artists to work and to dedicate their lives to the artistic practice in a manner that would not have been possible otherwise. Many artists did not stick to only one style, and instead they chose different elements from every movement and combined them with their own experiences developing their own particular manner. Hartigan has also pointed that this might have been one of the reasons for their lack of recognition, because "to the critic hoping to characterise their work under one particular label, an artist whose work appears to go in different directions, treating subject matter in certain styles but then occasionally reverting to an earlier style, serves often to confuse".[262] They, however, fought the rejection, the invisibility and the condescension. Their careers and their body of work broke the constriction of traditional art in favour of a manner that would serve as an expression of human emotions and not just an illusion.

The introduction of modernism in the Irish artistic scene did not happen in one day. The process took several years and many shows, the first significant one being the Dublin Sketching Club exhibition in December 1884 with works by John Singer Sargent and James McNeill amongst others.[263] This exhibition became a timid turning point in the Irish artistic arena that, until then, had rejected any external influence in the academic circles. In the 1920s, the Society of Dublin Painters was created around Paul and Grace Henry, Mainie Jellett, and a group of painters who had studied art in the Continent and later settled in Dublin. They were determined to find alternatives to the traditionalism of the Royal Hibernian Academy and to give open-minded artists a place to explore their avant-garde influences and their own ideas. Some of the Academy members who had studied abroad, such as Paul Henry and Charles Lamb, were involved in the beginnings of the Society of Dublin Painters as well. Again, the main characteristic of the Society was the preponderance of women, who included May Guinness, Eva and Letitia Hamilton, Hilda Roberts, Stella Frost, Joan Jameson, Brigid Ganly, Beatrice Glenavy, Harriet Kirkwood, Mary Swanzy, and Evie Hone. In many cases, these women came from a well-off background, had independent means or were married to prominent men, but they had to face social constraints. They rented rooms in the centre of Dublin where they organised both group and solo exhibitions, as each member was entitled to an annual solo exhibition. The members were unified in their distinctiveness and their interest in the avant-garde, from the strong Post-Impressionist influence in the work of Paul and Grace Henry, to the more formal approach to the work of Cézanne by Mary Swanzy. Members less attracted by the avant-garde, such as Jack B. Yeats or Letitia Hamilton, also prioritised colour over academic principles in their works exhibited at the Society, whose members were described as "the liveliest of the living painters, the explorers, the experimentalists".[264] As the 1930s went on, women dominated the Society of Dublin Painters in such a way that the *Irish Times* described the 1935 spring exhibition as "the first time that there has been a women artists' exhibition, as this show virtually may be taken to be".[265]

These exhibitions were followed by the return to Ireland of Mary Swanzy, Mainie Jellett and May Guinness who, after their time abroad, brought back with them the European avant-garde with long-lasting consequences. Eileen Gray (1878–1976) who, like Mary Swanzy, studied at the Académie Colarossi, created furniture designs and architecture that combined the Modernist aesthetic with comfort. She attended the Slade School of Art in London and became an exponent of the Japanese lacquer technique. She is now considered one of the earliest abstract artists in Ireland, and one of the most innovative designers of her time. Nano Reid (1900–1981) studied at the Dublin Metropolitan School of Art under Harry Clarke and Seán Keating, and later attended La Grande Chaumière Academy in Paris. Like Jellett and Grace Henry, she was also drawn to the West of Ireland and its wild spirit. Reid was one of the very few female artists of Catholic background, and became one of the most important painters of Irish landscape and Celtic heritage in the modernist manner. Recognisable national motifs such as megalithic tombs or Celtic crosses were recurrent in her artwork but, nevertheless, she also received adverse comments from the critics, with one writer claiming not to understand "what she gains by her murky colours, her graceless lumpy forms".[266]

These are only few of the many women who, as well as holding solo shows that often faced extremely negative reactions from the conservative Irish public, also took part in the organisation of ground-breaking exhibitions and groups that changed the course of Irish art. Norah McGuinness, Mainie Jellett, Evie Hone and Margaret Clarke amongst others were responsible for the creation of the Irish Exhibition of Living Art in 1943 that, progressively, relegated the Society of Dublin Painters to a second place as the vanguard of Irish painting. The IELA was established to fill the gap of exploration of contemporary Irish art and to respond to the public demand for such a forum. The catalyst of this organisation was the RHA's rejection of Louis Le Brocquy's painting *The Spanish Shawl* in 1942, a decision that encouraged several Modernist and Academicians to create an alternative venue for painters and sculptors who did not agree with the sterile vision of official institutions. Conceived by Sybil Le Brocquy following the incident between her son Louis and the RHA, the first organising committee of the IELA was formed by Louis Le Brocquy, Norah McGuinness, Evie Hone, Ralph Cusack, Elizabeth Curran as its secretary, Margaret Clarke, Laurence Campbell, and the Rev. Jack Hanlon with Mainie Jellett as its chairwoman, succeeded by Norah McGuinness after Jellett's death in 1944. The group aimed to "make available to a large public a comprehensive survey of significant work, irrespective of School or manner, by Irish living artists".[267] This initiative paved the way for the avant-garde to access the Irish artistic scene, but this only happened outside nationalist cultural institutions.[268] The IELA embraced more modernist and less academic trends and, despite its progressive perspective, many Irish painters exhibited their artwork both in more traditional institutions such as the Royal Hibernian Academy as well as at the IELA. Its first exhibition was held at the Dublin Metropolitan School of Art in 1943, and it included works by both academic traditionalists as well as artist of the avant-garde. The reaction to the first exhibition was mixed, and the organisation was often referred to as the Salon des Refusés of Irish Art. Most of the negative comments were related to an alleged exclusion of Irish artists in the IELA, and to what a critic described as a "strange foreign-ness" due to the "absence of contact between these artists and their native cultural background".[269] Thomas MacGreevy, one of the few critics who openly praised the IELA, described its first show as the "most vital and distinguished exhibition of work by Irish artists that has ever been held", and declared that "as is to be expected at an exhibition on the organisation of which women artists have had as much say as men, there is everywhere evidence of that elusive quality –good taste. Yet, it cannot be said that good taste has been regarded as a substitute for technical accomplishment".[270] Supporters or detractors, they overall agreed that the IELA was a turning point in the history of Modern Art in Ireland, and the group continued its adventure until the early 1990s.

The conflicts regarding female modernist artwork in Ireland exemplified the difficulty faced by the public in accepting the modernist ideas and the newest explorations of national and cultural identity. Well aware that these negative reactions would only be silenced by the international press, Irish modernists artists also made a great effort to continue exhibiting outside Ireland as a strategy for survival.[271] Thanks to their courage, their experimentation, and their active involvement in radical organisations like the Society of Dublin Painters of the Irish Exhibition of Living Art, artists like Mary Swanzy, Grace Henry, Guinness and especially Mainie Jellett prepared the ground for the arrival and development of modern art in Ireland.

# NOTES

1. See Elizabeth Cumming, *Phoebe Anna Traquair, 1852–1936* (Edinburgh: National Galleries of Scotland, 1993).

2. For studies on Beatrice Elvery's life and work, see Beatrice Lady Glenavy, *Today We Will Only Gossip* (London: Constable and Company, 1964); Nicola Gordon Bowe, "The Art of Beatrice Elvery, Lady Glenavy (1883–1970), *Irish Arts Review Yearbook,* vol. 11 (1995): 168–175; "Preserving the Relics of Heroic Time: Visualizing the Celtic Revival in Early Twentieth Century Ireland", in *Synge and Edwardian Ireland,* ed. Brian

Cliff and Nicholas Grene (Oxford University Press, 2012), 58–83; *The Arts and Crafts Movement in Dublin and Edinburgh, 1885–1925* (with Elizabeth Cumming, Dublin: Irish Academic Press, 1998).

3. Nicola Gordon Bowe, "Preserving the Relics of Heroic Time: Visualizing the Celtic Revival in Early Twentieth-Century Ireland", in *Synge and Edwardian Ireland,* eds. Brian Cliff and Nicholas Greene (Oxford: Oxford University Press, 2012), 66.

4. Gordon Bowe, 68.

5. Sir William Orpen, *Stories of Old Ireland and Myself* (London: Williams and Norgate, 1925), 69.

6. Gordon Bowe, "The Art of Beatrice Elvery, Lady Glenavy", 168–170.

7. Gordon Bowe, 170.

8. Gordon Bowe, "Symbolism in Turn-of-the-Century Irish Art", 137.

9. Paul Larmour, *The Arts and Crafts Movement in Ireland* (Belfast: Friar's Bush Press, 1992), 108.

10. Glenavy, *Today We Will Only Gossip,* 90–91.

11. Gordon Bowe, "Preserving the Relics of Heroic Time: Visualizing the Celtic Revival in Early Twentieth-Century Ireland", 66–67.

12. Larmour, *The Arts and crafts Movement in Ireland,* 109.

13. Rebecca Long, "Stories of Ancient Days. Mythological Constructs of Childhood on Independence Ireland", in *Constructions of the Irish Child in the Independence Period, 1910–1940,* eds. Ciara Boylan and Ciara Gallagher (Cham: Palgrave Macmillan, 2018), 195.

14. Steward, *When Time Began to Rant and Rage,* 130.

15. Emily Mark-Fitzgerald, *Commemorating the Irish Famine. Memory and the Monument* (Liverpool: Liverpool University Press, 2013), 173–176.

16. Steward, *When Time Began to Rant and Rage,* 130.

17. Quoted in Derek Warfield and Raymond Daly, *Celtic and Ireland in Song and Story* (Kildare: Derek Warfield, 2008), 130.

18. Maciej Ruczaj, "The Liturgy of Revolution: Political Theology of Patrick Pearse Between Catholicism and Modernism", PhD diss. (Prague: Charles University, 2015), 79.

19. Glenavy, *Today We Will Only Gossip,* 91.

20. Glenavy, 90.

21. Quoted in Patrick Pearse, *A Significant Irish Educationalist: The Educational Writings of P.H. Pearse,* ed. Séamas Ó Buachalla (Dublin: Mercier Press, 1980), 381.

22. Ruczaj, "The Liturgy of Revolution", 94.

23. Elaine Sisson, *Pearse's Patriots. St. Enda's and the Cult of Boyhood* (Cork: Cork University Press, 2004), 62–63.

24. Pearse, *Collected Works of Padraic H. Pearse,* 156.

25. Quoted in Larmour, *The Arts and Crafts Movement in Ireland,* 108.

26. Gordon Bowe, "Symbolism in Turn-of-the-Century Irish Art", 137.

27. Gordon Bowe, 137.

28. Gordon Bowe, "The Art of Beatrice Elvery", 170.

29. Glenavy, *Today We Will Only Gossip,* 52.

30. Orpen, *Stories of Old Ireland and Myself,* 69–70.

31. Glenavy, *Today We Will Only Gossip,* 112–114

32. S. Brian Kennedy, *Irish Art and Modernism, 1880–1950* (Dublin: Hugh Lane Municipal Gallery, 1991), 355.

33. Glenavy, *Today We Will Only Gossip,* 148.

34. Glenavy, 148.

35. Jenni Rogers et al, *Irish Women Artists from the Eighteenth Century to the Present Day* (Dublin: National Gallery of Ireland and the Douglas Hyde Gallery, 1987), 118.

36. Glenavy, *Today We Will Only Gossip,* 148.

37. Kennedy, *Irish Art and Modernism,* 184.

38. Gordon Bowe, "The Art of Beatrice Elvery", 175.

39. *The Irish Times,* 30 September, 1955. Quoted in Gordon Bowe, "The Art of Beatrice Elvery", 169.

40. McConkey, *A Free Spirit,* 142.

41. Nicola Gordon Bowe and Elizabeth Cumming, *The Arts and Crafts Movements in Dublin and Edinburgh: 1888–1925* (Dublin: Irish Academic Press, 1998), 126.

42. Publications on the biography and career of Margaret Clarke include: Hilary Pyle, "Darling Margaret. A Look at Orpen's Favourite Pupil", *Irish Arts Review Yearbook* (2007): 85–91; Carla Briggs, *Margaret Clarke. An Independent Spirit.* Exhibition Catalogue Essay (Dublin: National Gallery of Ireland, 2017); and "Margaret Clarke as a History Painter", in *Irish Women Artists 1800–2009. Familiar but Unknown,* ed. Éimear O'Connor (Dublin: Four Courts Press, 2010), 84–102; Fionna Barber, "Race, Irishness and Art History. Margaret Clarke's Bathtime at the Crèche, Motherhood and the Matter of Whiteness", in *Narratives Unfolding: National Art Histories in an Unfinished World,* ed. Martha Langford (Montreal and Kingston: McGill-Queen's University Press, 2017), 62–80; Ingrid Jenker, "Allegory, Portrait or Genre? 'Mary and Brigid', by Margaret Clarke", *Irish Arts Review Yearbook,* vol. 15 (1999): 148–151.

43. Orpen, *Stories of Old Ireland and Myself,* 78.

44. Marie Hammond Callaghan, "Margaret Clarke's Marie and Brigid, 1917: Mother Ireland in Irish Art and Nationalism", *Atlantis: Critical Studies in Gender, Culture and Social Justice,* Mount Saint Vincent University (1998): 101.

45. Pyle, "Darling Margaret", 90.

46. See Fionna Barber, "Race, Irishness and Art History. Margaret Clarke's Bathtime at the Crèche, Motherhood and the Matter of Whiteness", in *Narratives Unfolding: National Art Histories in an Unfinished World,* ed. Martha Langford (Montreal and Kingston: McGill-Queen's University Press, 2017), 62–80.

47. Barber, 68.

48. Rogers et al, *Irish Women Artists from the Eighteenth Century to the Present Day,* 129.

49. Pyle, "Darling Margaret", 87.

50. Fiana Griffin, "Margaret Clarke. Portrait of Eamon de Valera", Adam's Auctioneers, accessed on May 10th 2020, https://www.adams.ie/41253/Margaret-Clarke-RHA-1888-1961-Portrait-of-amon-de-Valera-Oil-on-canvas-50-5-x-40-5cm-20-x-16-Inscribed-

verso-sketch-of-Eamon-de-Valera-two-sittings-by-Margaret-Clarke-Provenance-The-sitter-and-t?view=lot_detail

51. Extract from a letter to Mr. Dwyer, Fitzwilliam square, regarding a commission, July 1932.Quoted in Fiana Griffin, "Margaret Clarke. Portrait of Eamon de Valera".

52. Hammond Callaghan, "Margaret Clarke's Mary and Brigid", 100.

53. Jenker, "Allegory, Portrait or Genre?", 148–150.

54. Quoted in Hammond Callaghan, "Margaret Clarke's Mary and Brigid", 106.

55. Hammond Callaghan, 100–103.

56. Hammond Callaghan, 100.

57. Schaus, *Women and Gender in Medieval Europe,* 210.

58. Lady Augusta Gregory, "Saint Brigit", in *Irish Folktales,* ed. Henry Glassie (New York: Pantheon Books, 1985), 59.

59. Gregory, 192.

60. Barber, "Race, Irishness and Art History", 70.

61. Hammond Callaghan, "Margaret Clarke's Mary and Brigid", 108.

62. Hammond Callaghan, 106.

63. H. L. Morrow, "Two Picture Exhibitions", *The Irish Statesman* (April 12th 1924). Quoted in Jenker, "Allegory, Portrait or Genre?", 150

64. Fionna Barber, ".The Vibrant Studio: Margaret Clarke's Performative Femininities and 1920s Painting", Art and Reality: The Role of Visual Culture in the Post-Independence State, UCD (Symposium, October 19th 2018), accessed on May 10th 2020, https://soundcloud.com/real-smart-media/fionna-barber-margaret-clarke-performative-femininities-and-1920s-painting

65. Barber, "The Vibrant Studio".

66. Pyle, "Darling Margaret", 90–91.

67. Barber, "Race, Irishness and Art History", 72.

68. For studies on the Magdalene Laundries, see Katherine O'Donnell, "Academics Becoming Activists: Reflections on Some Ethical Issues of the Justice for Magdalenes Campaign", *in Irishness on the Margins. Minority and Dissident Identities,* ed. Pilar Villar-Argáiz (Dublin: Palgrave Macmillan, 2018), 77–100; James M. Smith, *Ireland's Magdalen Laundries and the Nation's Architecture of Containment* (Manchester: Manchester University Press, 2008).

69. Barber, "Race, Irishness and Art History", 72–73.

70. Barber, 69–70

71. Carla Briggs, "Out of the Shadows", *Irish Art Review,* vol. 34, no. 2 (Summer 2017): 279.

72. Barber, "Race, Irishness and Art History", 69.

73. Briggs, "Out of the Shadows", 280.

74. See Lucy Costigan and Michael Cullen, *Strangest Genius. The Stained Glass of Harry Clarke* (Dublin: The History Press Ireland, 2010).

75. Pyle, "Darling Margaret", 91.

76. Niamh McNally, "Margaret Clarke: Portrait of the Artist as a (Young) Woman", *Totally Dublin* (June 24th 2017), accessed on April 25th 2020, https://www.totallydublin.

ie/arts-culture/margaret-clarke-portrait-artist-young-woman/

77. Hammond Callaghan, "Margaret Clarke's Mary and Brigid", 107

78. Recent exhibitions include *A Newry Artist, Margaret Clarke RHA (1884–1961)* (Newry, 2007); *Women in Newry and Mourne in the Twentieth Century* (Newry, 2016–2017); *Creating History: Stories in Ireland in Art* (Dublin, 2016–2017); and particularly *Margaret Clarke. An Independent Spirit* (Dublin, National Gallery of Ireland, 2017).

79. For studies on the life and work of Lilian Lucy Davidson, see Katherine Cahill, "In the Mainstream of Irish Naturalism: The Art of Lilian Lucy Davidson", *Irish Art Review Yearbook,* vol. 15 (1999): 34–45; Marie Bourke, *West of Ireland Paintings at the National Gallery of Ireland from 1800 to 2000* (Dublin: National Gallery of Ireland, 2014).

80. Katherine Cahill, "In the Mainstream of Irish Naturalism: The Art of Lilian Lucy Davidson", *Irish Art Review Yearbook,* vol. 15 (1999): 34–45.

81. Claire Dalton, *Irish Women Artists, 1870–1970* (Dublin: Adam's, 2014), 94.

82. Niamh O'Sullivan, "Lilian Lucy Davidson ARHA (1893–1954). Potato Harvest", *Important Irish Art* (Whyte's, May 27th 2019), accessed on May 5th 2020, https://www.whytes.ie/art/potato-harvest-1931/167705/?SearchString=&LotNumSearch=19&GuidePrice=&OrderBy=&ArtistID=&ArrangeBy=list&NumPerPage=15&offset=0

83. Morisson, "The Guise of Irishness", 67.

84. Connolly and Finucane, *Journeys Through Line and Colour,* 37.

85. Richard Kearney, *Transitions: Narratives in Modern Irish Culture* (Manchester: Manchester University Press, 1988), 163.

86. Burke, *West of Ireland,* 34.

87. Cahill, "In the Mainstream of Irish Naturalism", 40.

88. Kinmonth, *Irish Rural Interiors in Art,* 234–235.

89. Lara Marlowe, "Hunger Museum Puts Focus on Art About the Famine", *The Irish Times* (October 1st 2012), accessed on April 25th 2020, https://www.irishtimes.com/news/hunger-museum-puts-focus-on-art-about-the-famine-1.545793

90. Niamh Ann Kelly, *Imaging the Great Irish Famine. Representing Dispossession in Visual Culture* (London: Bloomsbury Academic, 2018), 124–125.

91. Cahill, "In the Mainstream of Irish Naturalism", 36.

92. Rogers et al, *Irish Women Artists from the Eighteenth Century to the Present Day,* 126.

93. Winifred M. Letts in *The Irish Times* (April 3rd 1954). Quoted in Katherine Cahill, "In the Mainstream of Irish Naturalism", 45.

94. See Hilary Pyle, "The Hamwood Ladies: Letitia and Eva Hamilton", *Irish Arts Review Yearbook,* vol. 13 (1997): 122–134.

95. Morgan O'Driscoll, *Irish and International Art Auction Catalogue* (December 4th 2017), 43.

96. Roger et al, *Irish Women Artists from the Eighteenth Century to the Present Day,* 165.

97. McConkey, *A Free Spirit,* 179.

98. McConkey, 178.

99. "Hamwood Ladies", Hamwood Estate, accessed on April 29th 2020, https://hamwood.ie/hamwood-ladies/

100. Dalton, *Irish Women Artists, 1870–1970,* 84.
101. See James G. Cruickshank, "Grace Henry", *Irish Arts Review,* vol. 9 (1993): 174–178; Delia Gaze, *Dictionary of Women Artists,* vol. 1 (London: Fitzroy Dearborn Publishers, 1997).
102. S. Brian Kennedy, *Great Irish Artists: From Lavery to Le Brocquy* (Dublin: Gill and MacMillan, 1997), 48.
103. Marianne Hartigan, "Irish Women Painters and the Introduction of Modernism", in *When Time Began to Rant and Rage. Figurative Painting of Twentieth-Century Ireland,* ed. James Christen Steward (Berkeley: Merrell Holberton, 1998), 67–68.
104. Cruickshank, "Grace Henry", 174–178.
105. Hartigan, "Irish Women Painters", 69.
106. *The Irish Times,* October 20th 1923.Quoted in Hartigan, "Irish Women Painters", 68.
107. Breda B. Gray and Louise Ryan, "Politics of Irish Identity and the Interconnections Between Feminism, Nationhood and Colonialism", in *Nation, Empire, Colony: Historicizing Gender and Race,* ed. Ruth Roach Pierson (Indiana: Indiana University Press, 1998), 121–138.
108. Catherine Nash, "Remapping the Body/Land: New Cartographies of Identity, Gender and Landscape in Ireland", in *Writing Women and Space. Colonial and Postcolonial Geographies,* eds. Alison Blung and Gillian Rose (New York and London: The Guildford Press, 1994), 236.
109. Linda Nochlin, "Women, Art and Power", *in Women, Art and Power and Other Essays* (New York: Harper and Row, 1988), 19.
110. Nash, "Remapping the Body/Land", 235.
111. Janet K. TeBrake, "Irish Peasant Women in Revolt: the Land League Years", in *Irish Historical Studies,* 28, 109 (1992): 63–80.
112. Antoinette Quinn, "Cathleen Ni Houlihan Writes Back: Maud Gonne and Irish National Theatre", in *Gender and Sexuality in Modern Ireland,* eds. Anthony Bradley and Maryann Gialanella Valiulis (Amherst: University of Massachusetts Press, 1997), 41.
113. For publications on Mary Swanzy, see Sean Kissane and Liz Cullinane, *Mary Swanzy: Voyages* (Dublin: Irish Museum of Modern Art, 2018); Brian Fallon, "Swanzy in Samoa", *Irish Arts Review,* vol. 30, no. 4 (2013–2014): 108–113; "Adventures in Art", *Irish Arts Review,* vol. 35, no. 4 (2018–2019): 74–79.
114. Quoted in Julian Campbell, "Mary Swanzy Collection", Christie's, accessed on May 10th 2020, https://www.christies.com/lotfinder/Lot/mary-swanzy-hrha-1882-1978-the-embrace-4902989-details.aspx.
115. Rogers et al, *Irish Women Artists from the Eighteenth Century to the Present Day,* 144–146.
116. Thomas MacGreevy, "'Fifty Years of Irish Painting 1900–1950", *Capuchin Annual* (1949): 497–512.
117. Hartigan, "Irish Women Painters", 64.
118. "Mary Swanzy. Voyages", Irish Museum of Modern Art, accessed on May 10th 2020, https://imma.ie/whats-on/mary-swanzy-voyages/

119. See Kissane and Cullinane, *Mary Swanzy: Voyages.*
120. Liz Cullinane, "Mary Swanzy. The Unsung Hero of Irish Modernism", *The Irish Independent* (October 21st 2018), accessed on May 10th 2020, https://www.independent.ie/entertainment/theatre-arts/mary-swanzy-the-unsung-hero-of-irish-modernism-37435424.html
121. See Selena Daly, "Mary Swanzy (1882–1978): A Futurist Painter from Ireland", *International Yearbook of Futurism Studies,* vol. 5 (Berlin/Boston: De Gruyter, 2015): 70–86.
122. See Richard Cork, *Vorticism and Abstract Art in the First Machine Age* (Berkeley: University of California, 1976).
123. Daly, "Mary Swanzy (1882–1978)", 71.
134. Daly, 71.
125. Róisín Kennedy, "Mary Swanzy HRHA (1882–1978). The Storm", *Important Irish Art* (Adam's, November 22th 2017), 20.
126. Kennedy, 20.
127. Julian Campbell, *An Exhibition of Paintings by Mary Swanzy, H.R.H.A., 1882–1978.* (Dublin: Pyms Gallery, 1986), 22.
128. Rogers et al, *Irish Women Artists from the Eighteenth Century to the Present Day,* 144.
129. Welten Ruud, "Paul Gauguin and the Complexity of the Primitivist Gaze", *Journal of Art Historiography,* no. 12 (2015): 1–13.
130. Sean Kissane and Liz Cullinane, "Mary Swanzy: Voyages", press release (Limerick City Gallery of Art, 2019), 3.
131. "Mary Swanzy, HRHA. 1882–1978", Sotheby's, accessed on April 28th 2020, http://www.sothebys.com/en/auctions/ecatalogue/2004/irish-sale-including-property-from-the-jefferson-smurfit-group-l04620/lot.32.html
132. Hartigan, "Irish Women Painters", 70.
133. Rogers et al, *Irish Women Artists from the Eighteenth Century to the Present Day,* 146.
134. Brian Fallon, "Adventures in Art", *Irish Arts Review* (2018/2019): 74–79.
135. Quoted in Edel Cassidy, "Mary Swanzy: Modern Irish Master", *Anthology,* 9 (2018): 36–39.
136. Hartigan, "Irish women Painters", 73.
137. Terence Brown, *Ireland: A Social and Cultural History. 1922 to the Present* (New York: Cornell University Press, 1981), 76.
138. For biographical information on Constance Markievicz, see Lindie Naughton, *Markievicz: A Most Outrageous Rebel* (Kildare: Merrion Press, 2018) and Anne Haverty, *Constance Markievicz: Irish Revolutionary* (Dublin: Lilliput Press, 2016). Studies about her artwork have been carried out by Patrick Quigley, *Sisters Against the Empire: Countess Constance Markievicz and Eva Gore-Booth, 1916–17* (Dublin: Liffey Press, 2016); and Constance Cassidy (ed.), *Countess Markievicz. Prison Poetry and Sketches* (Sligo: Lissadell Press, 2017).
139. McCoole, *No Ordinary Women,* 202.
140. Naughton, *Markievicz: A Most Outrageous Rebel,* 52.

141. Naughton, 38.
142. Anne Haverty, *Constance Markievicz: An Independent Life* (London: Pandora, 1988), 52.
143. Patrick Quigley. *The Polish Irishman: The Life and Times of Count Casimir Markievicz* (Dublin: Liffey Press, 2012), 55.
144. Quigley, *The Polish Irishman,* 55.
145. Lauren Arrington, *Revolutionary Lives. Constance and Casimir Markievicz* (Princeton: Princeton University Press, 2016), 45.
146. Quoted in A. Norman Jeffares, *A Commentary on the Collected Poems of W. B. Yeats* (London: Palgrave Macmillan, 1968), 246.
147. Quoted in McCoole, *No Ordinary Women,* 24.
148. Steele, *Women, Press and Politics,* 117.
149. Constance Markievicz, "James Connolly as I Knew Him", *The Nation* (March 26th 1927). Quoted in Conor Kostick and Lorcan Collins, *The Easter Rising: A Guide to Dublin in 1916* (Dublin: O'Brien Press, 2000), 76–77.
150. McCoole, *No Ordinary Women,* 203.
151. Marta Bustillo, "Two Girls in Silk Kimonos", Trinity College Dublin (2015), accessed on May 11th 2020, https://www.tcd.ie/library/1916/two-girls-in-silk-kimonos/
152. Rogers et al, *Irish Women Artists from the Twentieth Century to the Present Day,* 176.
153. Arrington, *Revolutionary Lives,* 152
154. Shonagh Hill, *Women and Embodied Mythmaking in Irish Theatre* (Cambridge: Cambridge University Press, 2019), 52.
155. Eva Gore-Booth, *The Death of Fionavar from The Triumph of Maeve* (London: Erskine Macdonald, 1916), 7.
156. Casey A. Jarrin, "The Prison Gallery: Exhibit Collaboration Between Kilmainham Gaol and Alcatraz", in *Irish Studies: Geographies and Genders,* eds. Marti D. Lee and Ed Madden (Cambridge: Cambridge Scholars Publishing, 2008), 49–59.
157. Anne Clare, *Unlikely Rebels: The Gifford Girls and the Fight for Irish Freedom* (Cork: Mercier Press, 2011), 73.
158. Clare, 268–269.
159. Clare, 234.
160. See "Markievicz, Constance de, 1868–1927". *National Library of Ireland Catalogue,* Prints and Drawings.
161. Arrington, *Revolutionary Lives,* 230.
162. Alison Martin, "Off to Fight for the Republic. Countess Markievicz's Propaganda Cartoons in the Irish Civil War", *The Irish Story* (January 8th 2018), accessed on May 11th 2020, https://www.theirishstory.com/2018/01/08/off-to-fight-for-the-republic-countess-markieviczs-propaganda-cartoons-in-the-irish-civil-war/#.XrkIvEQzbIU
163. Gavin M. Foster, *The Irish Civil War and Society Politics, Class and Conflict* (London: Palgrave Macmillan, 2015), 69.
164. Martin, "Off to Fight for the Republic", *The Irish Story* Website.
165. Arrington, *Revolutionary Lives,* 229.

166. All the cartoons mentioned here have been compiled by the National Library of Ireland in the Catalogue, http://catalogue.nli.ie/
167. McCoole, *No Ordinary Women,* 92.
168. McCoole, 203.
169. Marian Broderick, *Wild Irish Women. Extraordinary Lives from History* (Dublin: The O'Brien Press, 2012), 12–16.
170. Amelia O'Mahony-Brady, "Artsdesk: Markievicz and the Modernist", *Totally Dublin,* accessed on May 11th 2020, https://ww.totallydublin.ie/arts-culture/arts-culture-features/artsdesk-markiewicz-and-the-modernist/
171. For studies on the live and work of Kathleen Fox, see Jenni Rogers et al, *Irish Women Artists From the Twentieth Century to the Present Day* (Dublin: National Gallery of Ireland and the Douglas Hyde Gallery, 1987); the Solomons Papers in Trinity College Dublin; Deirdre Kelly, "Art as Social Commentary: Two Visual Interpretations of the 1916 Rising", *History Studies,* vol. 16 (2015): 20–31; John Clarke, "Kathleen's Story" and "Kathleen Fox Interview", *Footprints,* vol. 32, no. 2 (2017): 5–11.
172. Connolly and Finucane, *Journeys Through Line and Colour,* 45.
173. Clarke, "Kathleen's Story", 9–11.
174. Sikata Banerjee, *Muscular Nationalism. Gender, Violence and Empire in India and Ireland, 1914–2004* (New York: New York University Press, 2012), 90.
175. Kelly, "Art as social commentary", 23–24.
176. Bhreathnach-Lynch, *Ireland's Art, Ireland's History,* 141.
177. Kelly, "Art as social commentary", 23.
178. Bhreathnach-Lynch, "Landscape, Space and Gender".
179. "Kathleen Fox (1880–1963). Ruins of the Four Courts", *Important Irish Art* (Adam's, October 1st 2014), 184–185.
180. Bowe and Cumming, *The Arts and Crafts Movements,* 134.
181. For studies on Estella Solomons's life and work, see Hilary Pyle, *Estella Solomons: Portraits of Patriots* (Dublin: Allen Figgis, 1996) and "Notes from Estella", *Irish Arts Review,* vol. 25, no. 1 (Spring 2008): 96–99; Jane Maxwell, "Vita Brevis, Ars Longa", Manuscripts and Archives Research Library, Trinity College Dublin (https://www.tcd.ie/library/1916/vita-brevis-ars-longa/); Dalton, *Irish Women Artists, 1870–1970;* Rogers et al, *Irish Women Artists From the Eighteenth Century to the Present Day.*
182. Eoin O'Brien, "From the Waters of Sion to Liffeyside. The Jewish Contribution: Medical and Cultural", *Journal of the Irish Colleges of Physicians and Surgeons,* vol. 10, no. 3 (January 1981): 113.
183. See Angela Griffith et al, *Making their Mark: Irish Painters-Etchers and the Etching Revival 1880–1930* (Dublin: The National Gallery of Ireland, 2019).
184. Róisín Kennedy, "The Invisible Irish Etchers", *Art in Print,* vol. 9, no. 3 (September/October 2019): 38–40.
185. Nicola Gordon Bowe, "The Iconic Book in Ireland, 1891–1930", in *The Oxford History of the Irish Book. Vol. 5. The Irish Book in English, 1891–2000,* ed. Clare Hutton and Patrick Walsh (Oxford: Oxford University Press, 2011), 407.
186. Hilary Pyle, *Portraits of Patriots,* 6.

187. *Irish Women Artists,* 30.
188. Seumas O'Sullivan, *The Rose and Bottle: And Other Essays* (Dublin: Talbot Press, 1946), 97.
189. Pyle, "Notes from Estella", 96–99.
190. Lorcan Collins. *Ireland's War of Independence, 1919–21: The IRA's Guerrilla Campaign* (Dublin: O'Brien Press, 2019), 55.
191. Frank Shovlin, *The Irish Literary Periodical, 1923–1958* (Oxford: Oxford University Press, 2003), 41.
192. Seumas O'Sullivan, "Editorial", *The Dublin Magazine,* vol. 1, no. 2 (1926): 1. Quoted in Shovlin, *The Irish Literary Periodical,* 47.
193. Shovlin, *The Irish Literary Periodical,* 41.
194. Dalton, *Irish Women Artists, 1870–1970,* 60.
195. Mary Kenny, "Thoroughly Modern Mainie", in *The Irish Independent* (August 10th 2018), accessed on May 11th 2020, https://www.independent.ie/entertainment/theatre-arts/mary-kenny-thoroughly-modern-mainie-37218106.html
196. For publications on the life and work of Mainie Jellett, see Bruce Arnold, *Mainie Jellett and the Modern Movement in Ireland* (New Haven: Yale University Press, 1991) and *Mainie Jellett, 1897–1944* (Dublin: Irish Museum of Modern Art, 1991); Eileen McCarvill (ed.), *The Artist's Vision. Mainie Jellett: Lectures and Essays on Art* (Dublin: Dundalgan Press, 1958); Stella Frost, *A Tribute to Evie Hone and Mainie Jellett* (Dublin: Browne and Noland, 1957).
197. Dalton, *Irish Women Artists,* 40.
198. Arnold, *Mainie Jellett and the Modern Movement in Ireland,* 17.
199. Mainie Jellett, "An Approach to Painting", in *The Field Day Anthology of Irish Writing. Irish Women's Writing and Traditions. Volume 5,* eds. Angela Bourke et al. (New York: New York University Press, 2002), 1085–1086.
200. Jellett, 1085–1086.
201. Aoife Keogh and Fiona King, "Mainie Jellett", in *In Colour Exhibition Catalogue* (Fingal: Fingal Arts office, n.d.), 4–9.
202. Arnold, *Mainie Jellett and the Modern Movement,* 45.
203. Arnold, Bruce, "Mainie Jellett and Modernism", in *Irish Women Artists from the Eighteenth Century to the Present Day,* eds. Jenni Rogers, Wanda Ryan-Smolin and Elizabeth Mayes (Dublin: The National Gallery of Ireland and Douglas Hyde Gallery, 1987), 31.
204. Jellett, "An Approach to Painting", 1085.
205. Arnold, "Mainie Jellett and Modernism", 31.
206. Connolly and Finucane, *Journeys Through Line and Colour,* 92.
207. McConkey, *A Free Spirit,* 73.
208. Arnold, "Mainie Jellett and Modernism", 32.
209. Peter Brooke, "Albert Gleizes in 1934", in *Texts by Gleizes,* accessed on May 11th 2020, http://www.peterbrooke.org/form-and-history/texts/1934/introduction.html
210. Jellett, "An Approach to Painting", 1085.
211. Peter Brooke, "Albert Gleizes in 1934", in *Texts by Gleizes.*

212. Brooke.
213. Brooke.
214. Daniel Robbins, *Albert Gleizes, 1881–1953. A Retrospective Exhibition* (New York: The Solomon R. Guggenheim Foundation, 1964), 22.
215. Arnold, *Mainie Jellett and the Modern Movement in Ireland,* 75.
216. Keogh and King, "Mainie Jellett", 6.
217. Arnold, "Mainie Jellett and the Modern Movement in Ireland", 82.
218. A.E. Russell in *The Irish Statesman* (October 27th 1923). Quoted in Arnold, *Mainie Jellett and the Modern Movement in Ireland,* 80.
219. "Two Freak Pictures", The *Irish Times* (23 October 1923). Quoted in Hartigan, "Irish Women Painters", 72.
220. Arnold, *Mainie Jellett and the Modern Movement in Ireland,* 80.
221. Thomas MacGreevy. *Untitled Memories of Mainie Jellett* (TCD, MS 8002/7), 1–2. Quoted in Brown, *The Yeats Circle,* 79.
222. Quoted in Cullen, *Sources in Irish Art,* 254.
223. McConkey, *A Free Spirit,* 201.
224. Arnold, *Mainie Jellett and the Modern Movement in Ireland,* 100.
225. Arnold, 181.
226. Séan Kissane, *Analysing Cubism* (Cork: Crawford Art Gallery, 2013), 107.
227. Bruce Arnold, "Jack Yeats and the Making of Irish Art in the Twentieth Century", in *When Time Began to Rant and Rage. Figurative Painting from Twentieth-Century Ireland,* ed. James Christen Steward (Berkeley: Merrell Holberton, 1998), 59.
228. Barry Sloan, "The Redress of Imagination: Bernard MacLavery's Grace Notes", in *The Gift of Story. Narrating Hope in a Postmodern World,* eds. Emily Griesinger and Mark Eaton (Waco, USA: Baylor University Press, 2006), 303–315.
229. Belinda Loftus, *Mirrors: William III and Mother Ireland* (Dundrum: Picture Press, 1990), 50.
230. Brown, *The Yeats Circle,* 81.
231. Dalton, *Irish Women Artists,* 88.
232. Frost, *A Tribute to Evie Hone and Mainie Jellett,* 19–20.
233. James White, "Pictures of the Home", in *Irish Art: A Volume of Articles and Illustrations* (Dublin: The Parkside Press, 1944), 50.
234. O'Toole, *Modern Ireland in 100 Artworks,* 22.
235. McConkey, *A Free Spirit,* 77.
236. Quoted in Hartigan, "Irish Women Painters", 65.
237. Ciarán Benson, "Modernism and Ireland Selves", in *Circa,* 61 (January/February 2002): 18–23.
238. O'Toole, *Modern Ireland in 100 Artworks,* 22.
239. Jellett, "An Approach to Painting", 1085.
240. Arnold, "Mainie Jellett and Modernism", 30.
241. Kennedy, *Irish Art and Modernism,* 59.
242. See Hilary Pyle, "From the Vanguard", *Irish Arts Review,* vol. 34, no. 4 (2017/2018): 128–133; Rogers et al, *Irish Women Artists from the Eighteenth Century to the Present Day*

(Dublin: National Gallery of Ireland and the Douglas Hyde Gallery, 1987).
243. Pyle, "From the Vanguard", 130.
244. Dalton, *Irish Women Artists,* 92.
245. Luke Gibbons, "Visual Modernisms", in *The Cambridge Companion to Irish Modernism,* ed. Joe Cleary (Cambridge: Cambridge University Press, 2014), 129.
246. Pyle, "From the Vanguard", 130.
247. Pyle, "From the Vanguard", 130.
248. Hartigan, "Irish Women Artists", 65.
249. Milmo-Penny Fine Art, "May Guinness, 1863–1955", *Irish Gallery.* Accessed on April 27th 2020, http://www.mpfa.ie/irgallery.htm
250. Jack Flam, *Matisse on Art* (Berkeley: University of California Press, 1995), 81.
251. Séan Kissane, "Woman with Red Hair", *Irish and International Art* (Whyte's, September 16th 2019), 62.
252. Pyle, "From the Vanguard", 128.
253. Pyle, 128,
254. Pyle, 130.
255. Rogers et al, *Irish Women Artists from the Eighteenth Century to the Present Day,* 34.
256. Quoted in Elizabeth Mayes and Paula Murphy. *Images and Insights. Exhibition Catalogue* (Dublin: Hugh Lane Municipal Gallery of Modern Art, 1993), 76.
257. Dalton, *Irish Women Artists,* 92.
258. Luke Gibbons, "Visual Modernisms", 129.
259. Sean Kissane, "Analysing Cubism.", *Irish Arts Review,* vol. 30, no. 1 (Spring 2013), 65
260. Pyle, "From the Vanguard", 133.
261. Hartigan, "Irish Women Painters", 64.
262. Hartigan, 65.
263. Hartigan, 65–66.
264. Hartigan, 71
265. Kennedy, *Irish Art and Modernism,* 48.
266. Quoted in Hartigan, "Irish Women Artist", 76.
267. Kennedy, *Irish Art and Modernism,* 119.
268. McConkey, *A Free Spirit,* 66–67.
269. Clair Wills, *That Neutral Island: A Cultural History of Ireland During the Second World War* (Cambridge: The Belknap Press of Harvard University Press, 2007), 284–285.
270. Thomas MacGreevy, "Living Art – A New Departure", *The Irish Times* (September 16th 1943): 3.
271. McConkey, *A Free Spirit,* 77.

# Part Four

# Presence II. The Arts and Crafts

# The Arts and Crafts Revival in Ireland

The Arts and Crafts Movement in Ireland was only a part of the wider Irish Revival that, as we have already seen, affected many different cultural fields. Affected as well by nationalist ideals and the process of decolonisation, the development of the Arts and Crafts in Ireland was different to its evolvement in England. It, however, cannot be understood without taking into account its origins in London, where the movement flourished in the second half of the nineteenth century as a sort of a reaction to the Industrial Revolution and modern society. This would explain why the influence was deeper in the industrialised countries of the north of Europe as well as in the USA, reaching Japan in the 1920s. Through the recovery of applied arts, the movement aimed to improve the modern world in three ways: artistically, socially and morally. In the arts, the movement prioritised the experiences of the craftsman or craftswoman and their relationship to the materials and the manual process of creation. It encouraged the "truth to materials" and traditional craftsmanship as the manner to counteract the mass production of poor-quality goods in an industrialised society.[1] It also advocated the unity of the arts and wished to break the limits between the fine arts (easel painting and sculpture) and decorative arts.[2] In its aim to improve the design of everyday life objects, the Arts and Crafts had an effect on diverse areas like bookbinding, architecture, ceramic, graphic arts, illustration, stained-glass, leather work, porcelain, stone and marble carving, pottery, hammered ironwork or interior design. Its main influence was the Victorian interpretation of medieval and folkloric decoration, workshops and guilds. In the social and moral spheres, the movement advocated social reform and rejected the mass-production of objects that dehumanised and alienated the work process and the producer itself. For this reason, the movement attracted a great number of socialists into its ranks.

This questioning of industrial products and the aim to return to traditional craftsmanship was first articulated by the art critic and sociologist John Ruskin (1819–1900), the philosophical leader of the English Arts and Crafts Movement.[3] Ruskin became the most influential of the Victorian writers on the arts, and through his writing he challenged the moral basis of Victorian Britain and spoke out about the connection between art and society. He believed that artistic practice had the potential to modify the lives of people who, generally, were more oppressed by visual ignorance than by deficient material conditions. Ruskin rejected the possibility that mass-produced objects had any aesthetic quality. According to him, the products fabricated in industrialised societies had a negative impact, both on the producer –because the object was not a product of his or her hands, but of mechanical production– and on the buyer –because the products were of mediocre quality.[4] This combination of artistic reflections and morality inspired the work of William Morris (Essex, 1834–1896), the leader of the movement in England and also one of the most influential figures in the Irish Arts and Crafts Movement.[5] Morris became concerned with the threats of industrialisation to the well-being of the individual worker, and reacted against what he considered to be a decay of decorative arts in England. Despite his rejection of the contemporary world, his association of aesthetic quality and utility was a modern ideal influenced by socialism.[6] Morris had witnessed the bad working conditions suffered by the workers in the factories, as well as the consequences that this factory system had in nature and in the final products. He believed that if the quality of design of the final product improved, the well-being of the worker would also improve, and thus society would benefit from it. Like Ruskin, Morris had an especial interest in the Middle Ages and craftsmen guilds that had been substituted now by an industrial society corrupted by capitalism. He considered that creative brotherhoods would also have a positive effect on society, and aimed to achieve social reform through the guilds and applied arts.

During a trip to France in 1858, Morris and Philipp Webb ideated the Red House in Bexleyheath, one of the most important significant buildings of the Arts and Crafts Movement that summarised the movement's ideology through the use of traditional materials, natural beauty, functionality and configuration.[7] The building was soon to become the meeting point for the Pre-Raphaelite circle, and witnessed the creation of the English Arts and Crafts Movement as well. It was during the decoration of the house that Morris, Rossetti and Webb decided to convert their enterprise into business, and in 1861 they created Morris, Marshall, Faulkner and Co, which aimed to bring together architects, designers and artists in order to complement each other's talents. Another enterprise founded by Morris was the Kelmscott Press, a book printing and binding company that promoted the Arts and Crafts movement through book arts influenced by medieval illuminated manuscripts, and also through the publishing of works by Morris, Keats and Rossetti amongst others.[8] Those years also saw the foundation of many different associations such as the Home Arts and Industries Association, which promoted rural handicrafts, the Guild of Handicraft (1888) or the Arts and Crafts Exhibition Society (1887). The Society became a pioneer space for those applied-art artists who did not benefit from the developments in the venues for painting or sculpture such as the Royal

Academy. The main focus of the Exhibition Society was the acknowledgment of every craftsman and craftswoman involved in the production of the objects: designer and executants were to be identified in order to raise their status to the same level as that of fine artists, something Morris did not fully agree with.[9] He, however, was involved in the Society during the last years of the nineteenth century, becoming president in 1892. The main problem faced by the English Arts and Crafts Movement and Morris himself was how to produce useful and beautiful objects affordable also to the working classes. Morris never successfully solved this problem, and the Movement remained a domain of the upper-classes. But it inspired the creation of different associations of Arts and Crafts, and changed the status of applied arts in the cultural scene.

The Arts and Crafts Exhibition Society of London was the beginning of an international rethinking of the status of decorative arts especially in Ireland, where they were characterised by a nationalist and anti-colonialist spirit. Although with less international repercussion and of smaller scope than the movement in England and other wealthier European countries, the Arts and Crafts movement was paramount in Ireland's cultural history. Unlike England, Ireland had no industrial revolution to react against except for Belfast, to a certain extent.[10] However, inspired by the English applied arts, the Arts and Crafts became the counterpart of the Irish Literary Revival and one of the movements that came closest to the literary and language revivals that took part in the country.[11] Between the 1890s and the 1920s, this crafts Revival in Ireland focused on making Irish creations of high quality produced by local artists and materials. Like fine arts, the Arts and Crafts were also intertwined with the social and political issues of the time such as the Home Rule, the War of Independence and the Civil War, the foundation of the Irish Free State and the search for a national identity based on Ireland's pre-colonial past. Nationalist motifs were already popular in Ireland prior to the arrival of the Arts and Crafts Movement in the country. Due to its condition as a British colony, the nature of the movement in Ireland was different than in England. As an occupied country, the easel painting introduced under British rule was often negatively associated to colonialism, just like in Mexico.[12] Nationalist culture supported a national art based on the Irish tradition, local material and Irish workforce, just like Morris and Ruskin proclaimed. The first enterprises of the Arts and Crafts Movement in Ireland aimed to improve the conditions of the impoverished classes, affected by the uneven industrial development and the socio-political struggle. It had the support and the help of figures like Edward Martyn, Lady Gregory and W. B. Yeats, whose writing in *The Celtic Twilight* (1893) already addressed the desire to "attempt to find in folk literature and life, in places where the traditional order of life remains unbroken, an approach to experience that contravenes the modern materialistic approach […], a search for the traditions which lay buried in peasants' huts and cottages".[13] Applied arts became the vehicle for the transmission of nationalist ideas inspired by

Margaret Stokes's aforementioned book *Early Christian Art in Ireland,* the Book of Kells, the Ardagh Chalice and the Tara Brooch. This allowed craftsmen and women to study the early Irish metalwork on which their creations would be inspired. Irish guilds based their artistic creations on Celtic motifs of interlaced patterns and ornaments, high crosses, peltas, triskeles, stylised animals and plants.[14]

One of the main roots of the Irish Arts and Crafts Movement in Ireland were the several lace and crochet industries that proliferated after the Great Hunger of 1840, when many families found themselves in the deepest poverty. These industries provided jobs in the farming areas for women of any social class, and preceded the art industries that, from 1880 onwards, focused on reviving the use of diverse materials such as wood or metal, and techniques like embroidery.[15] These cottage industries, supported by convents and philanthropists, offered women the opportunity to be trained at the schools and then continue their work at home. Despite the differences between the Irish and the British Arts and Crafts movement, they had certain characteristics in common, as Ireland shared its art educational system with England. This South Kensington system was one of the reasons for the leading role of the domestic arts and also for women to be at the vanguard of the movement even before the creation of the Arts and Crafts Society of Ireland. Women had already been part of the artistic expression as weavers or embroiderers, and those who came from well-off families encouraged the post-Famine craft enterprises through their philanthropic activities. Countess Cowper founded the Royal Irish School of Art Needlework in Dublin, Mary Montgomery led the foundation of the Art Metal Industry, Florence Vere O'Brien founded the Limerick Lace School and Clare Embroidery in 1892, and Kenmare Convent helped to develop Celtic-design embroidery in Kerry.[16] In 1886, Mrs. Bagwell, the wife of a local landowner, created the Marlfield Embroideries in Clonmel, Co. Tipperary, to train and employ women after the Famine. The convents also engaged in industrial employment through the knitting and lace industries, and Mother Arsenius, Sister of Charity, opened a woollen factory in Foxford, Co. Mayo, in 1892.[17] These are just few of the many women who became involved in the revival of Irish cottage industries. These lace and crochet industries shown their work in Dublin at the 1853 Great Industrial Exhibition, at the 1865 Dublin International exhibition and in many other artisan shows.

One of the most important figures in the Irish Arts and Crafts was the Scottish philanthropist Ishbel Maria Hamilton-Gordon, Marchioness of Aberdeen (1857–1939).[18] In 1877 Ishbel married John Hamilton Gordon, 7th Earl of Aberdeen, who in 1886 was appointed Lord Lieutenant of Ireland. Before moving to the island, Lady Aberdeen was already president of the Aberdeen Ladies' Union and also leader of the Women's Liberal Federation which supported women's suffrage. In 1886, as soon as the couple moved to Ireland, she also became involved in the craft Revival of the country. She founded and economically supported several craft adventures such as the Leenane Lace Industry in Connemara (1886) or the Irish Lace Depot in Dublin (1887). Her most ambitious project was the inauguration of the Irish Home Industries Association in 1886, which aimed to encourage Irish home and cottage industries, to provide practical assistance for craft-makers, and to find a market for the products by improving distribution and attracting publicity.[19] The Association went on to become the central point of the different cottage industries scattered around Ireland. Soon after her arrival, Lady Aberdeen also began to organise an exhibition of different Irish crafts such as woven linens and needlework to be displayed at the Women's Home Industries Section of the Edinburgh International Exhibition of Industry, Science and Art in 1886. She was also a sympathiser of Home Rule and the Gaelic League and, at her inaugural party for the Irish Industries Association, "the guests were requested to appear in garments of genuine Irish manufacture",[20] while at the Viceregal Ball in 1907 guests were "expected to wear Irish lace-dresses in the case of women, cuffs and jabots in the case of men".[21] This fashion evolved to the point that more eccentric events later required guests to dress up in ancient Irish costumes often handcrafted in Irish cooperatives like the Dun Emer Guild. However, even though Lady Aberdeen was especially active in the promotion of Irish crafts and in the improvement of the conditions of Irish women, she always emphasised women's duty within the household.[22]

Following the interest and support encountered at the different exhibitions held in Chicago and London, and encouraged by the success of women like Vere O'Brien or Lady Aberdeen, Lord Mayo and a group of patrons decided to found the Arts and Crafts Society of Ireland in 1894. Lord Mayo had also founded the County Kildare Archaeological Society in Ireland in 1892, and his wife, Lady Geraldine Mayo, revived the Royal Irish School of Art Needlework that very same year. He had known William Morris, and was reported as saying that "he should never forget what it was to have known and conversed with such a great man. He did not, however, want to see Ireland imitating Morris or anyone else".[23] The Arts and Crafts Society of Ireland was created only a year after the foundation of the Gaelic League, after a series of lectures that aimed to educate the public about art production and wished "to make the exercise of handicraft even a more mental than a physical effort".[24] It focused on raising the status of the Irish goods, which would lead to more demand both by the public and by the shops:

> [the Society wishes] to promote and improve the practice of the Artistic Handicrafts in Ireland – and of all the work of an ornamental and decorative character. The Society hopes to be able to develop much natural talent which is now unused or misdirected – and in various ways to aid Irish Craftsmen in regaining for their work the high repute it once possessed for excellence of workmanship and artistic taste.[25]

The aims of social reform were also addressed by Lord Mayo by saying that "arts and crafts may be the means of leading us to a peaceful and friendly understanding of one another".[26] It fostered artistic industries in Ireland, promoted artistic culture and held exhibitions of Irish arts and crafts through a great variety of media, from book-binding and illustration to lace design, porcelain, pottery, stained glass, embroidery, ironwork, wood, stone and marble carving. Influenced by William Morris, Lord Mayo also wished to associate high art and daily life: "Our efforts are also directed to efface, as far as is possible, the distinction between the artist and the artisan, and to carry the contemplation of beauty from public galleries and buildings into the homes of the people and into their daily life".[27] The first exhibition was held a year after the foundation of the Society, inaugurated with the words: "Children of the Gaelic Race / Yours was once the gift divine / Masters of the magic line / Guard your heritage of Grace".[28] The works exhibited at the Society addressed the three main influences of the movement: first, the ideas of John Ruskin and William Morris through the British Arts and Crafts; Second, the legends of the High Kings of Ireland and the country's pre-colonial past; And third, themes from Celtic mythology, a recall of a romanticised pre-industrial past and a symbol of a purer and more authentic craft tradition.[29] Along with the Arts and Crafts Society of Ireland, another important institution regarding the development of applied arts in the country was the Dublin Art School which, after 1900, seceded from the hands of the South Kensington system and passed under the control of the Department of Agriculture and Technical Instruction and its secretary T. P. Gill. The aim of the School in this new period was the creation of a "national school of Art, encouraging freedom, aiming at distinctive national qualities" based on "the beautiful and suggestive objects in the museum" and through "art craft classes".[30] The School trained a whole new generation of students between 1901 and 1923. Many pupils from Mr. Child's class joined the An Túr Gloine cooperative, and other students decided to found their own guilds and industries.

Thanks to the development of organisations such as the Irish Industries Association or the Royal Irish School of Art Needlework, along with the support of convents and philanthropists, many women with no means found jobs in which they could use and improve their skills. Applied art had become an acceptable occupation for Irish women by the end of the nineteenth century, and many female crafters stood out in areas such as enamelling and stained glass, often competing favourably against British schools. They took part in many exhibitions around Europe before the First World War, culminating in 1914 with the *Exposition des Arts Décoratifs de Grande Bretagne et d'Irlande in the Louvre*. The Irish Arts and Crafts Movement was led by women who regarded it not only a as a way to share their knowledge, but also to provide jobs for those women who found themselves in unfavourable circumstances. Some pioneer women stepped into male domains, as Elizabeth Yeats did running a printing press. Phoebe Traquair, although internationally recognised as one of the leading figures of the Scottish Arts and Crafts Movement, was born in Kilternan, County Dublin, and had a deep impact on the work of her niece Beatrice Elvery, both on painting and applied arts. Other women who contributed to the Irish Arts and Crafts were also involved in the nationalist struggle: Mia Cranwill, who hid weapons in her studio during the war, was a leading figure of the Irish Revival who stood out thanks to metalworks such as the *Senate Casket*, commissioned in 1924 by the Irish nationalist and Senator Alice Stopford Green. The casket was to be placed on the Chariman's desk in the Irish Seanad during each session:

> "We should place no emblem before us in this Assembly that is not of Ireland" –Green wrote for its presentation in the Seanad–. "The form of the casket", she continues, "should go back in direct descent to the 'shrines' designed by the Irish over a thousand years ago [...]. A really living art has no need to copy in slavish routine, and can today be as free as original and distinguished as in the times of ancient renown, supposed to have been lost [...]. If we want to revive here an Irish nation we must dig our roots deep into its soil and be nourished by that ancient earth".[31]

All these women surpassed the aims of Irish nationalism and gave the Arts and Crafts an artistic, social and feminist perspective that prevailed in time. In 1903, two of the most important enterprises were founded: the Dun Emer Gild and An Túr Gloine. These cooperatives of artists fought against standardised artwork and wished to create unique and useful objects made of Irish materials using Irish workforce. While Dun Emer Guild was the pioneer, An Túr Gloine went on to become the longest adventure of the Irish Arts and Crafts movement.

## Dun Emer Guild and Cuala Industries

Many pages have been written about the innovative modernist paintings of Jack B. Yeats as well as about W. B. Yeats, praising him as the leading figure of the Irish Revival.[32] The Yeats sisters, on the contrary, became overshadowed by the prestige of the brothers despite their social and artistic innovation within the Arts and Crafts Movement of the Irish Revival. Alongside Evelyn Gleeson, Susan "Lily" Yeats and Elizabeth "Lolly" Yeats founded, ran and worked at the Dun Emer Guild, a pioneer cooperative enterprise comprised by women and characterised by it social conscience.

Lily (Sligo, 1866–Dublin, 1949) and Lolly (London, 1868–Dublin, 1940) were born to the painter John B. Yeats and Susan Pollexfen. Along with Jack B. and William B., the sisters were looked after by a governess, Martha Jowitt, until 1878. Their early life was not easy, especially due to their father's struggles to financially support the family.[33] The mother also suffered from health problems, and died at the age of 59 in 1900. Both Lolly and Lily attended the Metropolitan School of Art from 1883 and took classes at the Royal Dublin Society before moving to England in 1886. In London, the Yeats family became acquainted with William Morris and his family, and in 1888 Lily began to study embroidery and to work at Morris and Co. along with Ellen Wright and under the supervision of May Morris. "Lily is still very happy at the Morris's", wrote W. B. Yeats in 1888; "she makes cushion covers and mantelpiece covers without end".[34] However, in her personal diaries and letters Lily described her time in London as a rather dark period in her life due to her domineering employer, May Morris, and the oppressive family atmosphere.[35] In any case, at the Morris company Lily's skills were encouraged; she excelled at her work and soon she became an assistant embroiderer for May Morris. One of the most important works she contributed to was the bed hangings designed for Morris' Kelmscott Manor, also showed at the Arts and crafts Exhibition in 1893. In April 1894 Lily left the job due to her ill health and, after working briefly as a governess in France, she returned to London in 1896. As for Lolly, during her time in London she began to write fiction for *The Vegetarian*, and published her own home-made magazine entitled *The Pleiades* along with six other friends. She studied to be a kindergarten teacher and devoted herself to the teaching of art. She also learnt the art of typography and provided text and illustrations for four painting manuals: *Brushwork* (1896), *Brushwork Studies of Flowers, Fruits and Animals for Teachers and Advanced Students* (1898*), Brushwork Copy Book* (1899) and *Elementary Brushwork Studies* (1900).[36]

Evelyn Gleeson (1855–1944) was born in Cheshire, England, to an Irish doctor who worked hard in England in order to found the Woollen Mills in Athlone in 1859. Gleeson was raised in an "atmosphere charged with interest in industrial effort for the benefit of Ireland", as she described it.[37] She was trained as a teacher and studied portraiture at the Ludovici Atelier before being trained in design by Alexander Millar, a leading carpet designer and member of the English Arts and Crafts Movement. In London she became involved with the progressive Women's Pioneer Club, the Gaelic League and the Ladies Irish National Land League. In the early 1890s she was appointed secretary of the Irish Literary Society, co-founded by W. B. Yeats, where she became acquaintance with the Yeats family.[38] As addressed earlier in this book, Gleeson opened the debate about artistic hierarchy within the cultural nationalist movement and highlighted the importance of the visual arts in the Revival. In 1902 Gleeson bough a charming old house in Dundrum, Dublin, where she founded the Dun Emer Guild with the moral and economical support of her good friend, the famous botanist Augustine Henry. The Yeats sisters were approached by Gleeson to join her in the establishing of the craft workshop, where she wished to improve the standards in the crafting of Irish products created by Irish women. The Dun Emer Guild ("The Fort of Emer") took its name from the wife of the Irish mythological hero Cu Chulainn. She was a very well-known figure in the

Irish folklore for her beauty, her wisdom and her artistic skills.[39] The ideology of the cooperative was clearly addressed in its manifesto, published in 1903:

> Everything as far as possible is Irish: the paper of the books, the linen of the embroidery and the wool of the tapestry and carpets. The designs are also the spirit and the tradition of the country. The education of the work-girls is also part of the idea, they are taught to paint and their brains and fingers are made more active and understanding; some of them, we hope, will become teachers to others, so that similar industries may spread through the land. Things made of pure materials, worked by these Irish girls, must be more lasting and valuable than machine-made goods which only serve a temporary purpose. All the things made at Dun Emer are beautiful in the sense that they are instinct with individual feeling and have cost thought and care.[40]

The guild served both as domestic space and a place for business and commerce. The duties in the guild were divided between the three women from the beginning of the enterprise: Gleeson focused on the creation of tapestries and rugs in a style that developed from the influence of Turkish carpets to a more Irish spirit embracing the designs of Celtic manuscripts and the colours of the Irish landscape. Lily taught Gaelic and Irish culture, and was also responsible for the embroidery department. The workshop recalled May Morris's studio at Hammersmith Terrace, and much of May's influence was felt both in the atmosphere and in the style of Lily's artworks. The influence of the English Arts and Crafts was combined by Lily with a personal manner of expressive stitches and Celtic patterns made with local materials such as Irish wool, which led her work to be published in the *Art Journal* in 1906.[41] Lily's embroidery workshop, both in Dun Emer and in the Cuala Industries later, employed young Irish working-class girls such as Sarah Hyland who were often involved in nationalist circles. This caused the workshop to suffer the raid of the Free State Troops when they arrested two young female employees in 1923.

Lolly attended the Women's Printing Association in London, co-founded by Emily Faithfull who was an activist and publisher dedicated to improving the working conditions and employment opportunities for women.[42] She studied composition, type-setting, design and press mechanics, and after a few months at the Association she created her own printing department in an upstairs room in Dun Emer. She used an old Albion press –the same model used in Kelmscott Press– bought from a provincial newspaper following the advice of Emery Walker, who was the typographical advisor at Morris's press. Following the Irish Revival's ideal of unity between ancient and modern, the press combined a Gothic-influenced style with modern typographies. The guild embraced more political motives than other crafting organisations, as all the founders were connected to the Irish nationalist movement at some level. However, it did not share Kelmscott's concept of guilds' socialism. Lolly's press was based on a cooperative form and shared the ideology of the Arts and Crafts Movement. At the same time, it was influenced by Irish cultural nationalism, supported contemporary nationalist writers and published limited edition hand-press books of leading Irish authors of the period such as W. B. Yeats himself. The press followed traditional hand-methods of print and used locally sourced linen rag paper. Lolly also produced hand-coloured prints, bookplates, cards and newspapers illustrated by painters like Jack B. Yeats or the artist and occultist Pamela Colman-Smith. The long running series of Christmas cards, St. Patrick's Day cards and business cards were items offered to a wider public, as not everyone could afford other objects more exclusive and expensive. The books published by Dun Emer were not accessible nor aimed at a general audience, but "for people who really want something rather exclusive and are ready to pay for it".[43] This exclusivity was part of the problem of the Dun Emer Industries, which always struggled financially and had to explore other ways to gain access to the wider public. The books were hand-printed in Irish paper and linen casing, and were influenced by modern design and typography. Their clear and simple format of minimalist aesthetic helped the reader to focus on the text rather than on "superfluous" decorative elements.[44] The first hand-printed publication by the Dun Emer Press was *In the Seven Woods* (1903), by W. B. Yeats, who also acted as the press' literary editor. This volume of poems of the "Irish heroic age" was designed with care but contained no illustrations. Published in July, it was sold out by September. Its colophon, printed in Dun Emer's characteristic red ink, stated:

> Here ends *In The Seven Woods*, written by William Butler Yeats, printed upon paper made in Ireland, and published by Elizabeth Corbet Yeats at the Dun Emer Press, in the house of Evelyn Gleeson at Dundrum in the county of Dublin, Ireland, finished the sixteenth day of July in the year of the big wind, nineteen hundred and three.[45]

As well as books from Irish paper, the guild promoted political nationalism by reviving native cultural traditions in tapestries of Irish wool and Irish designs made by Lily and embroidered on Irish linen. Both Gleeson and Lily's creations were based on the combination between Celtic ornament and the European Art Nouveau, which led to an innovative form of Irish art. The works were framed or incorporated into cushions, table or bed linen and furnishing, and most of the objects were sold at nationalist art fairs or exhibitions in Dublin, London or New York, and acclaimed in the press.[46] The Dun Emer Guild also designed objects for public buildings like the Dáil, the Seanad or the Council Chamber of the Royal Dublin Society, as well as ecclesiastical works like altar carpets and vestments for the churches of Derry, Newry or Foxford. One of the guild's largest commissions was the decoration of the interior of St. Brendan's Cathedral in Loughrea (Galway), a building designed by Edward Martyn in a

Gothic Revival style and finished in 1902. Dun Emer was commissioned to create a set of twenty-four embroidered banners, most of them depicting Irish saints. The banners were designed by Jack B. Yeats, his wife Mary Cottenham Yeats and Pamela Colman Smith, and stitched by Lily and her seven female assistants using silk and wool on linen. The works featured the "primitive" patterns of the Irish stained-glass and the organic forms characteristics of the Art Nouveau. They combined medieval and contemporary styles through dramatic colours and simplified shapes surrounded by thick black lines of contour. The figures were portrayed as religious icons of Irishness created for contemplation and devotion and set against a golden background. Each panel contained an inscription with the name of the saint in Irish at the bottom. The confluence between the past and the present in the banners, both in style and symbolism, was addressed by a reviewer of *The Irish Monthly* in 1904:

> There is nothing of the conventional style about them [the Dun Emer banners], each figure being true to the traditions of the times in which the saint lived; so that perhaps to the untutored eye some of the figures might seem more quaint than beautiful in the ordinary sense – just as some people will prefer the conventional modern drawing-room style of picture to the work of the old masters. But one quickly realizes that these saintly little medieval figures carry with them the real atmosphere and feeling of ancient Ireland, the island of saints.[47]

The iconography of the Loughrea Cathedral has been read as an allegory of spiritual strength over failure.[48] The figures represented in the Loughrea banners are a symbol of Irish spiritual heroism in adverse circumstances, which are faced differently by the characters. The portrayal of the defiant St. Jarlath, who looks directly to the viewer, clashes with the depiction of St. Columcille, who appears seated, with his gaze turned down and his hand closed in a finch. The commission of the work, the process of creation and its reception meant to Evelyn Gleeson a triumph over foreign industries:

> Ecclesiastical art-work had until now been mainly supplied from Continental work-shops and it is with great satisfaction that we record the support given to us by a large order from Loughrea Cathedral, where embroidered banners from Dun Emer depicting Irish saints can now be seen. The embroidery is the mediaeval style which was received by William Morris.[49]

Although women often exhibited anonymously, female artistic practice in guilds had gradually become more acceptable with the time. Lily received great recognition for embroideries such as *The GPO* (n.d.) or *Foxgloves by a Stile* (n.d.), often exhibited through the Arts and Crafts Society of Ireland.[50]

Dun Emer's landscape embroideries addressed a very particular vision of rural Ireland in an original style with the green and purple colours of the Irish sky and scenery. These types of embroideries were warmly welcomed in the Irish Pavilion of Missouri's World's Fair, where the Dun Emer first exhibited in 1904, gaining international reputation for its needle works and cushions made from Irish wool and linen. The members of the guild also showed their work at the annual exhibitions of the Royal Dublin Society, the Oireachtas Exhibition in Dublin, the Gaelic League in London as well as in the New York Exhibition in 1907. Evelyn Gleeson and the Yeats sisters worked side by side with their assistants in the process of creation of every object, and developed a guild financially independent and "a little different from the dabbling of the wives of Lord Lieutenants of Ireland who took to arts and crafts as an occupation which kept them from direct involvement in Ireland's turbulent politics".[51] The strong involvement of women, either as craft workers, designers, artists or patrons became one of the main characteristics of the guild. Dun Emer was run and staffed by around thirty women, and had a political Home Industries aspect. According to Elaine Cheasley Patterson, "set against an industrial profile (low wages, sweated work at home for pennies), this artistic revival of Irish industries refined women's crafts as art and provided the women working in them with an alternative to these harsh conditions".[52] This female-only enterprise seems to clash with the ways in which Dun Emer addressed their advertising, and reveals the uneasy position of the guild at the confluence of Arts and Crafts, political nationalism and feminism. In 1904, Dun Emer launched a publicity campaign included in *Leabhar Dun Eimire* encouraging the Irish housewife to "decorate your house with Dun Emer tufted rugs, embroidered portieres and sofa backs, put Dun Emer tapestries on your walls and Dun Emer books in your bookcases. This is the duty of an Irishwoman".[53] The campaign echoed the discourses of the Catholic Church and Irish nationalism about female self-sacrifice, and invited Irish women to support the Irish economy while confining them in the domestic sphere. Yet, at the same time, Gleeson, Lily and Lolly stepped into the public sphere and successfully managed a culturally significant endeavour. The Dun Emer Industries became a pioneer enterprise in the Arts and Crafts of the turn of the century, and were as well highly influential in the visual arts of the Irish Revival. The success of the Yeats sisters was proved by the fact that even James Joyce addressed the guild in his novel *Ulysses* (1920), where he mocked some elements of the Irish Revival including the Dun Emer guild: "That's folk, he said very earnestly, for your book, Haines. Five lines of text and ten pages of notes about the folk and the fishgods of Dundrum. Printed by the weird sisters in the year of the big wind […]. To be printed and bound at the Druiddrum press by two designing females. Calf covers of pissedon green. Last word in art shades. Most beautiful book come out of Ireland my time".[54] The reference to "the year of the wind" is an allusion to W. B. Yeats's *In the Seven Woods*, a satirical comment about the pretensions of books with archaic colophons as well as a critique to the dominance of the Yeats family in the Irish cultural life during the Revival. However, Joyce's caricatures of Lilly and Lolly as mere handmaids to their more famous brother only proved the impact that Dun Emer had had in the cultural scene of Dublin at the beginning of the century.[55] Yet, despite its success, the cooperative faced several problems along the way like the poor conditions of the building and the financial struggles of its members. This was aggravated by the lack of business knowledge and experience of the Yeats sisters, W. B. Yeats and Gleeson, and the constant arguments between them.

Lolly travelled to New York to promote their products in October 1906. However, only a year after The Dun Emer Press would publish its last book: *William's Discoveries*. In 1907, Lily and her father also made a trip to New York in order to show the Dun Emer creations at the Irish Industrial Exhibition. She returned to Ireland a year after, but her father stayed for the rest of his life. 1908 was also the year when the Yeats sisters and Evelyn Gleeson split up the business due to the constant strain, and went separate ways. Gleeson kept the Dun Emer Industries and carried on with the work of the guild in Hardwick St., Dublin. She received many commissions for the decoration of churches and obtained artistic success, but she always struggled financially. She continued creating hand-knotted rugs, tapestries and embroidery works based on early Christian patterns and Celtic motifs. According to Nicola Gordon Bowe, Gleeson's artwork "reflected the nationalist, socialist industrial and ultimately political concerns in Ireland which had been gathering momentum since the early years of the nineteenth century".[56] Amongst the women that joined the workshops were May Kerley, who assisted with rugs and carpets, and the bookbinders Norah Fitzpatrick and Marie Walker, who was also an actress at the Abbey Theatre. Gleeson's sister also lived at Dun Emer with her children Grace, Edward and Kitty. Soon Kitty, an amateur actress, set designer and writer, began to work in the guild as a designer, creating Celtic costumes for nationalist women.[57] She also collaborated in the commissions for the Honan Chapel, St. Patrick's Church in San Francisco and worked in the carpet presented to Pope Pious XI in 1931. After her aunt's death in 1944, Kitty took over Dun Emer as its principal textile designer until the 1960s. Like Gleeson, Kitty's designs were also influenced by Irish medieval artworks, especially the Book of Kells, which she combined with Christian iconography. Evelyn Gleeson's accomplishments have often been eclipsed by the attention paid to the Yeats sisters due to their family background; however, she was also a pioneer of the Arts and Crafts Movement in Ireland and the main leader of one of the most important visual projects of the Irish Revival.

In 1908, the Yeats sisters took their part of the business and founded the Cuala Industries in Churchtown, Dublin. Lily continued working on embroidery and promoting national crafts made by Irish women with native materials like *The Proud and Careless Notes Live on, but Bless our Hands that Ebb Away* (ca. 1915)

Fig. 11. Lily Yeats and R. Brigid Ganly, ***The proud and careless notes live on, but bless our hands that ebb away***, 1915.
Embroidery therads on green silk (framed), 29.21 x 36.83 cm.
Image courtesy of Whyte's Auctioneers

(fig. 11), a distinctive work created in the guild. The embroidery illustrates the final stanza intoned by The Three Voices at the end of W. B. Yeats's poem entitled "The Prayers Ask for a Blessing on the Psalteries and Themselves", belonging to the collection *In The Seven Woods*. The scene was designed by Brigid Ganly (née O'Brien), the daughter of the painter Dermod O'Brien, who attended the Dublin Metropolitan School of Art under Margaret Clarke and was best known for her portraits and still lifes. The narrative detail of the composition was highlighted by the expressive stitches of Lily Yeats in a work that recalls the Dun Emer banners of the Loughrea Cathedral. The signatures of both artists are also stitched at the bottom corners of the embroidery. The three lamenting musicians are portrayed in an Irish hillside, dressed in imaginative and colourful cloaks that show the influence of Beatrice Elvery, Mary Cottenham Yeats, Wilhelmina Geddes and Jack B. Yeats. In 1935, Lily created a more primitive-styled version of this theme in black and white, also designed by Brigid Ganly and showing the same lines from the poem. During her time in the Cuala Industries, Lily often adapted the designs of other artists and produced a wide range of embroidered panels characterised by their narrative detail.

For her part, Lolly run the Cuala Press, another unique press within the Irish Arts and Crafts, as it was again run and staffed by women. The Cuala Press published seventy seven books between 1908 and 1946, the first one being *Poetry and Ireland* (1908), by W. B. Yeats and Lionel Johnson. The last one was Elizabeth Rivers's *Stranger in Aran* (1946). The press focused on contemporary works rather than classics, publishing books by W. B. Yeats –also the press editor– John Millington Synge, Ezra Pound or Patrick Kavanagh.[58] While the embroidery and tapestries created by Lily often contained text, image and elaborate decoration, the books were very modest, but they were praised for their typographical elegance and literary novelty. Even though W.B. Yeats advocated Morris's concept of "art unity", book design occupied a second place in the poet's editorial hierarchy. Unlike Morris' book designs, most of the books published in Cuala resisted illustration with the notable exception of *Reveries over Childhood and Youth* (1915), written by W. B. Yeats and with Jack Yeats's *Memory Harbour* (1900) as its frontispiece.[59]

According to the art critic W. B. Blaikie Murdoch (1880–1934), the Kelmscott volumes were "noble decorative items, rather than genuine masterpieces of typography, and it is here they differ with those from the Cuala".[60] While Lolly had studied the work of Morris, she surpassed him by recognising and developing the elegance of simplicity. The press also produced broadsides, cards and hand-coloured prints that aimed to attract those clients who could not afford the more expensive books or embroideries.[61] They also followed the iconography of the Revival in cards like *Greetings*, printed by Cuala Press in 1914 and designed by Eileen Booth, who illustrated two colleens in traditional clothes with Irish cottages on the background and set in the West of Ireland, following the iconography of the nationalist Revival. The Yeats sisters advertised these more economical goods in nationalist journals such as *Bean na hÉireann* which "recognised the poverty in which most people lived and had a column devoted to offering helpful hints for combating the drabness of life without spending a lot of money".[62] They also issued various series of *A Broadside*, a publication edited by Jack B. Yeats and published between 1908 and 1915, and then between 1935 and 1937.[63] The *Broadsides* displayed traditional and new ballads, as well as writing contributions by Lady Gregory, Douglas Hyde and Seamus O'Sullivan amongst others, and were often illustrated by Jack B. Yeats. The style applied to those publications was completely different from the typography and graphics of the Cuala and the Dun Emer books.

Disagreements continued amongst the members of the enterprise, especially between W. B. Yeats and Lolly. The latter found difficult to work with an editor who would not accept any questioning of his authority in the election of the literary artworks to be published. W. B. Yeats's stubbornness led his father to criticise his attitude regarding the Industries and to question the exclusivity of the publications:

> When you advise on books for the press, it should be advice and not haughty dictation [...]. After all, the press is Lolly's business and it means our means of living and she has other things to consider besides the literary excellence of a particular book –there are questions of convenience and commercial expediency and policy– matter for tactful consideration not to be decided offhand by a literary expert.[64]

However, despite the conflicts and the financial struggles following the flourishing of modern and more industrialised presses, the Cuala Industries made good progress for a while. After John Butler Yeats's death in 1922 the Cuala Press was moved to the basement of W.B.'s house in Merrion Square, and in 1935 the Cuala Industries were moved to Lower Baggot St, in Dublin. During this time Lolly published important works including Yeats's *The Bounty of Sweden* (1925) or Frank O'Connor's *The Wild Bird's Nest* (1935). Lily continued producing embroideries at Cuala Industries until illness caused her to be taken to a London clinic and later to France in order to recover. She returned to Dublin in 1925 and retired in 1931, when the Cuala embroidery workshop closed.

The guild struggled on throughout the 1930s with much assistance from W. B. Yeats's wife, George. The political activist Maire Gill, who was also a member of Sinn Féin and Cumann na mBan, and was jailed in Kilmainham Gaol in 1923 for possessing incriminating literature, had begun working at the Dun Emer Industries at the age of seventeen, and became the main compositor of the Cuala Press from the 1930s until 1969.[65] Lolly died of a heart failure in 1940 and Lily nine years later. Yeats's wife George took over and managed the press, publishing books until 1946 and producing prints and cards until her death in 1968. The Cuala Press was revived in 1969, when Anne and Michael Yeats –the children of W.B. and George Yeats– began printing books again. The context of guilds like Dun Emer or the Cuala Industries differed from the philanthropic upper-class movements of their time, and the Yeats sisters and Evelyn Gleeson had to face constant financial struggles. Unlike Gleeson, neither Lily nor Lolly were in any way directly involved in contemporary nationalist issues for independence and they did not take part in the women's campaigns for the right to vote.[66] The Dun Emer Press and the Cuala Press did not privilege female writers, and only four women writers (Lady Augusta Gregory, Katharine Tynan, Elizabeth Bowen and Elizabeth Rivers) were published during the guild's existence.[67] However, they worked tirelessly to maintain themselves as well as to provide employment for impoverished women. Lolly also became one of the main figures in the introduction of the Arts and Crafts printing methods in Ireland. By recuperating the traditional techniques of embroidery and hand-printing in Ireland and by publishing key books by contemporary authors, both the Dun Emer Guild and the Cuala Industries played a central part in sponsoring the Irish Revival, in the access of Irish women to the workforce and in the flourishing of the artistic scene in the country.

## An Túr Gloine

Sarah Henrietta Purser (Dun Laoghaire, 1848–Dublin, 1943) was the founder member of the stained-glass cooperative An Túr Gloine and one of the most influential patrons of the arts of her time.[68] She was born in Dun Laoghaire, Co. Dublin, to a middle-class Protestant family who was involved in the milling and brewing business. After being educated in Switzerland, Purser attended the Dublin Metropolitan School of Art between 1874 and 1875. In 1878, after the failure of the family business and when her father emigrated to America, Purser travelled to Paris and studied art at the Académie Julian. She focused on portraiture in order to make a living out of art and, through her training in France, her style became deeply influenced by the work of the Realists as well as Degas and the Impressionists.[69] Soon her early portraits and studies of the nude began to reveal a combination of the European manner with modernist trends and a personal use of expressive brushstrokes that she would later develop in her Irish themes, once back in Dublin.

Purser returned to Ireland in 1879 as an unknown figure in the artistic scene. However, by 1886 she had become a well-respected portraitist in her country and one of the few Irish women with a place in the front rank of the artists of the time.[70] She received frequent commissions, attended sessions at the Dublin Sketching Club long before women were accepted as members, exhibited regularly at the Royal Hibernian Academy from 1879 and, in 1891, she was appointed Honorary Member of the Academy, the first and only woman until then. Her study in Harcourt Terrace became one of the main venues for the Dublin literary and artistic circles, and was often visited by leading public figures such as Douglas Hyde, W.B. Yeats, Jane Barlow, Michael Davitt and John O'Leary, the sculptor John Hughes or Maud Gonne. Many of them were portrayed by Sarah Purser herself, who created a sort of imagery of the nationalist and artistic scene of her time. Her unique personality played an essential part in Purser's artistic success and led to a series of genuine and natural portraits. She was described by John O'Grady as an intelligent and sharp woman of "quiet benevolence",[71] rationalist and hostile to the mysticism surrounding the Irish Revival. She was well able to entertain her sitters and make them feel so comfortable that she could depict their deepest nature.[72] Her good sense and her honesty can be easily discerned in her art, something well admired both by the press and by the public. Thanks to this, by the end of the nineteenth century, Purser had become the leading and most prolific portraitist in Ireland.

Her first residential commission was a double portrait of Constance Gore-Booth and her sister Eva. It was painted in 1882 in an innovative style within Irish traditional portraiture and depicts a kneeled Eva picking primroses while

Constance stands behind her holding a bouquet of flowers.[73] This was only the first of many portraits of nationalist leaders that Purser carried out throughout her artistic career. *Michael Davitt Lying in State* was finished and exhibited at the New Gallery summer exhibition in London in 1892, and at the Royal Hibernian Academy only a year after. It represents the last days of the 'father' of the Irish League Michael Davitt. Born in Straide (County Mayo) in 1846, Davitt became a key figure of the Land War, the National Land League of Mayo and the Irish National Land League. He was also imprisoned for his activity in the Fenian movement. According to Beatrice Elvery, Purser had access to the nursing-home were Davitt was spending his last days and Elvery herself was sent there to do a drawing of Davitt that was given to his widow after his death.[74] Few years earlier, however, Davitt had been a sitter for Orpen, to whom he advised not to take any side:

> Just live and learn to try to understand the beauties of this wonderful world that God has been good enough to give us to live in. There is nothing that spoils its beauty more than party politics and intrigues or taking sides in any war against your fellow men. These things have ruined this beautiful world for me for years and years. Aye, take my advice. Live to love and never hurt a flea when he bites you. Remember it's his nature; he is only answering his call to live and love with as much right as you or I.[75]

It was Michael Davitt who arranged a meeting between Sarah Purser and Maud Gonne, another sitter of Purser's. Her life-size *Portrait of Maud Gonne* was painted in 1890 and exhibited at the Royal Hibernian Academy, first under the title *The New Pet*, and later on as *Lady with a Monkey*. Gonne was known for her love for animals and was often seen accompanied by her Irish wolfhound or her pet monkey 'Chaperone', whose name allowed her to go out unescorted but still stating, without lying, that she was indeed accompanied by her Chaperone.[76] It is not surprising that, through her many portraits of Gonne, Purser got to capture her unconventional life and her unique spirit. As John O'Grady described it, portraiture "suited Purser's temperament, letting her indulge her passion for conversation while she earned her living and bringing even more interesting sitters to her studio as her popularity grew".[77] Even her genre scenes developed into imaginative illustrations of little stories. Many of them showed only one figure, in many cases female, absorbed in a specific activity, such as *A Group Knitting* (1882), *Seated Lady Playing Chess* (1895) or *An important Letter* (1882). Many of Purser's paintings were modelled by Kathleen Kearney, who worked as secretary for Maud Gone and became Purser's favourite model from the 1920s until the end of her career.

Despite the fact that Purser evolved into Dublin's leading portraitist once John B. Yeats had left for America, some of her best paintings cannot be strictly classified as portraiture.[78] *An Irish Idyll* is an example of her interest in depicting the poor, and portrays a young woman in a brown dress and a shawl holding a child on her lap. The title derives from *Irish Idylls*, a collection of short stories about the Irish peasantry during the nineteenth century written by her friend the novelist Jane Barlow and published in 1892.[79] *Le Petit Déjeuner* (1881), although exhibited in several occasions, was never offered for sale, which clearly states Purser's feeling for this picture.[80] The model is the Italian musician Maria Feller, who became friends with Purser during their time in Paris. The painting depicts a moment of the daily life ("The Breakfast"), and captures a sense of ambiguity through the figure's pensive face portrayed lost in her own thoughts. The scene shows reminiscences of Degas's genre portraits as well as Berthe Morisot's female figures; Purser had met both artists in Paris. Through her genuine genre scenes and portraits, considered suitable for a female artist, Purser broke out the domestic confinement and became one of the main artistic patrons of the turn of the century. She also explored the philosophical, political and artistic ideas of her time, the richness of the Celtic and Early Christian Ireland, and the connection between art and nationalism. She harshly criticised the lack of support of Irish artists and crafters, especially by the Catholic Church, an institution that commissioned portraits of their bishops in Italy and imported low-quality stained-glass from Europe causing a great loss in the Irish craft.[81] A letter to the editor responded to Purser's critique by addressing that "it seems we [priests] are not endowed with aesthetic tastes or do not cultivate them. Thank god it is so", to which Purser answered back: "all right. I am not ashamed of not knowing the points of a horse, but then I don't accept the post of supplying mounts of the cavalry. If priests are no judges of beautiful things, of fine proportions, of stained class, of carved stone, why undertake the duty of filling the country with these very things".[82]

Purser was well aware of the creation of many new churches in Ireland, especially since the Catholic Emancipation in 1892, and of the demand of stained-glass windows to decorate them.[83] She wished to revive the greatness of the Irish art of the past, convinced that Ireland's duty was to recover its self-sufficiency in the arts. With the support of the nationalist and cultural activist Edward Martyn, Sarah Purser founded in 1903 the stained-glass cooperative An Túr Gloine ("The Tower of Glass"), where artists could work as individuals while making use of the common facilities. Edward Martyn had criticised the "imitation chromolithographs of mediaeval panelled saints", mass-produced, imported from abroad and created by foreign firms which neglected the truth to materials. He stated: "if we are determined to have bad work, it is better to have bad Irish than bad foreign".[84] He was willing to support any project that would employ native artists who would, where possible, depict Irish subjects to ornate the many ecclesiastical buildings created since the Catholic emancipation. Sarah Purser's studio was founded to restore the ancient craft of stained-glass in Ireland in order to heal the "demoralised" use of the materials in Ireland.[85] An Túr Gloine adhered to the ideal of the Arts and Crafts movement and the medieval standards, and promoted national windows of high quality and recognisable Irish iconography crafted by the hands of well-trained Irish artists using local materials. The classes began in 1903 under A. E. Child, a stained-glass artist and teacher at the Metropolitan School of Art thanks to the mediation of Edward Martyn and the support of the Department of Agriculture and Technical Instruction. Child was a pupil of Christopher Wall, a leading exponent of stained-glass in Britain and adviser to Purser's studio. His classes were attended by a young Harry Clarke, Michael Healy, Evie Hone, Catherine O'Brien and Wilhelmina Geddes, a group of students that created outstanding works for Irish churches as well as for international buildings during their time in An Túr Gloine.

Purser received the commissions and assigned them to the workers as she thought fit. In contrast to contemporary trade practice base on the division of labour, An Túr Gloine followed Purser's norm of "one artist, one window": According to her philosophy, each window carried out at the cooperative should be "in all its artistic parts the work of one artist, the glass chosen and painted by the same mind and hand that made the design and drew the cartoon".[86] She was one of the early artists who criticised the hierarchy of the arts within the Revival, and wished to raise the status of applied arts. In her studio all glass was considered "a work of free art as much as any other painting or sculpture".[87] Due to the lack of evidence of Irish medieval windows, stained-glass was seen as a field of exploration for a national school of artists working in an entirely new medium. Thus, the windows created in the studio combined the Celtic motifs of ancient metalwork, jewellery, sculpture or manuscripts in a modern idiom following the spirit of the Irish Revival. Purser's system, along with the innovative influence of A. E. Child, led to a revolutionary change in the Irish crafts. Thanks to her vast knowledge of the English medieval crafts and her good eye for artists, she ruled the cooperative with great success. Many of the leading artists and crafters of the time worked in the studio and genuinely revived the spirit and skills of the medieval artists in an atmosphere of freedom and support by their patron, who stated:

> I very often come upon, and which annoys me very much – that the artists in 24 Pembroke Street are in some way my pupils and under my directions. This, of course, is entirely not so. They are each born with their own imagination and sense of colour, and learned to draw before specializing in stained glass, and have each developed their technique on lines of their own for handling the materials, and are not interfered with anybody, and, as far as is possible, in this rather confusing business they get the credit or blame personally for their work.[88]

Two crucial figures in the success of An Túr Gloine were Harry Clarke (1889–1931) and Michael Healy (1873–1941). Harry Clarke (later the husband of Margaret Clarke), was the son of Joshua Clarke, who had established a stained-glass studio and church-decorating business in 1886.[89] Harry Clarke attended the Dublin Metropolitan School of Art, taking night classes under A.E. Child and later under William Orpen. During his time in London in the 1910s he focused on illustration and designed works for Hans Christian Andersen's *Fairy Tales* (1916) or the 1919 edition of Edgar Allan Poe's *Tales of Mystery and Imagination* amongst others. His work in illustration would later influence his stained-glass windows of vivid and exotic colours, imaginative compositions and meticulous attention to detail that he combined with his interest in Art Nouveau, Symbolism and the Celtic heritage. In 1921 he took over the family business and founded the Harry Clarke Studios, receiving important commissions for stained-glass windows. By the 1920s, Harry Clarke was the leading figure of An Túr Gloine followed by Michael Healy. Healy was too educated at the Dublin Metropolitan School of Art, and later attended the School of the Royal Hibernian Academy and the Accademia di Belle Arti in Florence. Like Clarke, Healy also worked as an illustrator, and later as a teacher at the Dominican College in Kildare.[90] He joined An Túr Gloine in 1903, where he too received lessons by A.E. Child. It was under the instruction of Child that the skills of the cooperative members flourished. The stained-glass and mosaics created in An Túr Gloine were shown in major exhibitions both in Ireland and abroad (e.g. the St. Louis World's Fair in 1904), but it was the third Arts and Crafts Society of Ireland exhibition in Dublin in 1910 the turning point in getting important public attention.[91]

The artists working in the studio during its first decade included major female glassmakers such as Wilhelmina Geddes, Ethel Rind, Catherine O'Brien and Beatrice Elvery. Elvery joined the cooperative only two years after its foundation, and worked there until 1912 when she left for the London's Slade School of Fine Art. After taking lessons in stained-glass from A.E. Child, her first work for An Túr Gloine was a series of windows for a convent in Enniskillen, although her designs can be seen all over Ireland.[92] She also created the windows for St. Stephen's Church in Mount Street, Dublin, St. Nicholas' Church in Carrickfergus and a war memorial at the Church of Ireland in Carrickmines.[93] Elvery developed a style that combined modern trends such as Fauvism or Expressionism with an Irish medieval aesthetic, creating symbolic religious images and folkloric scenes of the Irish people with intense colours. Like Michael Healy, she also adopted and adapted Irish Romanesque motifs and early Christian calligraphy in her works. During her time in An Túr Gloine, Elvery created some of the most evocative illustrations of the Irish Revival but, although her work was well received, she was not content with her stained-glass skills: "I never got the right feeling of glass or the detached, austere quality necessary for ecclesiastical art".[94]

It was through Beatrice Elvery that Wilhelmina Geddes was invited by Sarah Purser to join An Túr Gloine, thanks to an early work that Geddes showed in 1910 at the Arts and Crafts Society Exhibition and that caught the attention of the members of the studio.[95] Geddes' combination of watercolour and ink in

*Cinderella Dressing her Ugly Sister*, with its contrasts of tones, its simplifications of line and form and its inked outlines, was only a hint of what the artist would later achieve through the technique of stained glass. Despite being overshadowed by her more famous pupil Evie Hone, Geddes executed many outstanding windows of Expressionist taste for Irish churches in Dublin, Dun Laoghaire or Belfast, as well as abroad (e.g. St. Bartholomew's Church in Ottawa, Canada, or the Anglican All Saint's Church in Laleham, England).[96] Born in Leitrim in 1887, Geddes was a well-read artist educated as an illustrator and graphic designer at the Belfast School of Art. During her artistic training she won many prizes for her drawings from the life and from casts of antique sculpture, although she went also on to absorb the influence of Vorticism and German Expressionism. In the 1910s she attended Orpen's drawing classes at the Dublin Metropolitan School of Art and exhibited at the Arts and Crafts Society, the Royal Hibernian Academy, the Society of Scottish Artists and the Ulster Academy amongst others. Even though she had not been trained as a stained-glass artist, soon Geddes had learnt the techniques while working at the cooperative.

Her first stained-glass essay was a window illustrating the life of St. Colman MacDuagh, created between 1911 and 1912 in direct response to Purser's invitation to join An Túr Gloine.[97] The scene was highly influenced by El Greco in its expressive lines and draperies, colouring and monumentality. By combining the influences of the Renaissance painting and Greek sculpture with a religious subject-matter and a modern idiom, Geddes proved her ability in the craft. Shortly after, she created her first window for An Túr Gloine, a large scale dramatic composition of *The Angel of Resurrection* (1912) for St. Ninnidh's Church in Inishmacsaint (Co. Fermanagh). Thanks to her strict Methodist upbringing, Geddes had an outstanding command of biblical literature that she blended with her modern interpretations of religious themes and Celtic iconography. Her artistic mixture of myth and symbol can be seen in her allegories of the Presbyterian Church of Townsend, Belfast.[98] Even though she had expressed no interest in nationalism, following the inauguration of her window for Ottawa in 1919, she received a letter from the rector that said: "I do not know what Ireland means to you, but if you love Ireland I am sure that you will be glad". The commission was also described as a "triumph of Irish art" by the publication *Irish Life*.[99]

Although occasionally her manner had brought up controversy (as it happened in All Saints' Church, Laleham, where her window was placed at the back of the church in order to avoid "disturbing the congregation"),[100] her stained glass for the King Albert Memorial (1936–1938) in Belgium was considered one of the most important projects of the century in this technique.[101] Thomas MacGreevy also regarded Geddes, along with Jack B. Yeats, as the most "truly religious" of modern Irish artists.[102] She has been compared to Harry Clarke due to her capacity to synthesise the Irish tradition and her unique vision of Christian and Celtic heritage past towards modernism, and praised as one of the most inventive and talented artists of the Irish Arts and Crafts. Geddes often tended to suppress any detail that could divert the attention from the drama and strength of her figurative compositions. Her works were influenced by the Hiberno-Romanesque architecture of Ireland as well as by her meticulous antiquarian research, which developed in windows of especial Irish character (e.g., *The Fate of the Children of Lir,* 1930). Geddes had visited the great Gothic cathedrals of France, whose "archaic figures (of the thirteenth century)" she considered "not only more impressive, but more modern than anything that has been done since in the same medium".[103] Through her provocative use of colour, her Expressionist brushwork and her exaggerated chiaroscuro, Geddes explored the limits and potential of stained-glass and displayed imaginative interpretations of religious and historical topics in a modernist manner, becoming a progressive artist and a pioneer in the Irish crafts. When she died in 1955, *The Irish Times* described her as "the finest stained glass artist of our time", acclaiming her work as a "revival of the medieval genius".[104] Her *Crucifixion* (1922) was defined as "the most sincerely, passionately religious stained glass of our time",[105] although since then she has been largely forgotten.

Evie Hone was another artist who helped leading the studio's style into a more modern direction.[106] She was employed as Geddes's assistant in 1933, becoming one of the youngest members to have direct involvement with the decoration of churches and cathedrals in An Túr Gloine. Born in 1894 to a family of painters and artists, Hone studied in Ireland, England and finally France along with her lifelong friend Mainie Jellett, with whom she explored the philosophy and the manner of the Cubists under the teachings of Lhote and Gleizes. Hone's main stained-glass subject matters were religious and nationalist symbols which she depicted in blocks of bright colours, although in a less-abstract style than her paintings. She was an artist of Anglo-Irish Protestant background in search of an Irish Catholic identity, which probably explains why she refused to create cultural stereotypes through her work. She focused instead on a powerfully innovative, Expressionist style of strong colours, skilful technique and heavy symbolism that gained her both national and international recognition. Hone's interest in national issues and her search for an artistic expression of a national identity was clearly addressed in one of her most famous windows, *My Four Fields Green*, commissioned for the New York World Trade Fair in 1939. The window depicts the four provinces of Ireland through heraldic symbols in Hone's Cubist style, and nowadays it is displayed in the Government Buildings in Dublin.

In the early years of An Túr Gloine, the patronage of the stained-glass revival came from two sources: St. Enda's Church in Spiddal (Galway) and Loughrea Cathedral.[107] The latter became a showpiece for the crafters both from Dun Emer Guild and An Túr Gloine. This became the cooperative's first major project, executed under the guidance of Edward Martyn.[108] The Cathedral hosted stained-glass windows designed by Child himself, Michael Healy,

Sarah Purser, Catherine O'Brien and Evie Hone, as well as an *opus sectile* of the Stations of the Cross by Ethel Rind. The windows of the building portray the whole history of An Túr Gloine, from the first stained-glass of Sarah Purser to the window created by Evie Hone in 1941 depicting St. Brigid in an act of compassion offering bread to a starving peasant girl.[109] It was the first cathedral that was decorated under the influence of the new ideals carried out in the cooperatives and guilds of the crafts revival. Purser's little window of St. Brendan, in Loughrea, was, however, one of the very few windows of her creation.[110] Although she participated as an artist in the first years of An Túr Gloine with early works like her *Naomh Colmcille* (St. Columcille, 1910) or a window of the *King Cormac of Cashel* (1906) for the St. Patrick's Cathedral in Dublin, she gradually focused on managing the studio and continued canvassing for the development of the arts in Ireland, becoming a central figure in the foundation of the Dublin Municipal Gallery of Modern Art. Despite her duties managing An Túr Gloine and campaigning in the cultural arena, Purser found time to continue her painting career. Between 1903 and 1916, she showed annually at least two portraits at the Royal Hibernian Academy, plus ten other pictures. She was the first woman to be elected a full academician of the Royal Hibernian Academy in 1925, a year after Thomas MacGreevy criticised the Royal Hibernian Academy's attitude towards women.[111] A strong and independent spirit, Purser paved the way for many women to become independent professional artists. Until her death at the age of ninety-four she made significant contributions in the development of the Arts and Crafts. She fought tirelessly for a change in the status of craftsmanship and successfully managed An Túr Gloine, turning it into the most durable project of the Arts and Crafts Movement in Ireland.

# NOTES

1. Fiona MacCarthy, *Anarchy and Beauty. William Morris and his Legacy, 1860–1960* (New Haven and London: Yale University Press, 2015), 59

2. Vera Kreilkamp, *The Arts and Crafts Movement: Making it Irish* (Chicago: University of Chicago Press, 2016), 9

3. See Francis O'Gorman (ed.), *The Cambridge Companion to John Ruskin* (Cambridge: Cambridge University Press, 2015); Lawrence Goldman, *From Art to Politics: John Ruskin and William Morris* (London: William Morris Society, 2005); Tim Hilton, *John Ruskin* (New Haven: Yale University Press, 2002).

4. Wolfgang Kemp, *The Desire of my Eyes. The Life and Work of John Ruskin* (New York: Farrar, Straus and Giroux, 1900), 238–240.

5. See the aforementioned Fiona MacCarthy, *Anarchy and Beauty. William Morris and his Legacy, 1860–1960* (New Haven and London: Yale University Press, 2015); Charles Harvey and John Press, *William Morris. Design and Enterprise in Victorian Britain* (Manchester: Manchester University Press, 1991); William S. Peterson, *The Kelmscott*

*Press. A History of William Morris's Typographical Adventure* (Oxford: Oxford University Press, 1991).

6. Harvey and Press, 237.

7. MacCarthy, *Anarchy and Beauty,* 19–36.

8. See William S. Peterson, *The Kelmscott Press: A History of William Morris's Typographical Adventure* (Berkeley: Oxford University Press, 1991).

9. Elizabeth Prettejohn, *The Cambridge Companion to the Pre-Raphaelites* (New York: Cambridge University Press, 2012), 218.

10. Gordon Bowe, "The Irish Arts and Crafts Movement", 175.

11. Sheehy, *The Rediscovery of Ireland's Past,* 149.

12. See Róisín Kennedy, "Native Traditions and Modern Imperatives: Mexico and Ireland in the Imagination of Ernie O'Malley", in *Art History After Françoise Henry – 50 Years at UCD, 1965–2015,* eds. Carla Briggs, Nicky Figgis, Lynda Mulvin and Paula Murphy (Dublin: Gandon Editions, 2016), 126–139.

13. Quoted in Gordon Bowe, "The Irish Arts and Crafts Movement", 174.

14. Lloyd Laing and Jennifer Laing, *The Archaeology of Celtic Britain and Ireland. Art and Society* (London: The Herbert Press, 1995), 174.

15. Gordon Bowe, "The Irish Arts and Crafts Movement", 175.

16. Gordon Bowe, "The Irish Arts and Crafts Movement", 175.

17. Maria Luddy et al, "An Agenda for Women's History in Ireland, 1500–1900", *Irish Historical Studies,* vol. 28, no. 109 (May 1992), 32–33.

18. See Maureen Keane, *Ishbel: Lady Aberdeen in Ireland* (Newtownards: Colourpoint, 1999).

19. Sheehy, *The Rediscovery of Ireland's Past,* 147.

20. Larmour, *The Arts and Crafts Movement in Ireland,* 50.

21. Quoted in Maggie M. Williams, *Icons of Irishness from the Middle Ages to the Modern World* (New York: Palgrave Macmillan, 2012), 59.

22. Cathy Hartley, *A Historical Dictionary of British Women* (London: Europa Publications Limited, 1983), 1.

23. "Report on the Art and Crafts Society", *Cork Daily Herald* (May 27th 1901). Quoted in Vera Ryan, *Made in Cork. The Arts and Crafts Movement, 1880s-1920s* (Dublin: Gandon Editions, 2017), 5.

24. Horace Plunkett, "The Arts and Crafts Society of Ireland". Quoted in Cahill, "Crafting culture, fabricating identity", 33.

25. *First Journal and Proceedings of the Arts and Crafts Society of Ireland* (Dublin, 1896). Quoted in Nicola Gordon Bowe, "The Arts and Crafts Society of Ireland (1894–1925) with particular reference to Harry Clarke", *The Journal of the Decorative Arts Society 1850–the Present, no. 9, Aspects of British Design 1870–1930* (1985): 31.

26. Larmour, *The Arts and Crafts Movement in Ireland,* 58.

27. Larmour, 73.

28. Quoted in Gordon Bowe, "The Arts and Crafts Society of Ireland", 32.

29. Gordon Bowe, 29–30.

30. John Turpin, *A School of Art in Dublin since the Eighteenth Century: A History of the*

*National College of Art and Design* (Dublin: Gill and Macmillan, 1995), 197.

31. "Senator's gift to the Seanad". Seanad Éireann debate (November 26th 1924) 1924, accessed on May 12th 2020, https://www.oireachtas.ie/en/debates/debate/seanad/1924-11-26/8/

32. Patrick Crotty, "Swordsmen: W.B. Yeats and Hugh MacDiarmid", in *Modern Irish and Scottish Poetry,* ed. Peter Mackay et al (Cambridge: Cambridge University Press, 2011), 20; and Roche, *The Irish Dramatic Revival,* 7.

33. See Joan Hardwick, *The Yeats Sisters: A Biography of Susan and Elizabeth Yeats* (London: Pandora, 1996); Gifford Lewis, *The Yeats Sisters and the Cuala* (Dublin: Irish Academic Press, 1994).

34. Larmour, *The Arts and Crafts Movement in Ireland,* 151.

35. Peter Faulkner, "Dark Days in Hammersmith: Lily Yeats and the Morrises", *Journal of William Morris Studies,* vol. 11, no. 3 (Autumn 1995): 23.

36. "Yeats, Elizabeth Corbet", *Drawn to the Page. Irish Artists and Illustration 1830–1930.* Trinity College (2017), accessed on May 12th 2020, https://dttp.tcd.ie/artist/46

37. Sheehy, *The Rediscovery of Ireland's Past,* 158.

38. William Murphy, *Family Secrets, William Butler Yeats and his Relatives* (New York: Syracuse University Press, 1995), 89.

39. Caoilfhionn Ní Bheacháin, "The Dun Emer Press", *Modernist Archives Publishing Project,* accessed on May 12th 2020, https://www.modernistarchives.com/business/the-dun-emer-press

40. Quoted in Gordon Bowe and Cumming, *The Arts and Crafts Movements,* 124.

41. Dalton, *Irish Women Artists,* 20–23.

42. Ní Bheacháin, "The Dun Emer Press", *Modernist Archives* Website.

43. John Strachan and Claire Nally, *Advertising, Literature and Print Culture in Ireland, 1891–1922* (Hampshire: Palgrave Macmillan, 2012), 192.

44. Ní Bheacháin, "The Dun Emer Press", *Modernist Archives* Website.

45. William Butler Yeats, *In the Seven Woods* (Dublin: Dun Emer, 1903).

46. Gordon Bowe and Cumming. *The Arts and Crafts Movements,* 125.

47. Quoted in Strachan and Nally, *Advertising, Literature and Print Culture,* 192.

48. Marjorie Howes, "The Arts and Crafts Movement and the Irish Literary Revival", in *The Arts and Crafts Movement: Making it Irish,* ed. Vera Kreilkamp (Chicago: University of Chicago Press, 2016), 45–56.

49. Quoted in Strachan and Nally, *Advertising, Literature and Print Culture,* 195.

50. Dalton, *Irish Women Artists,* 20.

51. Hardwick, *The Yeats Sisters,* 111.

52. Elaine Cheasley Patterson, "Crafting a National Identity: The Dun Emer Guild, 1902–1908", *The Irish Review Reappraised,* eds. Betsey Taylor FitzSimon and James H. Murphy (Dublin: Four Courts Press, 2004), 110.

53. Quoted in Strachan and Nally, *Advertising, Literature and Print Culture,* 193.

54. James Joyce (1922), *Ulysses* (Dublin: Random House, 1961), p 12.

55. Lewis, *The Yeats Sisters and the Cuala,* 40.

56. Nicola Gordon Bowe, "Two Early Twentieth-Century Irish Arts and Crafts

Workshops in Context: An Túr Gloine and the Dun Emer Guild and Industries', in *Journal of Design History* 2, no. 2–3 (1989), 197.

57. Netzer, "Cloths of Ireland's New 'Golden Age'", 103.

58. Robin Skelton, "Twentieth-Century Irish Literature and the Private Press Tradition: Dun Emer, Cuala and Dolmen Presses, 1902–1963", *The Massachusetts Review,* vol. 5, no. 2 (Winter 1964): 370.

59. Brown, *The Yeats Circle,* 55.

60. Quoted in Strachan and Nally, *Advertising, Literature and Print Culture,* 192.

61. Skelton, "Twentieth-Century Irish Literature", 370.

62. Strachan and Nally, *Advertising, Literature and Print Culture,* 197.

63. Skelton, "Twentieth-Century Irish Literature", 370.

64. Strachan and Nally, *Advertising, Literature and Print Culture,* 193.

65. Kreilkamp, *The Arts and Crafts Movement,* 20.

66. Michael F. Suarez and Henry R. Woudhuysen, *The Oxford Companion to the Book, vol. 1* (Oxford: Oxford University Press, 2010), 681.

67. Simone Murray, "The Cuala Press: Women, Publishing and the Conflicted Genealogies of Feminist Publishing", *Women's Studies International Forum,* 27, no. 5/6 (2004): 492.

68. See John O'Grady, *The Life and Work of Sarah Purser* (Dublin: Four Courts Press, 1996).

69. O'Grady, *The Life and Work of Sarah Purser,* 31, 143.

70. O'Grady, 51.

71. O'Grady, 53.

72. O'Grady, 53–54.

73. O'Grady, 41.

74. Glenavy, *Today We Will Only Gossip,* 43.

75. Glenavy, 43.

76. "Miss Maud Gonne", Hugh Lane Municipal Gallery, accessed on May 13th 2020, http://emuseum.pointblank.ie/online_catalogue/work-detail.php?objectid=1675

77. O'Grady, *The Life and Work of Sarah Purser,* 60.

78. Arnold, *A Concise History of Irish Art,* 130.

79. O'Grady, *The Life and Work of Sarah Purser,* 222.

80. Dalton, *Irish Women Artists,* 18.

81. Sheehy, *The Rediscovery of Ireland's Past,* 155.

82. Quoted in O'Grady, *The Life and Work of Sarah Purser,* 94.

83. Nicola Gordon Bowe. "The Tower of Glass. An Túr Gloine and the Early Twentieth Century Stained Glass Revival in Ireland", in Building Conservation(2008), accessed on May 13th 2020, https://www.buildingconservation.com/articles/towerofglass/towerofglass.htm

84. Denis Gwynn, *Edward Martyn and the Irish Revival* (New York: Lemma Pub. Corp., 1930), 232.

85. Gordon Bowe, "The Tower of Glass"

86. O'Grady, The Life and Work of Sarah Purser, 101.

87. O'Grady, 101.
88. O'Grady, 101.
89. See Nicola Gordon Bowe, *The Life and Work of Harry Clarke* (Dublin: Irish Academic Press, 1994).
90. See Thomas David Caron, *An Túr Gloine and Michael Healy (1873–1941)* (Dublin: Trinity College Dublin, 1991).
91. Kreilkamp, *The Arts and Crafts Movement,* 119.
92. Trevor Roycroft, "Belleek Earthenware Plaque – Antwerp Belgium by Beatrice Elvery (Lady Glenavy)", in UK Belleek Collector's Group Newsletter, vol. 29, no. 3 (2008): 40–41.
93. Pauric J. Dempsey and Bridget Hourican, "Campbell, Beatrice Moss", in *Dictionary of Irish Biography,* accessed on May 13th 2020, https://dib.cambridge.org/viewReadPage.do;jsessionid=89772CF21263FB243273BF2F8E620070?articleId=a1410
94. Glenavy, *Today We will Only Gossip,* 40.
95. Gordon Bowe, "The Tower of Glass".
96. See Nicola Gordon Bowe, *Wilhelmina Geddes: Life and Work* (Dublin: Four Courts Press, 2015).
97. Nicola Gordon Bowe, "The Jewel in the Crown: The Art of Stained Glass in the Irish Arts and Crafts Movement, 1903–30", in *The Arts and Crafts Movement. Making it Irish,* ed. Vera Kreilkamp (Chicago: University of Chicago Press, 2016), 121.
98. Shirley Ann Brown, "Wilhelmina Geddes' Ottawa Window", *Irish Arts Review,* vol. 10 (1994): 181–188.
99. Quoted in Catherine Marshall, "Captured By Light", *Dublin Review of Books,* accessed on May 13th 2020, https://www.drb.ie/essays/captured-by-light-old
100. Mayes and Murphy. *Images and Insights,* 100.
101. Marshall, "Captured by Light", in *Dublin Review of Books* Website.
102. Thomas MacGreevy, "Stained Glass at An Túr Gloine", *The Irish Statesman* (December 13th 1924): 435.
103. Wilhelmina Geddes in "Making Stained Glass Windows", *Belfast News-Letter* (September 25th 1930). Quoted in Nicola Gordon Bowe, "Wilhelmina Geddes, Harry Clarke, and Their Part in the Arts and Crafts Movement in Ireland", *The Journal of Decorative and Propaganda Arts,* vol. 8 (Sprint 1988): 66.
104. Gordon Bowe, "The Tower of Glass", Building Conservation Website.
105. Thomas MacGreevy, "'Religious Art and Modern Ireland", *The Gaelic Churchman* (April 1922): 128–129.
106. Frost, *A Tribute to Evie Hone and Mainie Jellett,* 28.
107. Barrett and Sheehy, "Visual Arts and Society, 1900–21", 491.
108. Myra Hayes. *Seeing Ourselves in Stained Glass. A Comparative Study of Nineteenth and Twentieth Century Irish Stained Glass* (Limerick: University of Limerick, 2014), 101.
109. Thomas MacGreevy, "St. Brendan's Cathedral, Loughrea. 1897–1947", in *The Capuchin Annual* (1946–47): 353–373.
110. Gordon Bowe, "The Tower of Glass", Building Conservation Website.
111. Dalton, *Irish Women Artists,* 16.

# Afterword

The Irish Revival never witnessed the development of the national school of art that Thomas Davis campaigned for. Jeanne Sheehy has remarked that "there was no distinctive Irish style, and the Irish Revival did not pass on a living tradition in art as it did in literature",[1] and Hilary Pyle has observed that Irish art has always been marked by the authors' individualistic manners.[2] Even the Irish Exhibition of Living Art, which meant the development of a vibrant school of painting in Ireland, did not offer a common feature amongst the artists except for "the vital and progressive character of those independents".[3] This diversity is, indeed, what made the Irish artistic scene of the early twentieth century so fascinating. Each artist contributed in their own personal way to the complexity of discourse of the Irish cultural arena. In the end, the Irish school of painting developed in the Revival was, as Bruce Arnold described it, "the awkward strands of creative excellence not tied to the evocation of a harmonious world narrowly conforming to norms".[4] The IELA, however, did achieve Hugh Lane's goals. It established a dialogue between Modernism and tradition, the Irish heritage and the European trends. The development of this multifaceted artistic scene was only possible thanks to the innovations motivated by the artists explored in this book.

In 1950, the twenty-fifth Venice Biennale was inaugurated by Guido Gonnella. Amongst the contemporary artists who showed their work at the venue were the North Americans Jackson Pollock and Willem de Kooning, and the Mexican muralists Diego Rivera and David Alfaro Siqueiros. It was the first time that Ireland participated in the Biennale, and the country was represented by two important artists: Nano Reid and Norah McGuinness. The fact that two women had been chosen to show at the venue was rather overlooked; the *Irish Times* did not review the exhibition, and neither Reid nor McGuinness were mentioned by the British press.[5] However, their presence in the venue offered a new concept about Ireland's cultural identity, which developed throughout the century. Irish conservative art was being more challenged than ever by artists like Reid and McGuinness. In contrast with the idealisation of the west and the peasantry encouraged by the government of the Irish Free State, Irish artists of the mid-twentieth century began to focus on Dublin's "cosmopolitism". This encouraged the foundation and development of the Irish Exhibition of Living Art, whose direction was taken over by Norah McGuinness following the death of Mainie Jellett and until 1971. Curator David Britton has argued that the involvement of McGuinness and Reid in the Biennale was the voice of the Irish government saying: "Ireland is modern, we are progressive".[6] But was Ireland truly modern and progressive? Indeed, the participation of Reid and McGuinness in the Biennale meant another step in the country's path toward modernism. However, according to James White, the critics at the Biennale "were amazed to learn that Nano Reid was a woman".[7] This was a statement about a woman's place within the European avant-garde in the second half of the twentieth century. Female discrimination was not exclusive to the Abstract movement; even Surrealist art, a rather subversive and revolutionary trend, did not welcome women artists into its ranks. Surrealist painters like Remedios Varo or Leonora Carrington did not conform to the movement's ideal of the passive female muse, and subverted the Surrealist principles in order to become masters of their own creativity. Irish female artists of the second half of the twentieth century followed the same line.

The new generation of Irish artists were highly inspired by their predecessors. Mainie Jellett, May Guinness and Evie Hone were amongst those who had paved the way for new forms of expressions in Irish art. Norah McGuinness herself went to France and studied with André Lhote on Jellett's advice.[8] At her return, she developed a Fauvist manner influenced by Cubist principles. Nano Reid did not stick to Jellett's Cubist manner, and favoured a more Expressionist style. However, she often portrayed her beloved Boyne Valley, impregnated of important prehistoric Celtic heritage. Celtic crosses and megalithic tombs were recurrently included in her landscapes of Connemara, Donegal and Achill. However, the female artists who came to maturity in the 1940s held significant differences with the previous generation of painters. According to Fionna Barber, they personified a new type of woman in Ireland, developed after the foundation of the Irish Free State. These artists did not come from privileged backgrounds. They were middle-class, and chose an artistic career as a way of earning a living rather than in search of their own self-realisation. And they did not come from Anglo-Irish families.[9] They established themselves as professional artists in a time when Ireland was facing the economic and psychological consequences of the war. Commissions were scarce, and the heroic feeling inherent to the arts of the Revival had disappeared.[10] Nano Reid's portrayal of Irish subject matters linked Irishness with rural poverty, an image of an isolated country badly affected by the post-war economic consequences and the political instability.

Later, the Troubles marked a period of violence remarkably addressed in Micheal Farrell's *Madonna Irlanda: or The Very First Real Irish Political Picture* (1977).[11] The painting, a reinterpretation of Mother Ireland as a haloed prostitute, also speaks out about the treatment of women in the country. Ireland, highly influenced by Irish Catholicism, became an extremely polarised nation that emphasised women's domestic roles as wives and mothers. This also affected women artists and the whole artistic arena. With the retirement of May Guinness from the IELA in 1970, the organisation became an all-male committee, with the number of women showing their work dropping drastically.[12] However, female symbols such as the Virgin Mother or Mother Ireland had already been recognised for the "controlling and delimiting purpose they serve".[13] Through religious subject-matters, painters like Mainie Jellett, Mary Swanzy and Beatrice Elvery had begun to denounce the nationalist and Catholic rhetoric, and this continued to be challenged by the new generations throughout the century. The status of the visual arts in Ireland changed as the twentieth century passed, thanks to the growth of art colleges and venues (the Douglas Hyde Gallery or the Irish Museum of Modern Art amongst others), the foundation of the Arts Council in 1951 and the establishment of art history department in Trinity College Dublin and University College Dublin.[14]

Significant changes from the 1970s onwards, such as the accession of Ireland to the European Economic Community in 1972, paved the way for a more progressive country. Contemporary artists welcomed the outside influences and, at the same time, addressed contemporary issues such as gender and the Partition of Ireland.[15] Female artists have focused on issues like motherhood, sexuality and female allegories; they have explored the relationship between mother and daughter rather than between mother and son. And they have begun to replace the political and religious symbols that portrayed women as patronised and powerless.[16] In the 1990s, several exhibitions explored the connection between local and global and established a dialogue between the Irish past and the present. Vera Kreilkamp has highlighted the importance of two key shows in particular: "In a State" (1991) and "Re/Dressing Cathleen" (1997). The first one was held in Kilmainham Gaol, the site of the execution of the 1916 rebels. This symbolic venue displayed works by Alice Maher and Dorothy Cross that engaged with national identity. Cross had already criticised the nation's obsession with Mother Ireland in her show *Matriarchal* (1982). The second exhibition was also particularly relevant, as thirteen women artists "redressed" the traditional female allegories of Irish nationalism. In this show, held at the McMullen Museum of Modern Art (Boston), Rita Duffy exhibited *Becoming* (1995), a satirical portrayal of the sacred mother figure, in which an Irish woman appears draining her dead child in a colander. Kathleen Prendergast showed *Body Maps* (1983), an early series of work that address issues of colonisation by bringing together two key themes of the Irish Revival: the landscape and the female body. The body of work of Rita Duffy, Kathleen Prendergast, Alice Maher and Dorothy Cross, amongst others, offers a more confrontational perspective, especially regarding gender imagery. The exhibition *Irish Women Artists: From the Eighteenth Century to the Present Day* (National

Gallery of Ireland and Douglas Hyde Gallery, 1983) highlighted a key feature shared by the Irish Revival and contemporary visual arts: the high number of female artists in Ireland.

As Luke Gibbons states, "the function of art is not simply to represent people, but to empower people, to make people agents of their own representation".[17] Timeless art does not accept, but questions. It does not conform, but challenges. It evolves with society, and society evolves with it. The artists explored in this book carried out a quiet revolution in Irish art, some of them maybe even without being aware of it. They left an important legacy behind, which until very recently has been largely ignored. Recent publications and remarkable exhibitions on women artists have provided a wonderful material for further studies on women's cultural role in the Irish Revival and the revolutionary years. These women spoke out through their art, but also through their professional careers. They stepped into the public sphere, into the artistic institutions, and reclaimed a voice of their own. Their art was not unidirectional, but a compendium of individual expressions. Their creations became a dialogue between their past and their present; tradition and modernism; absence and presence.

# NOTES

1. Sheehy, *The Rediscovery of Ireland's Past,* 188.
2. Pyle, Hilary, *Irish Art, 1900–1950. Exhibition Catalogue* (Cork: Crawford Art Gallery, 1975), 9–16.
3. Elizabeth Curran, "Introduction", *Contemporary Irish Painting,* catalogue of an exhibition at Rhode Island, Boston and Ottawa (1950), 10.
4. Bruce Arnold, "Jack Yeats and the Making of Irish Art in the Twentieth Century", in *When Time Began to Rant and Rage. Figurative Painting from Twentieth-Century Ireland,* ed. James Christen Steward (Berkeley: Merrell Holberton, 1998), 54.
5. See Fionna Barber, "Excavating Room 50: Irish Painting and the Cold War at the 1950 Venice Biennale", in *A Shared Legacy: Essays on Irish and Scottish Art and Visual Adventure,* ed. Fintan Cullen and John Morrison (London and New York: Routledge, 2005), 207–219.
6. Chris Morrison, "Celebrating a Century of Irish Women's Art", *The Irish News* (July 31st 2014), accessed on May 10th 2020, http://www.irishnews.com/lifestyle/2014/07/31/news/celebrating-a-century-of-irish-women-s-art-98106/
7. Barber, "Excavating Room 50", 214.
8. Hartigan. "Irish Women Painters and the Introduction of Modernism", 73–76.
9. Barber, "Excavating Room 50", 210.
10. James Christen Steward, "The Irishness of Irish Painting", in *When Time Began to Rant and Rage: Figurative Painting of Twentieth-Century Ireland*" (Berkeley: Merrell Holberton, 1998), 21.

11. O'Toole, *Modern Ireland in 100 Artworks,* 184–186.

12. Éimear O'Connor (ed.), *Irish Women Artists, 1800–2009. Familiar but Unknown* (Dublin: Four Courts Press, 2010), 33.

13. Murphy, "Madonna and Maiden, Mistress and Mother", 100.

14. Fintan Cullen, "The Visual Arts in Ireland", in *The Cambridge Companion to Modern Irish Culture,* ed. Joe Cleary and Claire Connolly (Cambridge: Cambridge University Press, 2005), 315

15. Cullen, 315.

16. Murphy, "Madonna and Maiden, Mistress and Mother", 98.

17. Luke Gibbons, "Censorship and the Arts", in *Let In the Light: Censorship, Secrecy and Democracy,* ed. Patrick Smyth and Ellen Hazelkorn (Kerry: Brandon Books, 1993), 123.

# References

"Kathleen Fox (1880–1963). Ruins of the Four Courts", *Important Irish Art* (Adam's, October 1st 2014), 184. Irish Art", Adam's (October 1st 2014), 184–185.

"Markievicz, Constance de, 1868–1927". *National Library of Ireland Catalogue.* Prints and Drawings.

Allen, Richard and Trivedi, Harish. *Literature and Nation. Britain and India, 1800–1990.* New York: Routledge, 2000.

Allison, Jonathan. "Yeats and Politics". In *The Cambridge Companion to W. B. Yeats,* edited by Marjorie Howes and John Kelly, 185–205. Cambridge: Cambridge University Press, 2006.

Aodh de Blacam, "Mary of the Gael", in *The Irish Monthly,* vol. 67 (August 1939): 577–586

Armstrong Duffy, Shirley. "The role of women in Irish sketching clubs in the late nineteenth century". In *Irish Women Artists from the Eighteenth Century to the Present Day,* edited by Jenni Rogers, Wanda Ryan-Smolin and Elizabeth Mayes, 12–14. Dublin: National Gallery of Ireland and the Douglas Hyde Gallery, 1987.

Armstrong, Gordon S. *Samuel Beckett, W. B. Yeats and Jack Yeats: Images and Words.* London: Associated University Press, 1990.

Arnold, Bruce. "Jack Yeats and the Making of Irish Art in the Twentieth Century". In *When Time Began to Rant and Rage. Figurative Painting from Twentieth-Century Ireland,* edited by James Christen Steward, 52–62. Berkeley: Merrell Holberton, 1998.

Arnold, Bruce. *A Concise History of Irish Art.* London: Thames and Hudson, 1977.

Arnold, Bruce. *Mainie Jellett and the Modern Movement in Ireland.* New Haven: Yale University Press, 1991.

Arnold, Bruce. *Mainie Jellett, 1897–1944.* Dublin: Irish Museum of Modern Art, 1991.

Arrington, Lauren. *Revolutionary Lives. Constance and Casimir Markievicz.* Princeton: Princeton University Press, 2016.

Bain, Rowan et al. *May Morris. Art and Life. Exhibition Catalogue.* London: William Morris Gallery, 2018.

Banerjee, Sikata. *Muscular Nationalism. Gender, Violence and Empire in India and Ireland, 1914–2004.* New York: New York University Press, 2012.

Barber, Fionna. "Excavating Room 50: Irish Painting and the Cold War at the 1950 Venice Biennale". In *A Shared Legacy: Essays on Irish and Scottish Art and Visual Adventure,* edited by Fintan Cullen and John Morrison, 207–219. London and New York: Routledge, 2005.

Barber, Fionna. "Race, Irishness and Art History. Margaret Clarke's Bathtime at the Crèche, Motherhood and the Matter of Whiteness". *In Narratives Unfolding: National Art Histories in An Unfinished World,* edited by Martha Langford, 62–80. Montreal and Kingston: McGill-Queen's University Press, 2017.

Barrett, Cyril and Sheehy, Jeanne. "Visual Arts and Society, 1900–21". In *A New History of Ireland Under the Union, 1870–1921,* edited by William Edward Vaughan, 475–499. Oxford: Oxford University Press, 2010.

Barrett, Cyril. "Irish Nationalism and Art II: 1900–1970". *Studies: An Irish Quarterly Review,* vol. 91, no. 363 (2002): 223–238.

Beaumont, Caitriona. "Women, Citizenship and Catholicism in the Irish Free State (1922–1948)". *Women's History Review,* vol. 6, no. 4 (1997): 563–585.

Benson, Ciarán. "Modernism and Ireland Selves". *Circa,* 61 (January/February 2002): 18–23.

Bhreathnach-Lynch, Síghle. "Framing Ireland's History: Art, Politics and Representation 1914–1929". In *When Time Began to Rant and Rage: Figurative Painting from Twentieth Century Ireland,* edited by James Christen Steward, 40–51. Berkeley: Merrell Holberton, 1998.

Bhreathnach-Lynch, Síghle. "Landscape, Space and Gender. Their Role in the Construction of Female Identity in Newly Independent Ireland". *Canadian Women Studies,* vol. 17, 3 (1997): 26–30.

Bhreathnach-Lynch, Síghle. *Ireland's Art, Ireland's History: Representing Ireland, 1845 to Present.* Dublin: Creighton University Press, 2007.

Bhreathnach-Lynch, Síghle. "Imagining the Past: The Marriage of Strongbow and Aoife". *The Irish Review,* no. 29 (2002): 95–104.

Boland, Eavan. *Object Lessons. The Life of the Woman and the Poet in Our Time.* New York: Norton, 1996.

Bourke, Marie. *West of Ireland Paintings at the National Gallery of Ireland from 1800 to 2000.* Dublin: National Gallery of Ireland, 2014.

Bowles, Noelle. "Nationalism and Feminism in Lady Gregory's 'Kicora', 'Devorgilla', and 'Grania'". In *New Hibernia Review / Iris Éireannach Nua,* vol. 3, no. 3 (Autumn, 1999): 116–130.

Bradley, Anthony and Valiulis, Maryann Gialanella (Eds.). *Gender and Sexuality in Modern Ireland.* Massachusetts: University of Massachusetts Press, 1997.

Briggs, Carla. "Margaret Clarke as a History Painter". In *Irish Women Artists, 1800–2009. Familiar but Unknown,* edited by Éimear O'Connor, 62–80. Dublin: Four Courts Press, 2010.

Briggs, Carla. "Out of the Shadows". *Irish Art Review,* vol. 31, no. 2 (Summer 2017): 276–280.

Briggs, Carla. *Margaret Clarke. An Independent Spirit.* Exhibition Catalogue Essay. Dublin: National Gallery of Ireland, 2017.

Broderick, Marian. *Wild Irish Women. Extraordinary Lives from History.* Dublin: The O'Brien Press, 2012.

Brown, Karen E. "Thomas MacGreevy and Irish Modernism: Between Word and Image". In *Irish Modernism: Origins, Contexts, Publics,* 95–100. New York: Bern, 2010.

Brown, Karen E. *The Yeats Circle. Verbal and Visual Relations in Ireland, 1880–1939.* London: Routledge, 2011.

Brown, Shirley Ann. "Wilhelmina Geddes' Ottawa Window". *Irish Arts Review,* vol. 10 (1994): 181–188.

Bruce Arnold. "Jack Yeats and the Making of Irish Art in the Twentieth Century". In *When Time Began to Rant and Rage. Figurative Painting from Twentieth-Century Ireland,* edited by James Christen Steward, 52–62. Berkeley: Merrell Holberton, 1998.

Bruce, Arnold. "Mainie Jellett and Modernism". In *Irish Women Artists from the Eighteenth Century to the Present Day,* edited by Jenni Rogers, Wanda Ryan-Smolin and Elizabeth Mayes, 30–33. Dublin: The National Gallery of Ireland and Douglas Hyde Gallery, 1987.

Butler, Mary E. L. "Womanhood and its mission. Part 2". *Dublin University Magazine,* Vol. 53, no. 318, (May 1859): 623–640.

Cahill, Katherine. "In the Mainstream of Irish Naturalism: The Art of Lilian Lucy Davidson". *Irish Art Review Yearbook,* vol. 15 (1999): 34–45.

Cahill, Susan Elizabeth. "Crafting Culture, Fabricating Identity. Gender and Textiles in Limerick Lace, Clare Embroidery and the Deerfield Society of Blue and White Needlework", Master diss. Ontario: Queen's University, 2007.

Campbell, Julian. "Art Students and Lady Travellers". In *Irish Women Artists from the Eighteenth Century to the Present Day,* edited by Jenni Rogers, Wanda Ryan-Smolin and Elizabeth Mayes, 17–21. Dublin: The National Gallery of Ireland and Douglas Hyde Gallery, 1987.

Cardozo, Nancy. *Maud Gonne.* London: Victor Gollanez, 1979.

Caron, Thomas David. *An Túr Gloine and Michael Healy* (1873–1941). Dublin: Trinity College Dublin, 1991.

Carroll, Clare. "The Construction of Gender and the Cultural and Political Order in *The Faerie Queene* 5 and *A View of the Present State of Ireland:* The Critics, the Context and the Case of Radigund". *Criticism,* vol. 32, no. 2 (1990): 163–192.

Cassidy, Constance (ed.). *Countess Markievicz. Prison Poetry and Sketches.* Sligo: Lissadell Press, 2017.

Cassidy, Edel. "Mary Swanzy. Modern Irish Master". *Anthology,* 9 (2018): 36–39.

Cheasley Patterson, Elaine. "Crafting a National Identity: The Dun Emer Guild, 1902–1908".In *The Irish Review Reappraised,* edited by Betsey Taylor FitzSimon and James H. Murphy, 106–118. Dublin: Four Courts Press, 2004.

Clare, Anne. *Unlikely Rebels: The Gifford Girls and the Fight for Irish Freedom.* Cork: Mercier Press, 2011.

Clarke, John. "Kathleen's Story" and "Kathleen Fox Interview". *Footprints,* vol. 32, no. 2 (2017): 5–11.

Cleary, Joe. "Postcolonial Ireland". In *Ireland and the British Empire,* edited by Kevin Kenny. 251–288. Oxford: Oxford University Press, 2004.

Coffey, Thomas M. *Agony at Easter: The 1916 Irish Uprising.* Harmondsworth: PenguinBooks, 1976.

Collins, Lorcan. *Ireland's War of Independence, 1919–21: The IRA's Guerrilla Campaign.* Dublin: O'Brien Press, 2019.

Connolly, Maria and Finucane, Paul. *Journeys Through Line and Colour: Forty Irish Women Artists of the 20th Century.* Limerick: University of Limerick, 2010.

Connolly, Sean J. *Oxford Companion to Irish History.* New York: Oxford University Press, 1998.

Corbet, Mary Jean. *Allegories of Union in Irish and English Writing, 1790–1870: Politics, History and the Family from Edgeworth to Arnold.* Cambridge: Cambridge University Press, 2000.

Cork, Richard. *Vorticism and Abstract Art in the First Machine Age.* Berkeley: University of California, 1976.

Cormican, Anne. "William Orpen (1878–1931): A Voice for Pluralism in the Long Nineteenth Century". In *Travelling Irishness in the Long Nineteenth Century. New Directions in Irish American Literature,* edited by Marguérite Corporaal and Christina Morin, 81–102. New York: Palgrave MacMillan, 2017.

Costigan, Lucy and Cullen, Michael. *Strangest Genius. The Stained Glass of Harry Clarke.* Dublin: The History Press Ireland, 2010.

Crotty, Patrick. "Swordsmen: W.B. Yeats and Hugh MacDiarmid". In *Modern Irish and Scottish Poetry,* edited by Peter Mackay et al, 20–38. Cambridge: Cambridge University Press, 2011.

Cruickshank, James G. "Grace Henry". Irish Arts Review, vol. 9 (1993): 174–178.

Cullen Owens, Rosemary. "Votes for Women". In *The Irish Women's History Reader,* edited by Alan Hayes and Diane Urquhart, 37–43. London: Routledge, 2001.

Cullen, Fintan. "The Visual Arts in Ireland". In *The Cambridge Companion to Modern Irish Culture,* edited by Joe Cleary and Claire Connolly, 304–321. Cambridge: Cambridge University Press, 2005.

Cullen, Fintan. *A Shared Legacy: Essays on Irish and Scottish Art and Visual Culture.* London: Routledge, 2017.

Cullen, Fintan. *Ireland on Show: Art, Union and Nationhood.* New York: Routledge, 2016.

Cullen, Fintan. *Sources in Irish Art: A Reader.* Cork: Cork University Press, 2000.

Cullen, Maria and Luddy, Maria. *Women, Power and Consciousness in Nineteenth Century Ireland.* Dublin: Attick Press, 1995.

Cumming, Elizabeth. *Phoebe Anna Traquair, 1852–1936.* Edinburgh: National Galleries of Scotland, 2020.

Curran, Elizabeth. "Introduction". *Contemporary Irish Painting.* Catalogue of an Exhibition at Rhode Island, Boston and Ottawa.

Cusack, Tricia. "Introduction: Art, Nation and Gender". In *Art, Nation and Gender. Ethnic Landscapes, Myths and Mother-Figures,* edited by Tricia Cusack and Síghle Bhreathnach-Lynch, 1–11. Burlington: Ashgate, 2003.

Dalton, Claire. *Irish Women Artists, 1870–1970.* Dublin: Adam's, 2014.

Daly Mary E. "Women in the Irish Workforce From Pre-Industrial to Modern Times", in *The Irish Women's History Reader,* edited by Alan Hayes and Diane Urquhart, 192–198. London: Routledge, 2001.

Daly, Mary E. "Women and Irish trade Unions". In *The Irish Women's History Reader,* edited by Alan Hayes and Diane Urquhart, 222–228. London: Routledge, 2001.

Daly, Selena. "Mary Swanzy (1882–1978): A Futurist Painter from Ireland". *International Yearbook of Futurism Studies,* vol. 5 (Berlin/Boston: De Gruyter, 2015): 70–86.

Deepwell, Katy. *Dialogues: Women Artists from Ireland.* London and New York: IB Tauris, 2005.

Eavan Boland, "Outside History". *The American Poetry Review,* vol. 19, no. 2 (March/April 1990), 32–38.

Elgenius, Gabriella. *Symbols of Nations and Nationalism. Celebrating Nationhood.* Hampshire: Palgrave Macmillan, 2011.

Fallon, Brian. "Adventures in Art". *Irish Arts Review,* vol. 35, no. 4 (2018/2019): 74–79.

Fallon, Brian. "Swanzy in Samoa". *Irish Arts Review,* vol. 30, no. 4 (2013–2014): 108–113.

Faulkner, Peter. "Dark Days in Hammersmith: Lily Yeats and the Morrises". *Journal of William Morris Studies,* vol. 11, no. 3 (Autumn 1995): 22–25.

Figgis, Nicola (Ed.). *Painting, 1600–1900.Art and Architecture of Ireland. Vol. 2.* London: Yale University Press, 2014.

Finucane, Paul and Connolly Maria. *Journeys Through Line and Colour: Forty Irish Women Artists of the Twentieth Century.* Limerick: Limerick University Press, 2010.

Flam, Jack. *Matisse on Art.* Berkeley: University of California Press, 1995.

Foster, Gavin M. *The Irish Civil War and Society Politics, Class and Conflict.* London: Palgrave Macmillan, 2015.

Frost, Stella. *A Tribute to Evie Hone and Mainie Jellett.* Dublin: Browne and Noland, 1957.

Furman Adams, Wendy and James Tufte, Virginia."Saying it with flowers: Jane Giraud's ecofeminist Paradise Lost (1846)". In *Milton and Gender,* edited by Catherine Gimelly Martin, 223–253. Cambridge: Cambridge University Press, 2005.

Gaze, Delia. *Concise Dictionary of Women Artists.* New York and London: Routledge, 2001.

Gaze, Delia. *Dictionary of Women Artists, vol. 1.* London: Fitzroy Dearborn Publishers, 1997.

Bradley, Anthony and Valiulis, Gialanella (eds.). *Gender and Sexuality in Modern Ireland.* Amherst: University of Massachusetts Press, 1997.

Gibbons, Luke. "Censorship and the Arts". In *Let in the Light: Censorship, Secrecy and Democracy,* edited by Patrick Smyth and Ellen Hazelkorn, 121–124. Kerry: Brandon Books, 1993.

Gibbons, Luke. "Visual Modernisms". In *The Cambridge Companion to Irish Modernism,* edited by Joe Cleary, 128–144. Cambridge: Cambridge University Press, 2014.

Girvin, Brian. "An Irish solution to an Irish problem: Catholicism, contraception and change, 1922–1979". *Contemporary European History,* University of Glasgow, 27, no. 1 (2018): 1–22.

Glassie, Henry. *Irish Folktales.* New York: Pantheon Books, 1985.

Glenavy, Lady Beatrice. *Today we will only gossip.* London: Constable, 1964.

Goldman, Lawrence. *From Art to Politics: John Ruskin and William Morris.* London: The William Morris Society, 2005.

Gordon Bowe, Nicola and Cumming, Elizabeth. *The Arts and Crafts Movements in Dublin and Edinburgh, 1885–1925.* Dublin: Irish Academic Press, 1998.

Gordon Bowe, Nicola. "Preserving the Relics of Heroic Time: Visualizing the Celtic Revival in Early Twentieth-Century Ireland". In *Synge and Edwardian Ireland,* edited by Brian Cliff and Nicholas Greene, 58–83. Oxford: Oxford University Press, 2012.

Gordon Bowe, Nicola. "Symbolism in Turn-of-the-Century Irish Art". *The GPA Irish Arts Review Yearbook* (1989/1990): 133–144.

Gordon Bowe, Nicola. "The art of Beatrice Elvery. Lady Glenavy (1883–1970)". *Irish Arts Review Yearbook,* vol. 11 (1995): 168–175.

Gordon Bowe, Nicola. "The Arts and Crafts Society of Ireland (1894–1925) with particular reference to Harry Clarke". *The Journal of the Decorative*

*Arts Society 1850–the Present,* no. 9, Aspects of British Design 1870–1930 (1985): 29–40.

Gordon Bowe, Nicola. "The Iconic Book in Ireland, 1891–1930". In *The Oxford History of the Irish Book. Vol. 5. The Irish Book in English, 1891–2000,* edited by Clare Hutton and Patrick Walsh, 290–412. Oxford: Oxford University Press, 2011.

Gordon Bowe, Nicola. "The Irish Arts and Crafts Movement (1886–1925)". *Irish Arts Review Yearbook* (1990/1991): 172–185.

Gordon Bowe, Nicola. "The Jewel in the Crown: The Art of Stained Glass in the Irish Arts and Crafts Movement, 1903–30". In *The Arts and Crafts Movement. Making it Irish,* edited by Vera Kreilkamp, 117–126.Chicago: University of Chicago Press, 2016.

Gordon Bowe, Nicola. "Two Early Twentieth-Century Irish Arts and Crafts Workshops in Context: An Túr Gloine and the Dun Emer Guild and Industries". *Journal of Design History,* vol. 2, no. 2–3 (1989): 193–206.

Gordon Bowe, Nicola. "Wilhelmina Geddes, Harry Clarke, and Their Part in the Arts and Crafts Movement in Ireland". *The Journal of Decorative and Propaganda Arts,* vol. 8 (Sprint 1988): 58–79.

Gordon Bowe, Nicola. *The Life and Work of Harry Clarke.* Dublin: Irish Academic Press, 1994.

Gordon Bowe, Nicola. *Wilhelmina Geddes: Life and Work.* Dublin: Four Courts Press, 2015.

Gore-Booth, Eva. *The Death of Fionavar from the Triumph of Maeve.* London: Erskine Macdonald, 1916.

Gray, Breda B. and Ryan, Louise. "Politics of Irish Identity and the Interconnections Between Feminism, Nationhood and Colonialism". In *Nation, Empire, Colony: Historicizing Gender and Race,* edited by Ruth Roach Pierson, 121–138. Indiana: Indiana University Press, 1998.

Gray, Sara. *Dictionary of British Women Artists.* London: The Lutterworth Press, 2009.

Gregory, Lady Augusta. *Seventy Years.* New York: Macmillan, 1976.

Griffith, Angela et al. *Making their Mark: Irish Painters-Etchers and the Etching Revival,* 1880–1930. Dublin: The National Gallery of Ireland, 2019.

Grosz, Elizabeth. *Jacques Lacan. A Feminist Introduction.* London: Routledge, 1990.

Gwynn, Denis. *Edward Martyn and the Irish Revival.* New York: Lemma Pub. Corp., 1930.

Hammond Callaghan, Marie. "Margaret Clarke's Mary and Brigid, 1917. Mother Ireland in Irish Art and Nationalism". *Atlantis: Critical Studies in Gender, Culture and Social Justice,* Mount Saint Vincent University (1998): 99–111.

Hardwick, Joan. *The Yeats Sisters: A Biography of Susan and Elizabeth Yeats.* London: Pandora, 1996.

Hartigan, Marianne. "Irish Women Painters and the Introduction of Modernism". In *When Time Began to Rant and Rage. Figurative Painting from Twentieth-Century Ireland,* edited by James Christen Steward, 63–77. Berkeley: Merrell Holberton, 1998.

Hartley, Cathy. *A Historical Dictionary of British Women.* London: Europa Publications Limited, 1983.

Hartley, Lucy. "Art". In *The Cambridge Companion to John Ruskin,* edited by Francis O'Gorman, 83–99. Cambridge: Cambridge University Press, 2015.

Harvey, Alison. "West Indian Obeah and English 'Obee': Race, Femininity and Questions of Colonial Consolidation in Maria Edgeworth's *Belinda*". In *New Essays on Maria Edgeworth,* edited by Julie Nash, 1–29. London, Routledge: 2018.

Harvey, Charles and Press, John. *William Morris. Design and Enterprise in Victorian Britain.* Manchester: Manchester University Press, 1991).

Haverty, Anne. *Constance Markievicz: Irish Revolutionary.* Dublin: Liliput Press, 2016.

Hayes, Myra. *Seeing Ourselves in Stained Glass. A Comparative Study of Nineteenth and Twentieth Century Irish Stained Glass.* Limerick: University of Limerick, 2014.

Heilmann, Ann and Forward, Stephanie (eds.). *Sex, Social Purity and Sarah Grand,* vol. 1. London: Routledge, 2000.

Heilmann, Ann. "Wilde's New Women. The New Woman on Wilde". In *The Importance of Reinventing Oscar: Versions of Wilde During the Last 100 Years,* edited by Uwe Böker, Richard Corballis, Julie Hibbard, 135–146. Amsterdam: Rodopi, 2002.

Helmreich, Anne. "Domesticating Britannia: Representations of the Nation in Punch: 1870–1880". In *Art, Nation and Gender: Ethnic Landscapes, Myths and Motherfigures,* edited by Tricia Cusack and Síghle Bhreathnach-Lynch, 15–28. Aldershot: Ashgate, 2003.

Hill, Judith. *Lady Gregory. An Irish Life.* Dublin: The Collins Press, 2011.

Hill, Shonagh. *Women and Embodied Mythmaking in Irish Theatre.* Cambridge: Cambridge University Press, 2019.

Hilton, Tim. *John Ruskin.* New Haven and London: Yale University Press, 2002.

Holdeman, David. *The Cambridge Introduction to W. B. Yeats.* Cambridge: Cambridge University Press, 2006.

Howes, Marjorie. "The Arts and Crafts Movement and the Irish Literary Revival". In *The Arts and Crafts Movement: Making it Irish,* edited by Vera Kreilkamp, 45–56. Chicago: University of Chicago Press, 2016.

Howes, Marjorie. *Yeats's Nations: Gender, Class and Irishness.* Cambridge: Cambridge University Press, 1996.

Hyde, Douglas. "The Necessity for De-Anglicising Ireland". In *An Irish Literature Reader. Poetry, Prose, Drama,* edited by Maureen O'Rourke

Murphy and James MacKillop, 139–149. New York: Syracuse University Press, 2006.

Ingman, Heather. *Twentieth-Century Fiction by Irish Women: Nation and Gender.* Hampshire: Ashgate, 2007.

James Christen Steward, "The Irishness of Irish Painting". In *When Time Began to Rant and Rage: Figurative Painting from Twentieth-Century Ireland,* edited by James Christen Steward, 16–22. Berkeley: Merrell Holberton, 1998.

Jarrin, Casey A. "The Prison Gallery: Exhibit Collaboration Between Kilmainham Gaol and Alcatraz". In *Irish Studies: Geographies and Genders,* edited by Marti D. Lee and Ed Madden, 19–59. Cambridge: Cambridge Scholars Publishing, 2008.

Jeffares, A. Norman. *A Commentary on the Collected Poems of W.B. Yeats.* London: Palgrave Macmillan, 1968.

Jellett, Mainie. "A Word on Irish Art", in *The Artist's Vision: Lectures and Essays on Art,* edited by Eileen MacCarvill, 103–106. Dundalk: Dundalgan, 1958.

Jellett, Mainie. "An Approach to Painting". In *The Field Day Anthology of Irish Writing. Irish Women's Writing and Traditions. Volume 5,* edited by Angela Bourke et al, 1085–1086. New York: New York University Press, 2002.

Jenker, Ingrid. "Allegory, Portrait or Genre? 'Mary and Brigid', by Margaret Clarke". *Irish Arts Review Yearbook,* vol. 15 (1999): 148–151.

Joyce, James. *Ulysses.* Dublin: Random House, 1961.

Kain, Richard M. and O'Brien, James. *George Russell (AE).* London: Bucknell University Press, 1976.

Keane, Maureen. *Ishbel: Lady Aberdeen in Ireland.* Newtownwards: Colourpoint, 1999.

Kearney, Richard. *Transitions: Narratives in Modern Irish Culture.* Manchester: Manchester University Press, 1988.

Kearney, Richard. *Transitions: Narratives in Modern Irish Culture.* Manchester: Manchester University Press, 1988.

Kelly, Deirdre. "Art as Social Commentary: Two Visual Interpretations of the 1916 Rising". *History Studies,* vol. 16 (2015): 20–31.

Kelly, Niamh Ann. *Imaging the Great Irish Famine. Representing Dispossession in Visual Culture.* London: Bloomsbury Academic, 2018.

Kemp, Wolfgang. *The Desire of my Eyes. The Life and Work of John Ruskin.* New York: Farrar, Straus and Giroux, 1900.

Kennedy, Brian S. *Great Irish Artists: From Lavery to Le Brocquy.* Dublin: Gill and MacMillan, 1997

Kennedy, Brian S. *Irish Art and Modernism. 1880–1950.* Dublin: Hugh Lane Municipal Gallery, 1991.

Kennedy, Brian S. "An Enduring View of Irish Identity: Paul Henry and the Realism of Fiction". *Irish Arts Review Yearbook,* vol. 15 (1999): 98–107.

Kennedy, Róisín. "Mary Swanzy HRHA (1882–1978). The Storm". Adam's, *Important Irish Art* (November 22[th] 2017): 20.

Kennedy, Róisín. "Native Traditions and Modern Imperatives: Mexico and Ireland in the Imagination of Ernie O'Malley". In *Art History After Françoise Henry – 50 Years at UCD, 1965–2015,* edited by Carla Briggs et al, 126–139. Dublin: Gandon Editions, 2016.

Kennedy, Róisín. "The Invisible Irish Etchers". Art in Print, vol. 9, no. 3 (September/October 2019): 38–40.

Keogh, Aoife and King, Fiona. "Mainie Jellett". In *InColour Exhibition Catalogue.* Fingal: Fingal Arts Office, n.d.).

Kiberd, Declan and Matthews, Patrick J. *Handbook of the Irish Revival: An Anthology of Political and Cultural Writings,* 1891–1922. Dublin: Abbey Theatre Press, 2015.

Kiberd, Declan. "Irish Literature and Irish History". In *The Oxford Illustrated History of Ireland,* edited by Robert Fitzroy Foster, 275–305. Oxford: Oxford University Press, 1989.

Kiberd, Declan. *Inventing Ireland. The Literature of the Modern Nation.* Cambridge: Harvard University Press, 1995.

Kiberd, Declan. *The Irish Writer and the World.* Cambridge, Cambridge University Press, 2005.

Kinmonth, Claudia. *Irish Rural Interiors.* London: Yale University Press, 2006.

Kissane, Sean and Cullinane, Liz. Mary Swanzy: Voyages. Dublin: Irish Museum of Modern Art, 2018.

Kissane, Séan. "Woman with Red Hair". *Irish and International Art* (Whyte's, September 16[th] 2019): 61.

Kissane, Séan. *Analysing Cubism.* Cork: Crawford Art Gallery, 2013.

Kohfeldt, Mary Lou. *Lady Gregory: The Woman Behind the Irish Renaissance.* London: Andre Deutsch, 1985.

Kostick, Conor and Collins, Lorcan. *The Easter Rising: A Guide to Dublin in 1916.* Dublin: O'Brien Press, 2000.

Kreilkamp, Vera. *The Arts and Crafts Movement: Making it Irish.* Chicago: University of Chicago Press, 2016.

Laing, Kathryn et al. *Edna O'Brien: New Critical Perspectives. Dublin:* Carysfort Press, 2006.

Laing, Lloyd and Laing, Jennifer. *Celtic Britain and Ireland. Art and Society.* London: Herbert Press, 1995.

Laing, Lloyd and Laing, Jennifer. *The Archaeology of Celtic Britain and Ireland.* Art and Society. London: The Herbert Press, 1995.

Larmour, Paul. *The Arts and Crafts Movement in Ireland.* Dublin: Friar's Bush Press, 1992.

Ledger, Sally. *The New Woman. Fiction and feminism at the fin de siècle.* New York: Manchester University Press, 1997.

Lewis, Gifford. *The Yeats Sisters and the Cuala.* Dublin: Irish Academic Press, 1994.

Loftus, Belinda. *Mirrors: William III and Mother Ireland.* Dundrum: Picture Press, 1990.

Long, Rebecca. "Stories of Ancient Days. Mythological Constructs of Childhood on Independence Ireland". In *Constructions of the Irish Child in the Independence Period,* edited by Ciara Boylan and Ciara Gallagher, 187–206. Cham: Palgrave Macmillan, 2018.

Luddy, Maria et al. "An Agenda for Women's History in Ireland, 1500–1900". *Irish Historical Studies,* vol. 28, no. 109 (May 1992): 1–37.

Luddy, Maria. "Feminism". In *The Princeton History of Modern Ireland,* edited by Richard Bourke and Ian McBride, 484–486. New Jersey: Princeton University Press, 2016.

Luddy, Maria. "Gender and Irish History". In *The Oxford Handbook of Modern Irish History,* edited by Alvin Jackson, 193–213. Oxford: Oxford University Press, 2014.

Luddy, Maria. "Irish Women's Opposition to the 1937 Draft Constitution". In *Transactions of the Royal Historical Society,* vol. 15, edited by Aled Jones, 175–195. Cambridge: Cambridge University Press, 2005.

Luddy, Maria. "The Labour Movement in Ireland, 1800–2000". In *The Field Day Anthology of Irish Writing, vol. 4: Irish women's writing and traditions,* edited by Angela Bourke et al, 548–565. Cork: Cork University Press, 2002.

Luddy, Maria. *Women in Ireland, 1800–1918. A Documentary History.* Cork: Cork University Press, 1995.

MacCarthy, Fiona. *Anarchy and Beauty. William Morris and his Legacy, 1860–1960.* New Haven and London: Yale University Press, 2015.

MacGreevy, Thomas. "Fifty Years of Irish Painting, 1900–1950". *Capuchin Annual* (1949): 497–512.

MacGreevy, Thomas. "Living Art – A New Departure". *The Irish Times* (September 16th 1943): 3.

MacGreevy, Thomas. "Religious Art and Modern Ireland". *The Gaelic Churchman* (April, 1922): 128–129.

MacGreevy, Thomas. "St. Brendan's Cathedral, Loughrea. 1897–1947". *The Capuchin Annual* (1946–1947): 353–373.

MacGreevy, Thomas. "Stained Glass at An Tur Gloine", *The Irish Statesman* (December 13th 1924): 435.

MacGreevy, Thomas. "Three historical paintings by Jack B. Yeats". *Capuchin Annual* (1966): 238–51.

MacGreevy, Thomas. *Jack B. Yeats: an appreciation and interpretation.* Dublin: Victor Waddington, 1945.

Markale, Jean. *Women of the Celts* (Vermont: Inner Traditions, 1986).

Mark-Fitzgerald, Emily. *Commemorating the Irish Famine. Memory and the Monument* Liverpool: Liverpool University Press, 2013.

Marshall, Catherine. *Irish Art Masterpieces.* California: Hugh Lauter Levin Associates, 1994.

Mayes, Elizabeth and Murphy, Paula. *Images and Insights. Exhibition Catalogue.* Dublin: Hugh Lane Municipal Gallery of Modern Art, 1993.

McCarvill, Eileen (ed.). *The Artist's Vision. Mainie Jellett: Lectures and Essays on Art.* Dublin: Dundalgan Press, 1958.

McConkey, Kenneth. *A Free Spirit. Irish Art 1860–1960.* London: Antique Collectors Club, 1990.

McCoole, Sinéad. *No Ordinary Women: Irish Female Activists in the Revolutionary Years, 1900–1923.* Dublin: O'Brien Press, 2015.

Meehan, Niall. "Article 44 Reconsidered". *History Ireland,* vol. 27, no. 1 (January/February 2019): 44–47.

Morgan O'Driscoll. *Irish and International Art Auction Catalogue* (December 4th 2017).

Morisson, Valérie. "The Guise of Irishness: Irish Ethnographic and Folkloric Paintings from a European Perspective, 1880–1930". *Revue Miroirs,* 2 (2015): 61–87.

Murphy, Paula. "Madonna and Maiden, Mistress and Mother: Woman as a Symbol of Ireland and Spirit of the Nation". In *When Time Began to Rant and Rage. Figurative Painting from Twentieth-Century Ireland,* edited by James Christen Steward, 90–101.Berkeley: Merrell Holberton, 1998.

Murphy, William. *Family Secrets. William Butler Yeats and his Relatives.* New York: Syracuse University Press, 1995.

Murray, Simone. "The Cuala Press: Women, Publishing and the Conflicted Genealogies of Feminist Publishing". *Women's Studies International Forum,* vol. 27, no. 5/6 (2004): 489–506.

Nash, Catherine. "Remapping and Renaming: New Cartographies of Identity, Gender and Landscape in Ireland". *Feminist Review,* no. 44, Nationalisms and National Identities (1993): 39–57.

Nash, Catherine. "Remapping the Body/Land: New Cartographies of Identity, Gender and Landscape in Ireland". In *Writing Women and Space. Colonial and Postcolonial Geographies,* edited by Alison Blung and Gillian Rose. New York and London: The Guildford Press, 1994.

Naughton, Lindie. *Markievicz: A Most Outrageous Rebel.* Kildare: Merrion Press, 2018.

Nelson, Charles. "Irish Women Artists as Natural History Illustrators". In *Irish Women Artists from the Eighteenth Century to the Present Day,* edited by Jenni Rogers, Wanda Ryan-Smolin and Elizabeth Mayes, 28–29. Dublin: The National Gallery of Ireland and Douglas Hyde Gallery, 1987.

Netzer, Nancy. "Cloths of Ireland's New Golden Age": Creating Textiles for the Honan Chapel". In *The Arts and Crafts Movement. Making it Irish,* edited by Vera Kreilkamp, 101–116. Chicago: University of Chicago Press, 2016.

Nochlin, Linda. "Why Have There Been No Great Women Artists?". In *Women, Art and Power and Other Essays,* edited by Linda Nochlin, 145–178. London: Thames and Hudson, 1989.

Nochlin, Linda. "Women, Art and Power". In *Women, Art and Power and Other Essays,* edited by Linda Nochlin, 1–36. New York: Harper and Row, 1988.

Norman, Geraldine. *Nineteenth-Century Painters and Painting: A Dictionary.* Berkeley and Los Angeles: University of California Press, 1977.

Ó Céirin, Kit and Ó Céirin, Cyril. *Women of Ireland: A Biographic Dictionary.* Galway: Tír Eolas, 1996.

Ó Corráin, Donnchadh. "Prehistoric and Early Christian Ireland". In *The Oxford History of Ireland,* edited by Robert Fitzroy Foster, 1–43. New York: Oxford University Press, 1989.

O'Brien, Eoin. "From the Waters of Sion to Liffeyside. The Jewish Contribution: Medical and Cultural". *Journal of the Irish Colleges of Physicians and Surgeons,* vol. 10, no. 3 (January 1981): 113.

O'Connor, Éimear (ed.). *Irish Women Artists, 1800–2009. Familiar but Unknown.* Dublin: Four Courts Press, 2010.

O'Connor, Éimear. *Séan Keating. Art, Politics and Building the Irish Nation.* Newbridge: Irish Academic Press, 2013.

O'Donnell, Katherine. "Academics Becoming Activists: Reflections on Some Ethical Issues of the Justice for Magdalenes Campaign". In *Irishness on the Margins. Minority and Dissident Identities,* edited by Pilar Villar-Argáiz, 77–100. Dublin: Palgrave Macmillan, 2018.

O'Gorman, Francis (ed.). *The Cambridge Companion to John Ruskin.* Cambridge: Cambridge University Press, 2015.

O'Grady, John. *The Life and Work of Sarah Purser.* Dublin: Four Courts Press, 1996.

O'Leary, Eoin. "The Irish National Teachers' Organisation and he Marriage Bar for Women National Teachers, 1933–1958". *Saothar,* 12 (1987): 47–52.

O'Sullivan, Niamh. *Aloysius O'Kelly: Art, Nation, Empire.* Dublin: Field Day, 2010.4

O'Sullivan, Seumas. *The Rose and Bottle: And Other Essays.* Dublin: Talbot Press, 1946.

O'Toole, Fintan. *Modern Ireland in 100 Artworks.* Dublin: Royal Irish Academy, 2016

O'Toole, Tina. *The Irish New Woman.* London and New York: Palgrave Macmillan, 2013.

Orpen, Sir William. *Stories of Old Ireland and Myself.* London: Williams and Norgate, 1925.

Ortner, Sherry B. "Is female to male as nature is to culture?". In *Woman, Culture, and Society,* edited by Michelle Zimballist Rosaldo and Louise Lamphere, 68–87. Stanford, CA: Stanford University Press, 1974.

Owens, Cóilín D. and Radner, Joan N. (eds.). *Irish Drama, 1900–1980.* Washington: The Catholic University of America Press, 1990.

Parsons, Michael. "Cubist painting in a Monkstown gallery". *The Irish Times,* (July 30th 2011).

Pearse, Padraic. *A Significant Irish Educationalist: The Educational Writings of P. H. Pearse.* Edited by Séamas Ó Buachalla. Dublin: Mercier Press, 1980.

Pearse, Padraic. *Collected Works of Padraic H. Pearse. Political Writings and Speeches.* Dublin: The Éire-Gael Society, 2013.

Peterson, William S. *The Kelmscott Press. A History of William Morris's Typographical Adventure.* Oxford: Oxford University Press, 1991.

Pethica, James. 'Our Kathleen: Yeats's Collaboration with Lady Gregory in the Writing of Cathleen ni Houlihan'. In *Yeats Annual* no. 6, edited by Warwick Gould, 3–31. London: Macmillan Press, 1998.

Pollock, Griselda and Parker, Rozsika. *Old Mistresses. Women, Art and Ideology.* London and New York: I.B. Tauris, 2013.

Pollock, Griselda. *Vision and Difference. Feminism, Femininity and Histories of Art.* London and New York: Routledge, 2003.

Potter, Matthew C. (Ed.). *The Concept of the "Master" in Art Education in Britain and Ireland. 1770 to the Present.* London: Ashgate, 2013.

Prettejohn, Elizabeth. *The Cambridge Companion to the Pre-Raphaelites.* New York: Cambridge University Press, 2012.

Pyle, Hilary. "Darling Margaret.A Look at Orpen's Favourite Pupil". *Irish Arts Review Yearbook* (2007): 85–91.

Pyle, Hilary. "From the Vanguard". *Irish Arts Review,* vol. 34, no. 4 (2017/2018): 128–133.

Pyle, Hilary. "Notes from Estella". *Irish Arts Review,* vol. 25, no. 1 (Spring 2008): 96–99.

Pyle, Hilary. "The Hamwood Ladies: Letitia and Eva Hamilton". *Irish Arts Review Yearbook,* vol. 13 (1997): 122–134.

Pyle, Hilary. Irish Art, 1900–1950. *Exhibition Catalogue.* Cork: Crawford Art Gallery, 1975.

Pyle, Hilary. *Portraits of Patriots.* Dublin: Allen Figgis, 1996.

Quigley, Patrick. *Sisters Against the Empire: Countess Constance Markievicz and Eva Gore-Booth,* 1916–17. Dublin: Liffey Press, 2016.

Quigley, Patrick. *The Polish Irishman: The Life and Times of Count Casimir Markievicz.* Dublin: Liffey Press, 2012.

Quinn, Antoinette. "Cathleen Ni Houlihan Writes Back: Maud Gonne and Irish National Theatre". In *Gender and Sexuality in Modern Ireland,* edited by Anthony Bradley and Maryann Gialanella, 29–59. Amherst: University of Massachusetts Press, 1997.

Rappaport, Helen. *Encyclopedia of Women Social Reformers.* California: ABC-CLIO, 2001.

Kearney, Richard. *Postnationalist Ireland: Politics, Culture, Philosophy.* London: Routledge, 1997.

Roach Pierson, Ruth. "Nations: Gendered, Racialized, Crossed with Empire". In *Gendered Nations: Nationalisms and Gender Order in the Long Nineteenth Century,* edited by Ida Blom et al, 41–61. London: Bloomsbury, 2000.

Robbins, Daniel. *Albert Gleizes, 1881–1953. A Retrospective Exhibition.* New York: The Solomon R. Guggenheim Foundation, 1964.

Roche, Anthony. *The Irish Dramatic Revival,* 1899–1939. London: Bloomsbury, 2015.

Rogers, Jenni et al. *Irish Women Artists from the Eighteenth Century to the Present Day.* Dublin: National Gallery of Ireland and the Douglas Hyde Gallery, 1987.

Rosende Pérez, Aida. "La Iconografía Femenina de Irlanda. Creación y Re/Construcción de una Nación en Femenino". *Lectora,* 14 (2008): 251–267.

Ross, David A. *Critical Companion to William Butler Yeats. A Literary Reference to His Life and Work.* New York: Facts on File, 2009.

Roycroft, Trevor. "Belleek Earthenware Plaque – Antwerp Belgium by Beatrice Elvery (Lady Glenavy)". UK Belleek Collector's Group Newsletter, vol. 29, no. 3 (2008): 40–41.

Ruczaj, Maciej. "The Liturgy of Revolution: Political Theology of Patrick Pearse Between Catholicism and Modernism". PhD diss. Prague: Charles University, 2015.

Russell, George. "On Behalf of Some Irishmen Not Followers of Tradition". In *Penguin Book of Irish Verse,* edited by Brendan Kennelly, 314. Harmondsworth: Penguin, 1981.

Ryan, John. *Irish Monasticism. Origins and Early Development.* Dublin: Irish Academic Press, 1986.

Ryan, Vera. *Made in Cork. The Arts and Crafts Movement, 1880s-1920s.* Dublin: Gandon Editions, 2017.

Schaus, Margaret (ed.). *Women and Gender in Medieval Europe. An Encyclopaedia.* New York and London: Routledge Revivals, 2006.

Sharkey, Sabina. *Ireland and the Iconography of Rape: Colonisation, Constraint and Gender.* London: University of North London Press, 1994.

Sheehy, Jeanne. "The Training and Professional Life of Irish Women Artists Before the Twentieth Century". In *Irish Women Artists from the Eighteenth Century to the Present Day,* edited by Jenni Rogers, Wanda Ryan-Smolin and Elizabeth Mayes, 7–14. Dublin: The National Gallery of Ireland and Douglas Hyde Gallery, 1987.

Sheehy, Jeanne. *The Rediscovery of Ireland's Past. The Celtic Revival, 1830–1930.* London: Thames and Hudson, 1980.

Sheridan, Liz. "Women and Dublin's Municipal Collection". In *Irish Women Artists from the Eighteenth Century to the Present Day,* edited by Jenni

Rogers, Wanda Ryan-Smolin and Elizabeth Mayes, 15–16. Dublin: The National Gallery of Ireland and Douglas Hyde Gallery, 1987.

Shovlin, Frank. *The Irish Literary Periodical, 1923–1958.* Oxford: Oxford University Press, 2003.

Sisson, Elaine. *Pearse's Patriots. St. Enda's and the Cult of Boyhood.* Cork: Cork University Press, 2004.

Skelton, Robin. "Twentieth-Century Irish Literature and the Private Press Tradition: Dun Emer, Cuala and Dolmen Presses, 1902–1963". *The Masssachusetts Review,* vol. 5, no. 2 (Winter 1964): 368–377.

Sloan, Barry. "The Redress of Imagination: Bernard MacLavery's Grace Notes". In *The Gift of Story. Narrating Hope in a Postmodern World,* edited by Emily Griesinger and Mark Eaton, 303–315. Waco, USA: Baylor University Press, 2006.

Smith, Bonnie G. (ed.). *The Oxford Encyclopaedia of Women in World History.* Oxford: Oxford University Press, 2008.

Smith, James M. *Ireland's Magdalen Laundries and the Nation's Architecture of Containment.* Manchester: Manchester University Press, 2008.

Steele, Karen. *Women, Press and Politics During the Irish Revival.* New York: Syracuse University Press, 1997.

Steward, James Christian (ed.). *When Time Began to Rant and Rage: Figurative Painting from Twentieth-Century Ireland.* London: Merrell Holberton, 1998.

Strachan, John and Nally, Claire. *Advertising, Literature and Print Culture in Ireland, 1891–1922.* Hampshire: Palgrave Macmillan, 2012.

Suarez, Michael F. and Woudhuysen, Henry R. *The Oxford Companion to the Book, vol. 1.* Oxford: Oxford University Press, 2010.

TeBrake, Janet K. "Irish peasant women in revolt: the Land League Years". *Irish Historical Studies,* 28, 109 (1992): 63–80.

Thomas, Charles. *Christianity in Roman Britain to AD 500.* Berkeley and Los Angeles: University of California Press, 1981.

Tosh, Jemma. "'Rape me, I'm Irish': An Analysis of the Intersecting Discourses of Anti-Irish Racism and Sexual Violence". *Intersectionalities,* vol. 4, no. 1 (2015): 59–81.

Turpin, John. *A School of Art in Dublin since the Eighteenth Century: A History of the National College of Art and Design.* Dublin: Gill and Macmillan, 1995.

Turpin, John. "Visual Marianism and National Identity in Ireland: 1920–1960". In *Art, Nation and Gender. Ethnic Landscapes, Myths and Mother-Figures,* edited by Tricia Cusack and Síghle Bhreathnach Lynch, 67–78. Burlington: Ashgate, 2003.

Upstone, Robert et al. *William Orpen: Politics, Sex and Death.* London: Philip Wilson, 2005.

Villar-Argáiz, Pilar. *The Poetry of Eavan Boland: A Postcolonial Reading.* Dublin: Academica Press, 2008.

Walsh, Tom. "The National System of Education, 1831–2000". In *Essays in the History of Irish Education,* edited by Brendan Walsh, 7–44. Dublin: Palgrave Macmillan, 2016.

Ward, Margaret. "Marginality and Militancy: Cumann na mBan, 1914–36". In *The Irish Women's History Reader,* edited by Alan Hayes and Diane Urquhart, 58–63. London: Routledge, 2001.

Warfield, Derek and Daly, Raymond. *Celtic and Ireland in Song and Story.* Kildare: Derek Warfield, 2008.

White, James. "Pictures of the Home". In Irish Art: a Volume of Articles and Illustrations. Dublin: The Parkside Press, 1944.

William Butler Yeats. *Collected Poems of W. B. Yeats,* edited by Richard J. Finneran. New York: MacMillan, 2008.

Williams, Maggie M. *Icons of Irishness from the Middle Ages to the Modern World.* New York: Palgrave Macmillan, 2012.

Wills, Clair. *That Neutral Island: A Cultural History of Ireland During the Second World War.* Cambridge: The Belknap Press of Harvard University Press, 2007.

Wright, Julia M. *Representing the National Landscape in Irish Romanticism.* Syracuse: Syracuse University Press, 2014.

Yeats, William Butler. "An Irish National Theatre". In *The Collected Works of W. B. Yeats. The Irish Dramatic Movement, vol. VIII,* edited by Mary FitzGerald and Richard J. Finneran, 32–35. New York: Scribner, 2003).

Yeats, William Butler. *In the Seven Woods.* Dublin: Dun Emer, 1903.

Yeats, William Butler. *Selected Poems and Four Plays of William Butler Yeats,* edited by Marcha Louis Rosenthal. New York: Scribner, 1996.

## Website Content

"A Brief History", Irish Women Workers Union, accessed on May 8th 2020, https://womenworkersunion.ie/history/

"Abortion law in Ireland", Abortion Rights Campaign, 2019, accessed on April 29th 2020, https://www.abortionrightscampaign.ie/abortion-law-in-ireland/

"Eighth Amendment of the Constitution Act 1983", Irish Statute Book, accessed on April 29th 2020, http://www.irishstatutebook.ie/eli/1983/ca/8/schedule/enacted/en/html

"Hamwood Ladies". Hamwood Estate, accessed on April 29th 2020, https://hamwood.ie/hamwood-ladies/

"History", Irish Literary Society, accessed on May 8th 2020, https://irishlitsoc.org/home/about/history/

"Mary Swanzy, HRHA. 1882–1978", Sotheby's, accessed on April 28th 2020, http://www.sothebys.com/en/auctions/ecatalogue/2004/irish-sale-including-property-from-the-jefferson-smurfit-group-l04620/lot.32.html

"Mary Swanzy. Voyages". Irish Museum of Modern Art, accessed on May 10th 2020, https://imma.ie/whats-on/mary-swanzy-voyages/

"May Guinness, 1863–1955". Milmo-Penny Fine Art, Irish Gallery. Accessed on April 17th 2020, http://www.mpfa.ie/irgallery.htm

"Miss Maud Gonne". Hugh Lane Municipal Gallery, accessed on May 13th 2020, http://emuseum.pointblank.ie/online_catalogue/work-detail.php?objectid=1675

"O'Growney Memorial Lecture", published as *Gaelic League Pamphlet* no. 26, 2 (September 29th 1902).

"Senator's gift to the Seanad". Seanad Éireann debate (November 26th 1924) 1924, accessed on May 12th 2020.

"Yeats, Elizabeth Corbet", *Drawn to the Page. Irish Artists and Illustration 1830–1930.* Trinity College (2017), accessed on May 12th 2020, https://dttp.tcd.ie/artist/46

Amelia O'Mahony-Brady, "Artsdesk: Markievicz and the Modernist". *Totally Dublin,* accessed on May 11th 2020, https://ww.totallydublin.ie/arts-culture/arts-culture-features/artsdesk-markiewicz-and-the-modernist/

Barber, Fionna. "The Vibrant Studio: Margaret Clarke's Performative Femininities and 1920s Painting". Art and Reality: The Role of Visual Culture in the Post-Independence State, UCD (Symposium, October 19th 2018), accessed on May 10th 2020, https://soundcloud.com/real-smart-media/fionna-barber-margaret-clarke-performative-femininities-and-1920s-painting

Beale, Diana. "Time to give AE his Due". *The Irish Times* (August 23rd 2004). Accessed on May 9th 2020, https://www.irishtimes.com/culture/time-to-give-ae-his-due-1.1154481

Brooke, Peter. "Albert Gleizes in 1934". *Texts by Gleizes,* accessed on May 11th 2020,http://www.peterbrooke.org/form-and-history/texts/1934/introduction.html

Bustillo, Marta. "Two Girls in Silk Kimonos".Trinity College Dublin (2015), accessed on May 11th 2020, https://www.tcd.ie/library/1916/two-girls-in-silk-kimonos/

Campbell, Julian. "Mary Swanzy Collection". Christie's, accessed on May 10th 2020, https://www.christies.com/lotfinder/Lot/mary-swanzy-hrha-1882-1978-the-embrace-4902989-details.aspx.

Caoilfhionn Ní Bheacháin. "The Dun Emer Press". *Modernist Archives Publishing Project,* accessed on May 12th 2020, https://www.modernistarchives.com/business/the-dun-emer-press

Catherine Marshall, "Captured by Light", *Dublin Review of Books,* accessed on May 13th 2020, https://www.drb.ie/essays/captured-by-light-old

Cullen, Fintan. "Politics and the Painter". *The Irish Times* (May 1st 2010). Accessed on May 9th 2020, https://www.irishtimes.com/culture/books/politics-and-the-painter-1.659877

Cullinane, Liz. "Mary Swanzy. The Unsung Hero of Irish Modernism". The Irish Independent (October 21st 2018), accessed on May 10th 2020, https://www.independent.ie/entertainment/theatre-arts/mary-swanzy-the-unsung-hero-of-irish-modernism-37435424.html

Dempsey, Pauric J. and Hourican, Bridget. "Campbell, Beatrice Moss". *Dictionary of Irish Biography*, accessed on May 13th 2020, https://dib.cambridge.org/viewReadPage.do;jsessionid=FC21E9BF308122845DC58AA6EF517448?articleId=a1410

Gordon Bowe, Nicola. "Symbols of Ireland". Government of Ireland. Accessed on May 10th 2020, https://web.archive.org/web/20110614174614/http://www.gov.ie/en/essays/symbols.html

Gordon Bowe, Nicola. "The Tower of Glass. An Túr Gloine and the Early Twentieth Century Stained Glass Revival in Ireland". Building Conservation (2008), accessed on May 13th 2020.

Griffin, Fiana. "Margaret Clarke. Portrait of Eamon de Valera". Adam's Auctioneers, accessed on May 10th 2020, https://www.adams.ie/41253/Margaret-Clarke-RHA-1888-1961-Portrait-of-amon-de-Valera-Oil-on-canvas-50-5-x-40-5cm-20-x-16-Inscribed-verso-sketch-of-Eamon-de-Valera-two-sittings-by-Margaret-Clarke-Provenance-The-sitter-and-t?view=lot_detail

https://dib.cambridge.org/viewReadPage.do;jsessionid=89772CF21263FB243273BF2F8E620070?articleId=a1410

https://www.buildingconservation.com/articles/towerofglass/towerofglass.htm

https://www.modernistarchives.com/business/the-dun-emer-press

https://www.oireachtas.ie/en/debates/debate/seanad/1924-11-26/8/

https://www.royalacademy.org.uk/article/may-morris-art-and-life-william-morris-gallery

Kennedy, Maev. "Exhibition reveals London's admirable Irish". *The Guardian* (9 Mar. 2005). Accessed on May 9th 2020, https://www.theguardian.com/uk/2005/mar/09/arts.artsnews

Kenny, Mary. "Thoroughly Modern Mainie". *The Irish Independent* (August 10th 2018), accessed on May 11th 2020, https://www.independent.ie/entertainment/theatre-arts/mary-kenny-thoroughly-modern-mainie-37218106.html

Marlowe, Lara. "Hunger Museum Puts Focus on Art About the Famine". The Irish Times (October 1st 2012), accessed on April 25th 2020, https://www.irishtimes.com/news/hunger-museum-puts-focus-on-art-about-the-famine-1.545793

Martin, Alison. "Off to Fight for the Republic. Countess Markievicz's Propaganda Cartoons in the Irish Civil War". *The Irish Story* (January 8th 2018), accessed on May 11th 2020,https://www.theirishstory.com/2018/01/08/off-to-fight-for-the-republic-countess-markieviczs-propaganda-cartoons-in-the-irish-civil-war/#.XrkIvEQzbIU

Maxwell, Jane. "Vita Brevis, Ars Longa". Manuscripts and Archives Research Library, Trinity College Dublin, accessed on April 27th 2020, https://www.tcd.ie/library/1916/vita-brevis-ars-longa/

McAteer, Michael. "Celtic and Irish Revival", *Oxford Bibliographies,* accessed on May 8th 2020, https://www.oxfordbibliographies.com/view/document/obo-9780199846719/obo-9780199846719-0025.xml

McDayter, Ghislaine. "On the Publication of William Godwin's Memoirs of the Author of a Vindication of the Rights of Woman, 1978", in *BRANCH: Britain, Representation and Nineteenth-Century History.* Dino Franco Felluga. Extension of Romanticism and Victorianism on the Net Web. Accessed on May 7th 2020, https://www.branchcollective.org/?ps_articles=ghislaine-mcdayter-on-the-publication-of-william-godwins-memoirs-of-the-author-of-a-vindication-of-the-rights-of-woman-1798

McNally, Niamh. "Margaret Clarke: Portrait of the Artist as a (Young) Woman". *Totally Dublin* (June 24th 2017), accessed on April 25th 2020, https://www.totallydublin.ie/arts-culture/margaret-clarke-portrait-artist-young-woman/

Morrison, Chris. "Celebrating a Century of Irish Women's Art", *The Irish News* (July 31st 2014), accessed on May 10th 2020, http://www.irishnews.com/lifestyle/2014/07/31/news/celebrating-a-century-of-irish-women-s-art-98106/

O'Byrne, Robert. "The Man who Gave us Modern Art". *The Irish Times* (January 19th 2008). Accessed on May 19th, 2020, https://www.irishtimes.com/news/the-man-who-gave-us-modern-art-1.930285

O'Hanlon, Oliver. "An Irishman's Diary on the revolutionary art of May Guinness", in *The Irish Times* (March 20th 2017), accessed on May 11th 2020, https://www.irishtimes.com/opinion/an-irishman-s-diary-on-the-revolutionary-art-of-may-guinness-1.3014674?mode=sample&auth-failed=1&pw-origin=https%3A%2F%2Fwww.irishtimes.com%2Fopinion%2Fan-irishman-s-diary-on-the-revolutionary-art-of-may-guinness-1.3014674

O'Sullivan, Niamh. "Lilian Lucy Davidson ARHA (1893–1954). Potato Harvest". *Important Irish Art* (Whyte's, May 27th 2019), accessed on May 5th 2020, https://www.whytes.ie/art/potato-harvest-1931/167705/?SearchString=&LotNumSearch=19&GuidePrice=&OrderBy=&ArtistID=&ArrangeBy=list&NumPerPage=15&offset=0

www.ingramcontent.com/pod-product-compliance
Lightning Source LLC
Chambersburg PA
CBHW071357100726
47908CB00004B/1024